30043

The Bible on
Leadership

The Bible on Leadership

From Moses to Matthew—
Management Lessons for
Contemporary Leaders

Lorin Woolfe

AMACOM

American Management Association

New York • Atlanta • Brussels • Buenos Aires • Chicago • London • Mexico City
San Francisco • Shanghai • Tokyo • Toronto • Washington, D.C.

This publication is designed to provide accurate and authoritative information in regard to the subject matter covered. It is sold with the understanding that the publisher is not engaged in rendering legal, accounting,
or other professional service. If legal advice or other expert assistance is
required, the services of a competent professional person should be sought.

Library of Congress Cataloging-in-Publication Data

Woolfe, Lorin.
    The Bible on leadership : from Moses to Matthew : management lessons
for contemporary leaders / Lorin Woolfe.
      p.   cm.
    Includes bibliographical references and index.
      ISBN-10: 0-8144-0682-3 (hardcover)
      ISBN-13: 978-0-8144-0682-3 (hardcover)
    1. Leadership.   2. Executive ability.   3. Management.   4. Leadership
in the Bible.   I. Title.
    HD57.7 .W666   2002
    658.4'092—dc21   2002001991

Printing number

10   9

This book is dedicated to
Judy, Becca, Talia, and **Sascha,**
who daily remind me of my true purpose
and the divine in all of us.

Contents

Preface

What in heaven does the Bible have to do with leadership? Everything! The Bible is probably the most widely-read book in the world. It is revered for its religious precepts and guidance, its wisdom, and its literary beauty. Read carefully and with another perspective, it is also the greatest collection of leadership case studies ever written, with tremendously useful and insightful lessons for today's leaders and managers. Whatever our religious beliefs, most of us in the Western Hemisphere are familiar with the Bible's stories and heroes. They form some of the major archetypes of our collective consciousness and can serve as universal examples of leadership at its best (and worst).

Consider some of the managers and leaders of the Bible and the lessons they can impart to today's manager:

❖ Jacob, although inferior in strength to his macho brother Esau, was able to usurp his brother's birthright by appealing to "the power behind the throne" (his mother) to deceive the CEO (his father).

❖ Joseph, cast into corporate exile because of his brothers' jealousy of his close relationship with his father, Jacob, was forced to join the opposition, Egypt. There he was able to infiltrate the court, use his influence with Pharaoh, and ultimately bring his family and tribe to live with him, where they became a mighty force. However, the "merger" of the Israelites and Egyptians soon became extremely rocky, creating a whole new set of leadership problems.

❖ Moses, the man who inherited these problems, was a leader who spoke so poorly that his brother Aaron had to deliver most of his speeches for him. But the strength of his vision and his commitment to Israel's mission made him the ultimate visionary and a leader the people would follow through the most adverse circumstances. Many modern corporations experience adverse conditions, but few are condemned to wander in a desert (real or allegorical) for forty years. The Burning Bush is a corporate vision par excellence, and the Ten Commandments are the ultimate mission statement.

❖ Joshua succeeded Moses, and that transfer of power is an example of thorough succession planning, assisted by divine intervention. It would take a great and inspiring leader to replace Moses and lead the Israelites into the Promised Land. Joshua's motivational genius and strategic planning helped the Israelites literally knock down impregnable fortresses.

❖ Samson is one of the best "negative case studies" in history. He possessed great physical strength, but had some tremendous "blind spots" in his interpersonal judgment. The person he most desired was actually the person he had most to fear and who brought about his downfall. Samson was literally "blindsided" by an enemy he thought was a friend, and who also happened to be a member of the opposite gender. There are a lot of lessons in this story for today's business leader.

❖ Job had more troubles than any modern corporate executive, yet he stuck to his faith and his vision. His "case study" can teach the modern executive a lot about sticking to your vision despite obstacles, suffering, and doubters.

❖ Jesus, the son of a carpenter and born in a manger, rose to found the most populous religion on earth. Jesus' communication skills were consummate. He was able to cogently communicate new and revolutionary ideas using parables instead of direct explanation, and he was able to answer Pontius Pilate's loaded questions without appearing a traitor to Rome or a posturer to his own people. (Pilate: "Are you King of the Jews?" Jesus: "You say I am.") The Sermon on the Mount is a beautiful example of motivational communication, which influenced not just the small assembly there but millions of people in millions of assemblies since. His work with the disciples was some of the most astute team-building ever accomplished. And his mastery of the symbolic act gained him the largest following of any leader before or after him.

The Bible is full of these and other leaders—kings, prophets, warriors, strategists, and visionaries. It is a story of prophets true and false, fortunes gained and lost, organizations ascending and crashing. Its literal truth has been questioned, but its lessons and stories have been embraced as universal archetypes that influence the way we live our lives on a deep psychological, spiritual, and symbolic level.

So why shouldn't this biblical wisdom on leadership be applied on a business level? This book attempts to do just that, reviewing the most inspiring biblical "case studies" and comparing them to the challenges faced and conquered by some of today's most successful business leaders. It should come as no "revelation" that the traits and skills of successful Bible leaders are also those exhibited by the most successful modern leaders:

- ❖ Honesty and integrity
- ❖ Purpose
- ❖ Kindness and compassion
- ❖ Humility
- ❖ Communication
- ❖ Performance management
- ❖ Team development
- ❖ Courage
- ❖ Justice and fairness
- ❖ Leadership development

The emphasis of this book is on business, and most of the modern case studies depict business situations. But the Bible also has lessons for leaders in politics, athletics, the arts, and yes, even religion. You should find this book useful whether you are leading a business unit, a political committee or task force, an athletic team, a symphony orchestra, or a religious institution such as a church or synagogue (you have one of the world's best management tools, the Bible, at your fingertips—why not use it to help you lead your "stakeholders"?).

Whatever your arena for leadership, it is my most fervent wish that in studying the leadership challenges of the great figures of the Bible, you will receive the instruction and inspiration to meet your own leadership challenges.

Acknowledgments

A book is never the result of just one person. I'd like to thank Kevin Barron and Meldron Young. Their enthusiastic response to my idea and also to the chapter drafts kept me "on purpose." Thanks to Bill Hill for reminding me of the intersection of business and the spirit. Adrienne Hickey asked for my best and helped me focus my efforts. Erika Spelman ushered the book into final production with patience and biblical forbearance.

Thanks to all the modern leaders I've included; perhaps some of you may be surprised to find yourselves in a book that compares you to biblical leaders, but to me the connections were readily apparent.

And last but perhaps most important, thanks to my family, who did without me while I spent countless hours at the computer, in the library, and in my "study" digesting and merging biblical verse and management wisdom. You provide my inspiration and purpose.

The Bible on Leadership

Honesty and Integrity

"An honest answer is like a kiss on the lips."

—Prov. 24:26

"Judge me, O Lord, according to my . . . integrity."

—Ps. 7:8

 od's honest truth. Actions that back up the words and words that are congruent with the actions. People of integrity and honesty. People we can trust. That's what we look for in our leaders.

James Kouzes and Barry Posner, one of the best-known teams of management experts in the United States and authors of *The Leadership Challenge*, performed a survey of several thousand people around the world and several hundred case studies. They found that honesty was the most frequently cited trait of a good leader, so frequently cited that they wrote a separate volume about it, called *Credibility: How Leaders Gain and Lose It, Why People Demand It*.

It doesn't matter how noble or worthwhile your cause; if you haven't earned people's trust by constantly keeping your word and being true

1

to your values, people won't follow you too far. They may follow you to a point, but when the going gets tough, they'll start to hang back or look around for another leader. You may tell followers that despite the obstacles, the goal is achievable and that you will back them up 100 percent. But if you have failed to back them up in the past (or even if you simply lack a track record of trust and honesty), no one is going to line up to follow you through a deep mud puddle, let alone the Red Sea.

Lately, managers and leaders across the world have often left us wanting in this key area. Richard Nixon hired people to break into the headquarters of the opposing political party, then lied and claimed he had nothing to do with it. Bill Clinton had an affair with a White House intern a few years older than his daughter, then promptly denied that he had ever participated in any sexual activity with her.

Morton Thiokol, the aerospace company, failed to listen to a scientist's warnings that the *Challenger* spacecraft was unsafe, causing the entire crew to go crashing to a fiery death just minutes after the launch. Executives at Texaco engaged in a systematic pattern of discrimination against minority employees and tried to hide it, but audiotapes provided incontrovertible evidence of their actions.

The leaders in the Bible were cut from a different cloth. Even when their visions seemed unrealistic, people followed them because of their integrity and honesty. The Bible is full of examples of individuals who kept their words despite incredible natural and human obstacles, and of leaders who risked loss of power, money, and even their lives to keep their integrity intact. Noah was selected and rewarded for his integrity; Lot was saved from the hellfire and ashes of Sodom and Gomorrah for his honesty.

Moses, who brought God's warnings against lying, stealing, and coveting to his followers in dramatic fashion, was a man of great integrity himself. The Ten Commandments are very explicit: "Thou shalt not steal." "Thou shalt not murder." "Thou shalt not give false testimony against thy neighbor." "Thou shalt not covet they neighbor's house . . . wife . . . manservant or maidservant . . . or anything belonging to thy neighbor." That's four commandments out of ten that deal directly with integrity and honesty.

Isaiah, Jeremiah, and the other prophets, at great risk and with much unpopularity, warned an entire people when they were departing from their original precepts of truthfulness and morality. Jesus Christ brought the message that "the truth shall set you free," and he was willing to die for the truths he embodied. And fortunately today we have been blessed with a number of modern business leaders who realize that without honesty and integrity, material "success" rings hollow indeed.

HONESTY (AND DISHONESTY): ROLE MODELS

Fortunately for those of us who must work under modern leaders, integrity and honesty have not gone totally out of style. David Hunke, advertising director for the *Miami Herald* of the Knight-Ridder chain, notes: "We don't keep secrets very well around here, which is our own kind of joke. It is impossible to keep secrets, largely because of the issue of integrity. You can't imagine somebody at the very top of this corporation telling you something that wasn't true."[1]

Now we all know that, at least officially, journalists have a code of ethics. But what about Internet executives? CEO Robert Knowling of Covad Communications, an Internet provider, puts every employee through a three-day vision and values process, this in a fast-moving environment where time (measured in nanoseconds) is indeed money. An anchor of this process is the concept of integrity. "That's not an earthshaking aspiration but we give it some bite," notes Knowling. "We once had to dismiss a highly visible manager for a violation of our values. But, as Jack Welch says, you must be public about the consequences of breaking core values. I don't want to wake up one day with a profitable corporation that does not have a soul."[2]

Compare the integrity of Hunke and Knowling with that of monarchs Ahab and Jezebel, that "dirty duo" of the Bible whose lack of integrity would rival modern-day "monarchs" Leona and Harry Helmsley. For the uninitiated, Leona Helmsley was the New York "hotel queen" who, when caught paying almost no income taxes on a vast business empire, cavalierly stated that "only the little people pay taxes." There is a story, perhaps apocryphal, that she posted one of the "little people" on each side of her swimming pool with a bucket of iced shrimp so that she could partake while she swam her laps.

But Ahab and Jezebel's lack of integrity certainly rivals "Queen Leona's." A man named Naboth possessed a vineyard, which was close to Ahab's palace. Ahab wanted to buy it to use as a vegetable garden, but Naboth refused to sell: Ahab became angry and sullen, refusing to eat, but at least his first impulse was to obey the law, however distasteful and frustrating this might have been.

However, Jezebel saw no need for him to sulk or be disappointed: "Is this how you act as king over Israel? Get up and eat! Cheer up! I'll get you the vineyard." (1 Kings 21:7) She devised a simple yet totally amoral solution. She got two scoundrels (presumably through bribery or intimidation, since she was capable of both) to publicly testify that Naboth had cursed both God and the king (she wanted to cover all the bases).

Jezebel succeeded in getting Naboth stoned to death. As soon as she heard the "good news," she said to her husband, "Get up and take possession of the vineyard of Naboth the Jezreelite that he refused to sell you." (1 Kings 21:15) Ahab, man of integrity that he was, was only too happy to comply.

Compare Ahab and Jezebel's approach with that of King David, who wanted to build an altar to the Lord on the threshing floor of a fellow named Araunah the Jebusite. David forthrightly approached Araunah to humbly ask him to sell the threshing floor at full price (Ahab had Naboth killed so he could appropriate Naboth's vineyard at no cost).

Araunah offered David the threshing floor for free: "Take it! Let my lord the king do whatever pleases him." (1 Chron. 21:23) But David insisted on paying full price despite the fact that as King he could easily have appropriated the property by executive fiat.

By comparison, here is a modern example of a "vineyard" that was certainly coveted but not seized from its rightful owner because of an executive's integrity. David Armstrong of Armstrong Industries wanted to build a new plant next to the old one. In order to do so, the company would have to buy the home of a retired employee in his seventies and force him to relocate. The president vetoed the plan, exclaiming, "When we bought it (the company parcel), I promised he could stay there as long as he liked. Making him move now might upset him to the point where it shortens his life."[3] The new plant was built on the other side of the property.

And consider the integrity of Jean Maier, director of policy services for Northwestern Mutual Life. In a sense, she is watching over the "vineyards" (financial resources) of thousands of policyholders. Before she took the job, she told her boss, " 'I can't do this job unless I know I can do the right thing. I can't take some old lady's policy away . . . if I think it's not honorable.' And my boss said to me, 'You will never have to do that.' And I have never been put in that position."[4] Naboth would have been safe with her as a neighbor.

Too often, it seems honesty and integrity don't pay off in the short term, whereas dishonesty and lack of integrity do. How often have we heard sayings like "Do unto others before they can do unto you" or "No good deed will go unpunished"? In the Bible (as in business and organizational life), wrongdoers ultimately receive their proper consequences and virtuous people their just rewards, although not without a lot of needless suffering. If only people could be more honest from the beginning.

For instance, there's the ancient case study of Pharaoh, whose lack of integrity rivals any modern leader. This absolute ruler of Egypt could not tolerate any threat to his power. To keep his Hebrew slaves and build his vast monuments to himself, he was willing to rain destruction and death on his own people. When he refused to let the Hebrews go, God visited ten progressively destructive plagues on the Egyptians, starting with frogs (a relatively benign affliction) and moving to the killing of the firstborn (talk about progressive discipline!).

Pharaoh relented, probably because his own son was one of those killed. The story of the Israelites' hurried packing and exodus (resulting in the world's fastest-baking bread, matzoh) is well known to Jews and Christians alike. And it's a good thing that they were able to "bake and run" so quickly, because Pharaoh's "integrity" lasted only a few days. He went back on his word and pursued the Hebrews into the desert.

We're all familiar with what happened to Pharaoh's men when they tried to pursue the Israelites across the dry bed of the Red Sea, which had been parted for the fugitives. Seas may part for people of honor and integrity, but they often rush back to drown those whose word means nothing to themselves or others.

One test of a leader's integrity is his or her attitude toward "public" property. Some leaders take it all with them; others refuse to take a penny of the funds with which they have been entrusted. In recent times we know of leaders like Ferdinand Marcos and his wife, Imelda (she of the thousands of pairs of shoes), who appropriated much of their country's wealth before absconding to foreign shores. Compare their leave-taking to that of Samuel, who presided as the high priest of Israel for several decades. Not only did he refuse to take anything not belonging to him, he also asked his countrymen to identify anything that he had accumulated through the power of his office, and he would quickly and cheerfully return it!

> Here I stand. Testify against me in the presence of the Lord . . . Whose ox have I taken? Whose donkey have I taken? Whom have I cheated? Whom have I oppressed? From whose hand have I taken a bribe to make me shut my eyes? If I have done any of these, I will make it right.
> "You have not cheated or oppressed us," they replied. "You have not taken anything from anyone's hand." (1 Sam. 12:1–4)

Now, how many of today's business or political leaders would willingly open themselves up to such scrutiny? Michael Milken and Ivan Boesky certainly would not pass the test. Neither would many of the third-world leaders like the Sultan of Borneo, who made off with $1 billion worth of his country's oil wealth. But the third world is not the only place where political leaders fail to measure up in this area: Just ask the driver of the truck that pulled up to the Clintons' new Westchester County mansion to quietly remove and return to the White House a large collection of expensive furniture that had been donated—not to them personally but to "the Office of the President."

Samuel didn't passively respond or react to an investigation of his possessions. He initiated it himself! He *invited* investigation of his honesty and integrity, down to the last ox and donkey, promising to return anything that might have been immorally appropriated, no matter how insignificant. And he promised to rectify the least evidence of impropriety or dishonest gain.

This type of integrity runs throughout the Old and New Testaments. Consider the farewell speech of the disciple Paul to his followers:

> *I have not coveted anyone's silver or gold or clothing. You yourselves know that these hands of mine have supplied my own needs and the needs of my companions . . . They all wept as they embraced him and kissed him. What grieved them most was his statement that they would never see his face again.* (Acts 20:32–37)

Is it any wonder that such a profession and display of integrity and honesty provoked such heartfelt loyalty from Paul's followers, or that their grief was so great over the thought of losing him? If you left your organization today, would your followers grieve so openly about losing you, and if they did, would any of their grief relate to losing a leader of integrity?

But is integrity really attainable at the highest levels in modern business? Can't it be an impediment to material success? Charles Wang, chairman of Computer Associates, sees no such conflict. Wang is head of a $4.7 billion company, but he argues that effectiveness often boils down to truth telling, not dollars.

> *To be a successful person . . . you have to have integrity. Your word has to be everything you've got. You must have a moral compass. That's especially true if you're a leader because you're exposed more. People will get a sense of you, and if you are not true . . . they'll get a sense that you are sleazy . . . We buy a company, there's a contract that's just terrible, but you inherit all the contracts. You can argue the guy had no authority to sign it, but you . . . honor the contract.''*[5]

But leadership doesn't always have to be on a grand scale or come from the very top. John Boten, commercial systems manager of John Deere, feels that every transaction, no matter how large or small, should be conducted with integrity. When his company was undercharged by a vendor, he acted like King David, not King Ahab. "There was no question about it, we paid the vendor the amount that was due . . . it was taught to me early in my career that I have to have integrity in everything I do."[6] This one transaction was not going to "make or break" the company. Boten elected to follow his conscience and the words of Luke 16:10: "Whoever is dishonest with little will be dishonest with much."

INTEGRITY DESPITE TEMPTATION AND ADVERSITY

The story of Zacchaeus shows us that people who have lost their integrity can find it again. Zacchaeus was a tax collector for the Roman government, one of the least popular professions in ancient Israel. But he was not beyond rehabilitation. Because he was a short man, he climbed a tree so he could more clearly see and hear this mysterious prophet, Jesus. Jesus' response was to invite himself to the home of this social outcast:

> "Zacchaeus, come down immediately, for I must stay at your house today" . . . All the people saw this and began to mutter, "He has gone to be the guest of a sinner." But Zacchaeus stood up and said . . . "Look Lord! Here and now I give half of my possessions to the poor, and if I have cheated anybody out of anything, I will pay him back four times the amount." (Luke 19:1–8)

That's a pretty big turnaround for a tax collector. Even Samuel, Israel's high priest, promised to give back only what he had taken, not four times what he had taken!

Sometimes the integrity of those who have sinned outshines that of

those who have always taken the high road. In the early 1990s, audiotapes revealed that a group of Texaco executives had racist attitudes and
were systematically denying the hiring and promotion of African Americans. Texaco denied the problem at first, but finally CEO
Peter Bijur decided to take an approach with more integrity. He fired
one of the offending executives, denied retirement benefits to another,
established a plan to hire more African Americans at all levels of the
organization, and settled a lawsuit for $140 million. That's a pretty big
turnaround for an oil executive.

Rick Roscitt of AT&T Solutions might have been tempted to mis-
represent his organization's capabilities, since his new venture represented a huge financial risk for the organization and a personal risk to
his professional future. Although he needed every bit of new business
he could get, he turned away clients he didn't feel he could serve correctly, and admitted errors immediately, without the all-too-common
hemming and hawing. "What inspired me most about Rick was how
honest he was about the business," notes Chief Technology Officer
Dick Anderson. "He wouldn't hesitate to say to a client, 'You know,
we didn't do this right' or 'We don't think we should work for you'
. . . His aim wasn't to smell like a rose all the time, but instead to make
things right." Adds a client, "He engaged us in good faith give and take
. . . he was honest, a man of his word, and courageous, and I'll only
work with a partner like that."[7]

Warren Buffett, who has risen to the top in the rough and tumble
world of investing, notes that lack of honesty can *create* adversity. You
might think that his hiring criteria would be aggressiveness and hard-
headed numbers-crunching. But listen to his real hiring criteria: "integrity, intelligence, and energy. Hire someone without the first, and the
other two will kill you."[8]

The Bible is very specific about doing business honestly: "Do not
have two differing weights in your bag—one heavy, one light. Do not
have two differing measures in your house—one large, one small. You
must have accurate weights and measures, so that you may live long in
the land." (Deut. 25:13–15)

If you want to "live long in the land" of Merrill Lynch, integrity is expected. Chairman Emeritus John Tully called brokers when they made a large "killing" of $2 million or $3 million. "They thought I was calling to congratulate them," he muses. "But I was really calling to ask them a few questions. 'How did you make all that money? If the *New York Times* put how you did it on the front page, would you be proud?' I wanted to remind them of the culture of this firm and I wanted to make sure they lived it."

Tully also made integrity the first order of business in the performance appraisals of the firm's top 200 people. "The first question we always asked was never, 'How much did Dan produce?' It was always, 'Have you ever known Dan to distort or color the truth?' "

Tully also insisted that the firm display its integrity during the 1987 stock market crash. Some firms elected to minimize the damage by "hiding" from their customers during that period. "I said today's going to be a day when we're remembered for how we act. I want you folks to get out there . . . answer the phones, treat your clients with respect, give them good counsel . . . Do what's right for people and . . . you will be awash in clients. It never works the other way around."[9]

Another man who adhered to the same principles of integrity under adversity as Tully but predates him by about four thousand years was Job. You may argue that those Bible leaders had it easy, that they lived in a much less complex world and traded in a few camels, not billions of dollars. The issues of right and wrong were much more clear-cut then, and ethical decisions could be made a lot more easily.

Tell that to the protagonists in the Book of Job. It is one of the longest books in the Bible, an extended debate on integrity, humility, and discipline and how these are to be applied in the "real world."

The "patience of Job" is legendary. What is often forgotten is his integrity. Job was a recipient of every calamity known to God and man. First, he had every single one of his oxen and donkeys carried off by a marauding tribe called the Sabeans, who then "put to the sword" every one of his servants. To compound matters, all his sons and daughters were killed when a windstorm collapsed the house in which they were feasting. Finally, Satan afflicted Job with painful sores "from the soles of his feet to the top of his head. Then Job took a piece of broken pottery and scraped himself with it as he sat among the ashes." (Job 1, 2)

Talk about hitting "rock bottom"! Here is a man whose trials paralleled or surpassed any modern leader's sufferings. He had owned seven thousand sheep, three thousand camels, five hundred yoke of oxen, five hundred donkeys, and a large number of servants. He had lost all seven of his sons and daughters. If any man could be pardoned for temporarily (or permanently) deserting his principles, it would be Job. Even his wife suggested he was a gullible fool for sticking to these principles: "Are you still holding on to your integrity? Curse God and die!" (Job 2:9–10)

But Job repeatedly refused to give up his integrity: "You are talking like a foolish woman. Shall we accept good from God and not trouble? . . . as long as I have life within me . . . my lips will not speak wickedness . . . I will not deny my integrity." (Job 2:10, 27:2–5)

The modern leader may undergo many trials, but few of them as devastating as Job's. In a sense, all that he had left was his integrity, and he was determined to hold onto it. Leaders in all ages should realize that whether the coffers are bulging or empty, whether the flock is increasing or dwindling, integrity is the measure of leadership.

Consider Randall Tobias, CEO of Eli Lilly. When his company went through some difficult times in the mid-1990s, he did not seek a pure mathematical model for cutting costs. He considered the overall impact on the company and on the individuals who had in many cases spent their whole lives working for the company. Rather than dismiss them, he offered early retirement and one year's pay.

Bill Adams, CEO of Armstrong World Industries, takes an extremely personal and proactive approach to integrity at his company. He gives every employee his personal phone number and tells them, "Call me personally if you are ever asked to do something you consider wrong." His motto is not "Let the buyer beware" but "Let the buyer have faith."[10]

But some people never learn. One of the most dishonest men in the Bible is Judas Iscariot, one of Jesus' disciples who betrayed him, mostly out of greed and perhaps also out of jealousy. Judas realized he had none of the healing powers, communication skills, or ability to inspire others positively that his "boss" had. He knew he was never going to be "the boss" or even the boss's right-hand man. But he could make an impact by betraying the man many believe to be the son of God.

Judas' lack of integrity was noticed even before he betrayed Jesus. People who lack integrity usually show it in a variety of situations. At a dinner in Jesus' honor, a woman took a pint of expensive perfume and poured it on Jesus' feet. Guess which disciple objected on the basis of "integrity"? The one who lacked it the most: Judas Iscariot, who complained, " 'Why wasn't this perfume sold and the money given to the poor? It was worth a year's wages.' He did not say this because he cared for the poor but because he was a thief; as keeper of the money bag, he used to help himself to what was put into it." (John 12:4–6)

The example of Judas shows how it takes only one dishonest person or malcontent to severely derail a cooperative effort, particularly when that person is at or near the top.

A modern leader who feigned empathy toward the poor while he was enriching himself at their expense was William Aramony, former CEO of The United Way, the organization that historically has helped the modern equivalent of the widow, the orphan, the blind, the halt, and the lame. Aramony, who was making $400,000 per year, was discovered to have misappropriated a large amount of the organization's funds and resources for his own personal benefit.

ACTING WITH INTEGRITY

Words are not exactly cheap, but actions are dearer. Matthew emphasized that long speeches and "oaths" were not necessary to impress people with one's integrity.

> Do not swear at all: either by heaven, for it is God's throne; or by the earth, for it is his footstool; or by Jerusalem, for it is the city of the Great King. And do not swear by your head, for you cannot make even one hair white or black. Simply let your "Yes" be "Yes" and your "No," "No."
> (Matt. 5:33–37)

In recent years, we have been treated to leaders like Bill Clinton asking interrogators to "clarify" the meaning of the word *is,* and Bill Gates questioning the meaning of the word *concerned.* In the face of obfuscations like these, it is sometimes difficult to believe these men's "yeses" and "nos."

But let's go back a few thousand years, to Nehemiah, whose integrity inspired the people of Judah to rebuild the temple in less than two months. Appointed governor by King Artaxerxes, Nehemiah could have enriched himself and used any means at his disposal to complete the temple. But:

> *Neither I nor my brothers ate the food allotted to the governor. But the earlier governors . . . placed a heavy burden on the people and took forty shekels of silver from them in addition to food and wine. But . . . I did not act like that. Instead I devoted myself to the work on this wall . . . we did not acquire any land . . . Furthermore, a hundred and fifty Jews and officials ate at my table . . . Each day one ox, six choice sheep and some poultry were prepared for me . . . in spite of all this, I never demanded the food allotted to the governor, because the demands were heavy on these people. (Neh. 5:14–18)*

Note that Nehemiah refused to appropriate more than he was entitled to. He didn't even ask for the full amount of what he was entitled to, but shared what he had with his followers. This was for the sake of the morale of the people and for rapid completion of the task. Compare his philosophy to that of Russ Baumgardner, president of Apogee Enterprises, a glass manufacturer cited as one of the one hundred best companies to work for in America: "We pay the taxes that are due. We don't pay more than we owe, but we never cheat the government . . . And as long as we're on the subject, we never cheat our suppliers, or our employees, or our customers."[11]

The prophets were the people who kept the nation of Israel "honest." Again and again the people lost sight of the commandments dealing with honesty and integrity. Again and again, prophets arose to remind them where "true north" lay on the compass when the whole nation was taking a moral turn to the south.

Ezekiel prophesied against false prophets, those with "false words, lying visions . . . and utter lying divinations." (Ezek. 13:8–9) Today we speak of those who "varnish" or "whitewash" the truth by putting a pleasing patina on top of a weak or faulty structure. Several thousand years ago, Ezekiel addressed this universal problem using a very similar analogy:

> *When a flimsy wall is built, they cover it with whitewash, therefore tell those who cover it with whitewash that it is going to fall . . . When it falls, you will be destroyed in it . . . So I will spend my wrath against the wall and against those who covered it with whitewash. I will say to you, "The wall is gone, and so are those who whitewashed it." (Ezek. 13:10–16)*

Ezekiel proclaims there can be no true peace and harmony, either in business or politics, without true honesty and integrity. "Whitewashes" may seem to work in the short run, but they rarely do in the long run.

In 1985, Federal prosecutors charged GE's Re-Entry Systems with a mammoth whitewashing job, claiming they had committed $800,000 in fraud by altering workers' time cards. At first, GE refused to admit guilt, but Jack Welch says, "we got to the point where we concluded that someone did cheat . . . Until we got to that point, we were chasing ourselves around in a circle." He might have added that they were just adding coats of whitewash to a flawed structure. When Welch and GE finally saw that the problem was one of "basic integrity," they admitted their transgressions and set up an ethics program to make sure that the problem was addressed.[12]

The times of Jeremiah the prophet were corrupt, perhaps even more corrupt than America in the late twentieth century! He continuously spoke out about the lack of integrity that permeated the entire society, which did not make him a revered guest of honor at the king's court or banquets. But a leader who points out other leaders' lack of integrity is not necessarily going to be popular in any society or business:

> *Go up and down the streets of Jerusalem, look around and consider, search through her squares. If you can find but one person who deals hon-*

estly and seeks the truth, I will forgive this city. Although they say "As surely as the Lord lives," still they are swearing falsely. (Jer. 5:1–2)

Like the Greek philosopher Diogenes, Jeremiah could not find one honest man in the entire city. But he reasoned that he had looked only among the rank and file, not the exalted and moral heads of the metropolis. But, to a man, "with one accord they too had broken off the yoke and torn off the bonds. Therefore a lion from the forest will attack them, a wolf from the desert will ravage them . . . for their rebellion is great and their backslidings many." (Jer. 5:5–6)

Back then, the likelihood of an actual lion or ravaging wolf was a more literal likelihood, and a more compelling metaphor. Today, lack of honesty and integrity in our business and political leaders has fewer direct physical consequences, but just as great an impact on the business and political climate in our country. The "wolves" and "lions" that attack a leader or company that lacks integrity include loss of purpose, disaffection, and discouragement from the janitorial closet to the boardroom, and ultimately loss of trust from the consumer of the product or service.

Compare the long-term effects of Johnson & Johnson's proactively and voluntarily removing millions of dollars worth of Tylenol from the shelves when a tiny number of cyanide-contaminated containers were discovered with Ford's begrudging acknowledgement (after many articles, Congressional hearings, and speeches by Ralph Nader) that the location of the Mustang's gas tank had been responsible for many fiery deaths. Which company acted with more integrity? Which realized better short- and long-term economic and public relations results?

The prophet Isaiah lived in an era where honesty and integrity were not the foundations of the nation of Israel. He saw a vision of the Lord surrounded by angels, looked down at himself, and realized just how morally far he and his nation had sunk:

" 'Woe to me!' I cried. 'I am ruined! I am a man of unclean lips, and I live among a people of unclean lips.' " (Isa. 6:5)

Isaiah was probably the "cleanest-lipped" guy in town, but even he knew he was lacking. In a corrupt organization, all get corrupted. Once a company gets a reputation for "dirty dealing," even the most honest of its employees get tarred with the same brush. Perhaps Isaiah had nowhere else to go, or perhaps he had a supreme dedication to his people, but he decided to stay and reform the organization, despite the fact that he was preaching his message as forcefully as he could while no one seemed to be listening or responding.

Every organization has at least one Isaiah, someone who reminds the organization of its original mission and principles each time it strays from them. The wise and courageous leader permits the existence of "Isaiahs" as a safety valve and a warning sign. The wisest leaders protect their Isaiahs from harm or even become Isaiahs themselves. Some organizations even have a position called "corporate ombudsman," a person whose role is to challenge the wisdom and integrity of the status quo, which is supported by those in power but may not always be of long-term benefit to the organization.

Over 90 percent of the Fortune 500 have a statement of ethics. But to many, these statements are just writing on the wall. How many operationalize them like Northrup Grumman, which has an ethics department with a full-time staff that trains and counsels employees on the complex and daunting issues often faced in the aerospace industry?[13]

Or consider a CEO who takes it upon himself to be his own "Isaiah." Bill Hewlett of Hewlett-Packard once found the door to a supply room locked. He didn't like what that said about the honesty of the company's employees, so he snapped the lock open with a bolt cutter and left a note that said, "Don't ever lock this door again."[14] That act probably communicated more about company integrity than a hundred speeches at corporate gatherings.

Sir Adrian Cadbury, CEO of a company whose name is associated with sweetness, not toughness, stands firm in his belief that actions, not words, are the key measures of integrity. "The ethical standards of a company are judged by its actions, not by pious statements of intent put out in its name." This is probably a direct criticism of companies that actually hire outside consultants to "design" an "ethics statement," which has little or nothing to do with the way business is actually conducted. A company's true ethics are reflected by "where we stand as individual managers and how we behave when faced with decisions which require us to combine ethical and commercial judgments. What are our personal rules of conduct? Who else will be affected?"[15]

How important is it for leaders to have actions congruent with their stated beliefs and "good intentions"? Don't just ask the head of a chocolate company. Put the question to James, one of the twelve disciples of Jesus: "Anyone who listens to the word but does not do what it says is like a man who looks at his face in a mirror and, after looking at himself, goes away and immediately forgets what he looks like." (James 1:22–24)

SYSTEMS, SAFEGUARDS, STANDARDS

Individuals tend to exercise increased integrity and honesty when the group culture supports these behaviors. It takes very strong individuals to maintain these traits, particularly when they are in a position of power, with no checks, balances, or rules.

The rule of law is repeated many times over in the Bible, as are the actual laws. There are particularly strong warnings about abuses of power by those in high authority, as well as commands for leaders and followers at all levels to behave ethically.

The following passage was written by Moses, centuries before Saul was anointed the first king of Israel. Moses was keenly aware of the potential for abuse of power by any leader, no matter how upright. Therefore, he suggested some safeguards, which we have too often ignored in selecting our modern business and political leaders (or which they have ignored even when they were in place):

The king . . . must not acquire great numbers of horses for himself or make the people return to Egypt to get more of them . . . He must not take too many wives or his heart will be led astray. He must not accumulate large amounts of silver and gold. When he takes the throne of his kingdom, he is to write for himself on a scroll a copy of this law . . . It is to be with him, and he is to read it all the days of his life . . . [He should] not consider himself better than his brothers and turn from the law to the right or the left. (Deut. 17:14–20)

If only our modern business leaders paid more attention to these guidelines! Moses realized what Lord Acton centuries later expressed so succinctly, that "power corrupts and absolute power corrupts absolutely." He recognized the intrinsic threat that too much power might pose to a leader's honesty and integrity. Moses' warning addresses the dangers of greed (too many horses or large amounts of silver and gold can dull a leader's ability to spot injustice in other places), lust (too many wives or affairs can also hurt a leader's judgment and credibility), and arrogance (no leaders, corporate or political, are to hold themselves above the law).

Even kings and CEOs (or perhaps especially kings and CEOs) need written standards and guidelines to help remind them how to act ethically. When Solomon was about to succeed David on the throne of Israel, David's biggest priority and most fervent prayer was for his son to continue his tradition of integrity: "I know, my God, that you test the heart and are pleased with integrity . . . And give my son Solomon the wholehearted devotion to keep your commands, requirements and decrees . . ." (1 Chron. 29:17–19)

A company with a well-developed system of ethics—which is *actually used* rather than merely stated—does not spend a lot of time deciding the ethicality of each decision. In fact, a strong code like Johnson & Johnson's credo makes the decisions easier. An action either fits the code or it doesn't, and the stronger the code and the more often it has been put into practice, the clearer the ethical path.

John Pepper, chairman of Procter & Gamble, believes that "ethical business is good business." Moreover, it tends to attract and retain ethical people.

There are any number of people in this company who came here—and stay here—because of our ethical standards. When we move into places like Eastern Europe and ask new employees why they sought us out, it's wonderful to hear them say, "Because of what you stand for." I remember a former P & G chairman saying if it ever got to a point where we didn't think we could uphold good ethics and stay in a country, we'd leave that country . . . It's wonderful to have things you don't have to talk about. When we are discussing a product and there's something wrong with it, you know it's not up for discussion anymore until it's fixed.[16]

Herb Kelleher, CEO of Southwest Airlines must be sitting in the same tent as Pepper. He also feels that maintaining an ongoing set of ethical standards

. . . makes everything a lot easier. If someone makes a proposal, we don't spend a lot of time on it if it's contrary to our values. We just say, "No, we're not going to do that!" You might be able to make a lot of money, but it doesn't make any difference. It's not what we stand for. We can move quickly and say, "Okay, what's the next item?"[17]

There are probably a lot of business and political leaders who wish they had "moved on to the next item" rather than embarked on a course of action that was ethically questionable. But it takes a set of standards to be able to know when to "move on."

It also helps to "select capable men . . . trustworthy men who hate dishonest gain," Jethro's instructions to Moses in selecting his "officials over thousands, hundreds, fifties and tens." (Exod. 18:21) But just in case a few "bad apples" have fallen into the barrel, it's good to set up a system for detecting and removing them. After the Minuteman nose cone scandal in which they were found guilty of padding payroll records, GE instituted an ethics program, a component of which was a booklet called "The Spirit and the Letter of Our Commitment." The booklet, reproduced in all languages, explained that an ombudsman and hotline had been placed in every facility to field reports of potentially unethical activities. Says Welch, "We tell employees exactly who to call . . . Out of the messes you create new levels of excellence. Something has to come out of every serious event . . . How do you take it to the next step?"[18]

A system of ethics and standards can even cut across seemingly impregnable religious boundaries. Gary Heavin is the founder of Curves for Women, an international franchisor of health clubs for women. Heavin, a conservative Christian, has based his company largely on New Testament principles. But ironically, he has attracted Chasidic Jews as franchisees. Why? "They tell me, 'We appreciate your value system and your integrity. We wouldn't trust someone without a value system.' "[19]

Dennis Bakke and Roger Sant, leaders of AES, a giant electric utility, also feel that the special "buy-in" they get from their employees is based on their value system: "Our main goal . . . was to build a company that embodied the four principles that we felt mattered in any kind of community, be it a business, church, village or whatever: fairness, integrity, social responsibility, and fun."[20] (Who said an ethical company has to be boring?)

WHO'S WATCHING, ANYWAY?

In an old folk tale, a farmer tells his hired man to take a chicken and kill it "where no one can see." The hired man returns in a few hours with a live chicken. "Why didn't you kill it?" asks the farmer. "Everywhere I go, the chicken sees," answers the hired man.

Behind this humorous story is a subtle message: Someone is always watching, even if it is only the victim, the perpetrator, or the perpetrator's conscience. King David's forces were aligned against the forces of his own son, Absalom, who was trying to take over his father's throne a few years before the father was ready to hand it over. (Sounds like a typical family business.) David commanded his troops, "Be gentle with the young man Absalom for my sake." (2 Sam. 5:5) Absalom, riding his mule, got his hair caught in a tree and was hanging by it when a common foot soldier from David's side came upon him, but did not harm him. He reported this to his commander, Joab:

> Joab said to the man, "What? You saw him? Why didn't you strike him to the ground right there? Then I would have had to give you ten shekels of silver and a warrior's belt." But the man replied, "Even if a

thousand shekels were weighted out into my hands, I would not lift my hand against the king's son. In our hearing the king commanded you, 'Protect the young man Absalom for my sake.' " (2 Sam. 18:11–12)

This low-ranking foot soldier showed true integrity, refusing to be swayed by material reward or the wrath of his immediate superior. He knew he was not "alone" in the woods; whatever he did, Absalom (and perhaps a higher power) would see.

The New Testament also has many references to honesty and integrity, such as this passage from Matthew: "Live as though God were watching. Don't do your good deeds in front of men only." I worked in an organization where one work group had put up a sign that said, "Do nothing you would not do if Jesus were coming. Say nothing you would not say if Jesus were coming. Think nothing you would not think if Jesus were coming." The sign was needed, because there was a lot of tension and dissension in the unit, due at least as much to the nature of the work as to the personalities of the people. I can only imagine how the unit would have functioned *without* the sign!

Paul Galvin, former CEO of Motorola, went by this credo: "Tell them the truth, first because it's the right thing to do and second because they'll find out anyway." Whether in the short run or in the long run, dishonesty has a way of being exposed. And often, exposure happens just at the time when its purveyors can least afford it.

Employees are watching, not just in the electronics industry, but in the airlines too. Gordon Bethune took over Continental Airlines at a time when morale and trust were extremely low. He burned the procedures manual, painted the planes, made the first profits the airline had experienced in years, and delivered on a promised $65-per-employee bonus for on-time performance. Employees were watching carefully to see if he could be trusted; any failure to deliver on any of these promises could have spelled the end of Continental's revitalization.

And if you are a leader with a conscience, *you are watching yourself* (you don't need a chicken). Chris Graff, founder of Marque, an Indiana-based ambulance manufacturer, says, "I guess it's just a moral or ethical decision for me. When we make a decision, we should be able to explain that decision in the same way to anybody who asks, be it our spouse, our business partner, an employee, a creditor, or a customer. I have to sleep at night."[21]

James Burke, former CEO of Johnson & Johnson, made many of his biggest decisions based on Johnson & Johnson's famed credo, which has been in effect for almost six decades. The basic message of the credo is: Be straight with your employees, your customers, the public, and yourself, and you will achieve long-term success. During the Tylenol crisis, the company made an ethical decision that before risking even one more life to potential cyanide poisoning, economic sacrifice was necessary. Large amounts of product were destroyed, but Johnson & Johnson was not.

No one could ever accuse Jack Welch of being "soft-headed." But even Welch, the ultimate hardball player, believed that "excellence and competition are totally compatible with honesty and integrity. The A student, the four-minute miler, the high-jump world record holder—all strong winners—can achieve those results without resorting to cheating. People who cheat are simply weak."

Welch was taken aback when almost half of a group of business students, in a hypothetical case situation, said they would deposit $1 million in a Swiss bank account to an agent in order to book a $50 million order. "I was shocked! Shocked! I told the students someone was teaching them the wrong things. This was not one of those cases where you had to interpret the law; this was a simple bribery case."[22]

Bill O'Brien, president of Hanover Insurance, declared that though "once the morals of the workplace seemed to require a level of morality in business that was lower than in other activities, we believe there is no fundamental tradeoff between the higher virtues of life and economic success. We believe we can have both. In fact, we believe that, over the long term, the more we practice the higher virtues of life, the more economic success we will have."[23] At the time he spoke, the company was in the top quartile of its industry and had grown 50 percent faster than the industry standard over a ten-year period.

Honesty and integrity are not easy traits to implement over the long-term, but they've stood the test of time—over 5,000 years if we want to take a true "strategic" (biblical) view of this issue. Frances Hesselbein, former CEO of the Girl Scouts of America has noted that the longest-lasting organizations are usually blessed with leaders who have a sense of ethics and personal integrity. She may have been thinking of the Girl Scouts or century-old companies like Procter & Gamble, but her comments could equally apply to the organizational leaders of the Old and New Testaments.

Whether the time is 5000 B.C. or the twenty-first century, honesty and integrity ensure organizational success in the way it matters most—in the long term!

BIBLICAL LESSONS ON HONESTY AND INTEGRITY

- ❧ People won't follow leaders they think are dishonest.
- ❧ You can't expect honest followers if you model dishonesty.
- ❧ The higher you go, the more visible your integrity or lack of it becomes.
- ❧ "Insignificant" dishonest acts usually beget larger acts of dishonesty.
- ❧ In times of crisis, adversity, and temptation, a leader's integrity becomes most evident.
- ❧ Integrity is exhibited in actions, not pronouncements of intention.
- ❧ Honesty and integrity pay off long-term, though they may involve losses and sacrifices short-term.
- ❧ An organization with an ethical code and system of safeguards can create more consistently honest leaders.
- ❧ Act as if someone else with more power than you is watching.

CHAPTER TWO

Purpose

"Therefore we do not lose heart. Though outwardly we are wasting away, yet inwardly we are being renewed day by day."

—2 COR. 4:16

"I consider my life worth nothing to me . . . if only I may finish the race and complete the task . . ."

—THE DISCIPLE PAUL, ACTS 20:22

ll of us need a purpose. Work without purpose (even if it takes great skill) can become mindless, heartless drudgery. Add purpose, even to so-called grunt work, and our work lives take on an expanded, even inspired dimension.

Noah, a novice shipbuilder if ever there was one, was spurred on by an ennobling purpose—the knowledge that he was going to save enough of the sinful world so that it could continue to survive after the most catastrophic natural disaster it had ever experienced.

Abraham's purpose was to establish and spread the radical belief that there was one God whose spirit permeated and unified the entire universe. Until his time, the universe was thought to be split into many compartments, each of which had its own reigning force or "god."

Moses' great goal was to lead the Hebrews out of Egyptian slavery to the edge of the Promised Land. Joshua's goal was to lead them in. Solomon's was to build a temple, not for his own glory, but for the glory of a higher power and purpose. And the goal of the prophets was that each in his own way would keep an entire nation from straying from its original purpose.

For the modern corporate leader, the ability to formulate a clear, compelling purpose and stay "on purpose" is often the difference between success and failure, between an inspired and inspiring work life and the mere pursuit of profit or a paycheck. All the recent emphasis on mission and vision is something that the leaders of the Bible would have resonated with; indeed, they invented the terms, or at least lived with them daily.

Can you imagine Moses visiting the ten plagues on Pharaoh, fleeing a hostile country with a few bundles of flat bread, and trying to lead thousands of people through a parted sea without having a mission to sustain him and his followers? Steve Jobs of Apple also threw down a gauntlet of purpose to John Sculley when he convinced him to leave Pepsi to join a tiny company with few resources and little name recognition. Jobs did not offer Sculley more money (at least to start) or security. What he offered him was purpose: a chance to change the world. Jobs pointed out that all Sculley was doing was manufacturing more and more "sugar water" at Pepsi, whereas at Apple, he would have the chance to radically change the way the world communicates, learns, and exchanges information.

Of course, Moses did not always have an easy time of it, nor did Sculley or Jobs. Without an ongoing sense of mission and vision, Jobs's failures (such as the Lisa) could have been as demoralizing as the near starvation of the Israelites during forty years in the desert. Jobs was thrown out of the CEO slot in the company he had so courageously created because the company had outgrown his leadership style and business skills. Moses was also denied the honor of leading the Israelites into the Promised Land. Like Jobs, he was a great leader in times of calamity and innovation, but he was not the best man to lead a maturing group to the next stage of its development (and into its new offices).

While wandering in the literal desert (not just the proverbial one) both Moses and his successor, Joshua, had to hang on to their purpose for dear life in the face of physical calamity and psychological doubt. Of course, it helped to have manna from heaven when the food was about to run out. But still the people questioned the wisdom of their course and actively rebelled: "All the Israelites grumbled against Moses and Aaron [Moses' brother], and . . . said, 'If only we had died in Egypt! Or in this desert! . . . We should choose a new leader and go back to Egypt!' Moses and Aaron fell face down in front of the people and Joshua tore his clothes." To these dramatic nonverbal communications, they added some strong verbals: "The land we passed through is exceedingly good." The loyal assembly's reaction? "The whole assembly talked about stoning them." (Num. 14)

The executive triumvirate of Moses, Aaron, and Joshua was able to turn the situation around, but only with a strong appeal to a higher power and a reminder of their purpose. And Moses died there in the desert. Steve Jobs may have been sent into exile, but at least he got a second chance ("Next" indeed, and then more Apples!)

After Joshua had led the Israelites into the Promised Land and accomplished his purpose of settling it, he resoundingly reminded the nation of the continuity of its purpose and the need to carry that purpose to its next stage of development. He urged them to be strong, to obey all that was written in the Book of the Law of Moses, and not to intermarry with other nations or to form too close an alliance with any nation, since that would threaten their identity and, ultimately, their sense of purpose.

A few centuries later, King David's purpose was to consolidate the power of Israel and strengthen it ideologically. In a sense, he was the great builder of corporate culture for the new nation. A renaissance man equally at home with a sword and a harp, he made certain that the kingdom was strong culturally, monetarily, and militarily.

His son, Solomon, further built on that sense of purpose, the manifestation of which was the first temple in Jerusalem. It took seven years to build (presumably longer than any of today's corporate headquarters), but the *process* of building it was just as important to the nation as the actual completion. The mobilization of people and resources was just as galvanizing as the launch of a landmark new product like the Boeing 707.

THINKING BIG

Alan Mullaly was the leader of the team that built that pioneering aircraft. Here is how he describes the experience: "We wanted everyone to feel that, oh boy, building a brand-new airplane would be worth contributing to! The mission has to be bigger than any one of us, and it has to feel good . . . So that became our mission: building the best new airplane we could." One of the engineers of the project noted, "Alan energized us."[1]

Like Solomon, Mullaly wasn't just building a product; he was leading a mission with a purpose. And the best leaders approach all tasks that way. John F. Kennedy galvanized a nation by proclaiming his purpose of landing a man on the moon by the end of the 1960s. Martha Stewart grew her vast culinary/fashion empire from a small catering business, with her ultimate mission in mind from day one. Meg Whitman, founder of eBay, could have been knocked "off purpose" when her computer systems crashed in 1999. Instead, she worked 100-hour weeks for a month until the problem was solved. Fred Smith of Federal Express could easily have been deterred from the Promised Land; his blueprint for the company was dismissed as unworkable when he submitted it to his business school professor. But he intuitively felt that using one airport as a "hub" to achieve twenty-four–hour guaranteed delivery was an idea that would actually work.

When a leader is dedicated to a purpose, and when all the "troops" see that dedication is unwavering and "for real," great things happen. King David, faced with the daunting task of the construction of a temple, handed it over to his son Solomon, who admittedly lacked experience in the construction business. But David had also given himself wholeheartedly to this project: "With all my resources have I provided for the temple . . . gold for the gold work, silver for the silver . . . bronze . . . iron . . . onyx . . . stones of various colors. Besides I now give my personal treasures of gold and silver, over and above everything I have provided for this holy temple . . . Now who is going to consecrate himself today to the Lord?" (1 Chron. 29:2–5)

What David really meant was, "Who is going to follow my example

and give of their wealth and labor to help build this temple?" And
because he put his money where his purpose was (like Fred Smith of
Federal Express, who invested large amounts of his own money), he got
a tremendous response: "Then the leaders of the families, the officers of
the tribes . . . the commanders of the thousands and commanders of
hundreds . . . gave willingly. They gave toward the work on the temple
. . . five thousand talents . . . of gold, ten thousand talents of silver . . .
eighteen thousand talents of bronze . . . The people rejoiced at the
willing response of their leaders . . ." (1 Chron. 29:6–9)

No leader ever unified the efforts of thousands of people or raised
large amounts of capital without an unwavering sense of purpose. King
David serves as a shining example.

PURPOSE AND MODERN BUSINESS

But are we "pushing the analogy" a little too far? Can today's prag-
matic, secular business leader be compared to a biblical prophet or king?
Aren't most executives' "purposes" focused squarely on the bottom
line, with such intangibles as group solidarity, "mission," and "vision"
placed firmly at the rear?

Not always. Herb Kelleher, CEO of Southwest Airlines, says his vision is to have a company where "kindness and the human spirit are
nurtured," where you "do what your customers want and are happy in
your work." Of course, this is backed up by tremendous effort and a
carefully conceived niche strategy: a low-cost airline connecting out-
of-the-way routes with a minimum of frills. At Southwest, a rational
plan and an inspirational vision add up to one tremendously potent
purpose.

We all know that Herb is not exactly your typical Rotarian. But he
is not the only business leader who talks about Purpose with a capital P,
meaning it is about more than just profit. Consider the philosophy of
Konosuke Matsushita, founder of the giant Japanese conglomerate that
bears his name: "The mission of a manufacturer should be to overcome
poverty, to relieve society as a whole from misery, and bring it wealth."

Further, it should contribute to the "progress and development of society and the well-being of people . . . thereby enhancing the quality of life throughout the world."[2]

Matsushita's first really successful product was a bicycle light in the 1920s. Perhaps his purpose at that time was to make the world's best bicycle light. He could not have built his multibillion-dollar business empire without having developed a larger purpose.

"A" PLAYERS WITH AUDACIOUS GOALS

Jack Welch of GE wrote that the effective leader leads through a vision. Like King David, he constantly sought to field teams of "A" players. Central to being an "A" player is a sense of purpose: "At the leadership level, an 'A' is a man or woman with a vision and the ability to articulate that vision to the team, so vividly and powerfully that it becomes their vision."[3]

The Bible is full of A's, all of whom had a specific role to play in forwarding the purpose of their people. If you look closely at what each accomplished, you will agree that most of the leaders of the Bible committed themselves to what James Collins and Jerry Porras call BHAGs (Big Hairy Audacious Goals), in their book *Built to Last* (a title that certainly applies to the Judeo-Christian tradition and the Bible itself). The Bible abounds with players who would have easily qualified for Jack Welch's "A" team. And each of these A's has modern counterparts who also dare to challenge the limits of the possible and sometimes accomplish the seemingly impossible. Our modern leaders often have to cross the Red Sea, navigate vast wildernesses, and fight off larger, better-equipped armies before they are able to march into the Promised Land.

Daniel was a man with unshakeable purpose. He worshiped the God he believed in despite the punishment he knew he would receive for it. He believed the Lord would deliver him from the lions' den, but he vowed he would keep his faith in the Lord and maintain his purpose even if he was *not* delivered.

For Daniel's modern counterpart, listen to CEO Ralph Larsen of Johnson & Johnson, talking similarly about his company's core values: "The core values embodied in our credo might be a competitive advantage, but that is not *why* we have them. We have them because they define for us what we stand for, and we would hold them even if they became a competitive disadvantage for us in certain situations."

Being a Jew and believing in one God rather than a collection of idols was not a particular competitive advantage for Daniel in idolatrous, corrupt Babylon. But his purpose was unwavering, and it carried him even when it did not seem to have a likely short-term payoff. Several thousand years later, Daniel's "organization" is still thriving. Can anyone today find an airline route (or even a bus route) to a kingdom called "Babylon"? Johnson & Johnson, which has sustained substantial short-term losses through its devotion to its "credo," has also outlasted and out-profited many of its competitors.

MODERN LEADERS, TIMELESS PURPOSE

Fortunately, many modern companies have purposes that sustain them, perhaps not as strongly as Daniel's purpose, but with more staying power than Nebuchednezzar's. These purposes often go far beyond the mere provision of a product or service. Herman Miller's former chairman, Max De Pree wrote, "My goal is that when people look at us . . . not as a corporation but as a group of people working intimately within a covenantal relationship, they'll say, 'These folks are a gift to the spirit.' " His successor, J. Kermit Campbell, adds that the company's true mission is not to create products but to "liberate the human spirit."[4]

Supercomputer company Cray Research's CEO, John Rollwagen, likens working at Cray to being on "a mission for God." The comparison is apt when you consider the goals of many of the company's activities: to help cure AIDS, to patch up the hole in the ozone layer, to simulate car crashes without actually crashing cars, saving thousands of lives in the process. Says Vice President Deborah Barber, "It's different than attaching yourself to a tube of toothpaste."[5]

Tell that to Tom Chappell, creator of the world's leading "alternative toothpaste," Tom's of Maine. Chappell is definitely a "man on a mission," and Tom's of Maine is a "toothpaste with a mission." If Ben & Jerry's is about much more than ice cream, Tom's of Maine is about much more than toothpaste. Once a month, the whole company spends half a day focusing on one aspect of their mission: diversity, profitability, and the environment. The cost to the company? Some $75,000 in lost production time. "And it's worth every penny," says Chappell.

What exactly is gained? First of all, the company gains a lot of very practical recommendations for improving the operation while keeping it "on course." Secondly, it boosts morale, builds teamwork, and shows that the company practices what it preaches. Says Chappell, "When we need to call upon the reserves of our people—to dig in deeper, meet extraordinary goals—we can expect it here." These people aren't attaching themselves to a tube of toothpaste, they're attaching themselves to a larger business and social mission.[6]

In 1991, Larry Bossidy, CEO of Allied Signal, found himself in a position similar to that of Moses. The company lacked purpose, morale was suffering, and the bottom line was showing it. Like Moses, Bossidy had to take some drastic action and ask his people to make some hard sacrifices. No, he did not ask them to wander in the desert for forty years subsisting on matzoh and manna. But he did cut $225 million in capital spending, sold some divisions, and cut 6,200 jobs.

What made Allied Signal's people want to make these sacrifices? Bossidy's sense of purpose. *Fortune* magazine noted that Bossidy was able to paint a picture of the future as compelling as the one Moses had painted for the Israelites. The remaining employees "could see the Promised Land and know when they got there."[7] Bossidy made sure he constantly communicated his purpose to all levels of the company. And unlike Moses, he was able to "cross over" with his troops.

Moses' leadership capabilities did not just stem from a dynamic personality or communication style (indeed, he was "slow of tongue" and often needed his brother Aaron to speak for him). He had a tremendous well of power and purpose because he had been handed the law by a powerful figure. Wise corporate leaders also realize that they must codify their purpose if it is to go beyond the mere cult of personality and become a sustaining vision for the entire organization.

Listen to Emily Duncan, director of global diversity and work life, as she describes the power of a common purpose at Hewlett-Packard: "We have been fortunate at Hewlett-Packard, because we have had the strength of the HP way to help us cope . . . It represents our deeply held values, shared practices, and policies that have always guided the company." Those values? "Trust and respect for the individual, high achievement, uncompromising integrity, teamwork . . ."[8] Note that the loyalty is to the values and the overall purpose, not to the company founders themselves.

PURPOSE MEANS COMMITMENT TO THE RIGHT PRIORITIES

"What good is it if a man gains the world but forfeits his soul?" This quote from Matthew reminds us that for many leaders and companies, the ultimate success is not just in "the numbers" or even the spread of a radical new product or concept. Anita Roddick, CEO of The Body Shop, felt that a purpose of being merely "the biggest or the most profitable" would not sustain her company or inspire the employees to reach the ambitious goals the company has attained.

Says Roddick, "If your aspirations come from the values of your culture or church or temple or mosque, you have something beyond your livelihood creation. You're coming to work not as a nine-to-five sort of death but a nine-to-five sort of living." (Actually, it's about as hard to imagine Roddick's troops sticking to a nine-to-five schedule as it is to imagine the troops at Jericho announcing that they were not about to blow any rams' horns, thank you, because they had already marched around the city several times, they were tired, and it was quitting time.)

What is Roddick's purpose, which has driven the growth of The Body Shop and created incredibly loyal customers and supremely motivated employees? It is the creation of products that are natural and whose production protects rather than destroys the ecosystem, a belief that women are already beautiful and do not need artificial products to enhance that beauty, and a devotion to empowering the employees and customers (almost all of whom are women) rather than manipulating their insecurities about their appearance.

When Roddick talks about mission and purpose, she barely mentions products: "What has kept us going from all regions of the world . . . is our common set of values—our human rights campaigning, our social justice. That's the glue that keeps us together."[9]

Another aspect of purpose is a "no-exit strategy." When you truly believe in a purpose, you don't look for a back door (or a side door) to make your escape when the going gets rough. Daniel didn't enter the lions' den and then immediately look for the emergency exit in case the Lord couldn't pull him through. And many modern leaders founded their businesses with the same "no exit" attitude. Steve Jobs had a mission to make computers enjoyable and accessible to the general public at a time when only "geeks" could really run or enjoy computers. Bill Gates envisioned "a computer on every desk in every home, running Microsoft software." It is hard to conceive what Jobs and Gates would be doing today if they had failed. Their "no exit" strategy meant that they themselves could not conceive of such an outcome!

PEOPLE AS A PRIORITY

Many of the leaders in the Bible found their purpose in saving individuals or large groups of people from suffering and death. The Book of Esther tells us about a beautiful Jewish maiden who became Queen of Persia when she found favor with King Xerxes. She was chosen not just for her youth and beauty (she was little more than an adolescent, as were many leaders and heroes of the Bible). Ironically, she was also chosen for her obedience: The previous queen had been dethroned and exiled because she refused to appear when the king commanded.

The "irony" is that this young woman was thrust into a royal position so that she could risk it all to save her people. Haman, the king's evil prime minister, had hatched a plot to exterminate all the Jews, after he had been insulted by the Jew Mordechai, Esther's cousin. Mordechai's crime? Holding fast to his purpose, he refused to bow down to Haman and would bow down only to God.

Mordechai knew that there was only one person in the entire kingdom who could save the Jews—his cousin, the newly appointed queen. He also knew that she would have to have a strong sense of purpose to accomplish her mission. After all, the previous queen had been exiled for daring to assert herself in the smallest way. Esther could have taken the easy way out by hiding her Jewish identity, letting her people be destroyed but continuing to live royally herself.

Mordechai appealed to his young cousin's larger sense of purpose and destiny. His inspirational speech to her called her to a higher purpose, much like Steve Jobs asking John Sculley if he wanted to be remembered for sugar water or for revolutionizing the way people communicate: "If you remain silent at this time . . . you and your father's family will perish. And who knows but that you have come to royal position for such a time as this?" (Esther 4:14)

The young queen immediately responded to the challenge of purpose. "I will go to the king, even though it is against the law. If I perish, I perish." (Esther 4:16) She alerted the king to Haman's plot against her people. The king, no doubt moved by the purposefulness and bravery of his young wife (not to mention her beauty), hanged Haman on the very gallows that Haman had intended for Mordechai. Esther had saved the lives of thousands of people and the future of a great nation.

A modern example of someone who also saved the lives of thousands of people, even when those people were in far-away lands and there was (believe it or not) little or no chance to make a profit is Roy Vagelos, ex-chairman of Merck. Vagelos was not saving anyone he knew personally when he decided to develop Mectizan, a drug to cure "river blindness" (onchocerciasis), a disease peculiar to river regions of Africa, which resulted in "crocodile skin," lesions, and ultimately, blindness. Whole villages were devastated by this scourge, and often people committed suicide rather than suffer the disease.

Ironically, the people of these villages were so poor they could not even afford the small cost of the drug Merck proposed to develop. Merck typically discontinued research on a drug if it was expected to earn only $20 million or less in its first year. Here was a drug whose target market was completely impoverished. Clinical trials were risky and had many obstacles, both scientific and political. The World Health Organization refused to fund the trials and, because the affected areas were so remote, on-site testing was impossible. So Vagelos decided to develop the drug and give it away to the villagers!

Pharmaceutical companies have become the targets of criticism because their "purpose" often appears to be making money first and healing second. Vagelos and Merck made absolutely no profit on their cure for river blindness. But they established themselves as a company with a heart and with a purpose. Vagelos explained that Merck had introduced streptomycin (forsaking profit) into Japan four decades earlier and helped eliminate tuberculosis in that country and added, "It's no accident that Merck is the largest American pharmaceutical company in Japan today." Queen Esther qualifies as a Bible hero and a leader because she saved the future of her own people. Vagelos and Merck stand out as modern business heroes for saving the lives and futures of people not their "own."

In the best companies, the purpose continues, even when the leadership changes, as it inevitably must. The Israelites' basic purpose remained constant even as the leadership passed from Joseph to Moses to Joshua to David and Solomon. Ray Gilmartin, Vagelos's successor, has continued Merck's sense of purpose. Upon assuming the helm, Gilmartin studied the company's core values as espoused by George Merck, the founder and CEO from 1925 to 1950. "One of the things he said was, 'Medicine is for the people and not for profits. If you remember that, the profits will follow.' And the more we remember that, the more profits we have made."

Gilmartin has put this purpose into actions, such as pricing an AIDS

drug affordably so that it is accessible to more suffering people. "*Fortune*
has consistently ranked Merck as one of the best companies to work for
and in their summary they said employees liked the fact that we are
working toward a higher purpose," says Gilmartin. "So not only do we
talk about this stuff having a higher purpose, we base our actions on
it."[10]

Another company with a strong sense of purpose is Medtronic.
Founder Earl Bakken, who is also described as "still the spiritual leader
or 'soul' of Medtronic" even after his retirement, first stated that the
company's purpose was "to restore people to the fullness of health and
life." Medtronic's 9,000 employees are devoted to "full health, quality
products, personal worth of employees, fair profit and good citizen-
ship." That's a lot more "purpose" than just "making a profit" or manufacturing pills. Says current CEO Bill George, "At Medtronic, we
don't mix religion and business, but we certainly do not shy away from
the spiritual side of our work and the deeper meaning of our mission to
save lives."[11]

PURPOSE: GALVANIZING FORCE, COMPETITIVE ADVANTAGE

King David also had a purpose—to ascend to the throne of Israel and to
further his country's political and cultural ascendancy. Ironically, David
began his political career as an outcast. He was driven away from the
palace by Israel's first king, Saul, who, motivated by jealousy, vowed
not only to keep David from succeeding him but also to kill him if he
could ever catch up with him again.

David needed supporters and companions if he was ever to achieve
his purpose of ascending to the throne and forwarding the interests of
the nation. He was able to assemble a group of four hundred "mighty
men." This was a ragtag crew, most of them outcasts who were low in
political power and influence, but they were high in purpose and desire.
And the person with the highest purpose and desire was David himself.

Many times King Saul pursued him with intent to kill, and every time David escaped. Eventually, he succeeded Saul as king of Israel, even winning over Saul's son Jonathan as his strongest ally.

For a modern-day David with an equally ragtag group of "mighty men" (and women) who were transformed by purpose, we can turn to Jack Stack of Springfield Remanufacturing. When Stack was dispatched to this antiquated manufacturing facility in a remote area of Missouri, the staff was demoralized and purposeless. The facility had twenty days to ship an order of 800 tractors to the Soviet Union, with a huge cash penalty to the company if the order was not delivered. Up to that point they had been turning out tractors at the rate of five per day!

Stack did what King David had done. He "shared the mess." Like David challenging his "mighty men" to help him take over the kingdom, Stack held out a goal: 800 tractors in twenty days. He didn't minimize the difficulties; he acknowledged them and gave his people freedom in deciding how to overcome them. He freed them from the rigid job descriptions in effect at the plant and helped them to become more of a team with a unifying purpose.

What happened was a miracle similar to that of the loaves and the fishes or a poor shepherd boy's ascendancy to the throne of Israel. With limited resources and the same "ragtag" group that had been making five tractors a day, Stack's "mighty men and women" assembled and shipped over forty tractors per day to meet their goal. Like David, Stack had no choice but to rely on his people to join his sense of purpose: "People participate in something larger than themselves, something that has a powerful meaning, both individually and collectively." One of Stack's "mighty men" put it this way: "I'm not just a name on a time card. I'm a person, and what I have to say means something. I matter."[12]

Purpose is often manifested in physical acts. Hezekiah was a young king who ascended the throne of Israel at age 25. His father, King Ahaz, had strayed dramatically from the original purpose of his people. He even ordered his own sons to be sacrificed to placate the idols Baal and Molech.

Hezekiah, one of the sons spared this sacrifice, realized that strong symbolic measures were necessary to put the people of Israel back "on purpose." The first thing he did was to open the doors of the temple and repair them. This was not just the repairing of pieces of wood; it was a rededication of purpose. He then exhorted his subjects: "Listen to me, Levites! Consecrate yourselves now and consecrate the temple of the Lord . . . remove all defilement from the sanctuary." (2 Chron. 29:1–11) Many of the sacred items had become impure or unclean, and Hezekiah wanted to restore the temple to its former level of cleanliness.

For a modern parallel, let's segue for a moment to the "golden arches" of McDonald's, the modern version of a fast-food "temple." If there was one thing Chairman Ray Kroc couldn't stand to see, it was the defilement of one of his temples because it deviated from the cleanliness standards for which his chain had become known throughout the world.

One day, Kroc drove into a McDonald's franchise near corporate headquarters in Oakbrook, Illinois and observed a strong deviation from McDonald's purpose of offering an attractive, sanitary environment. The flowering bushes were littered with paper cups, Happy Meal boxes, napkins, and other trash. The manager was not present, so Kroc had the assistant manager call the manager in from his house. More than a little shocked, the manager asked Kroc what he could do for him. Kroc's answer: "Look, we don't want trash around our sites!" That's a simple but effective statement of purpose from the head of a multibillion-dollar corporation to the manager of a unit. An even more effective statement was Kroc himself helping the manager to pick up the trash.[13]

Whether it's young Jack Stack, young King Hezekiah, or old Ray Kroc, when the right leader shows commitment to purpose in the right way, people respond emphatically. We've seen how the unit manager at McDonald's responded to Ray Kroc's leadership. Here's how the Israelites responded to Hezekiah: "Then these Levites set to work. They brought out of the courtyard . . . everything unclean that they found in the temple of the Lord." They purified the entire temple and all the articles in it: "We have prepared and consecrated all the articles that King Ahaz removed in his unfaithfulness . . . they are now in front of the Lord's altar." No trash in front of or in that site either!

King Hezekiah also knew the power of ritual in establishing purpose: "As the offering began, singing to the Lord began also, accompanied by trumpets . . . The whole assembly bowed in worship, while the singers sang and the trumpeters played. All this continued until the sacrifice of the burnt offering was completed." (2 Chron. 29)

Anyone who has ever been to a sales meeting or corporate "pep rally" can see some parallels here. The clothes are different (Brooks Brothers and Armanis rather than linen robes), as are the musical instruments, and hopefully there are fewer live sacrifices. But the major commonality remains: dedication to and celebration of purpose.

Nehemiah was another biblical leader with a purpose: to rebuild the wall of Jerusalem, and with it the will of its people. The wall had been destroyed while the Hebrews were in exile. In rebuilding the wall, Nehemiah would also be rebuilding the symbol and fabric of a nation. "Then I said . . . 'You see the trouble we are in: Jerusalem lies in ruins, and its gates have been burned with fire. Come, let us rebuild the wall of Jerusalem, and we will no longer be in disgrace . . .' They replied, 'Let us start rebuilding.' " (Neh. 2:17–19)

This could be the battle cry of any corporation or team that has suffered a disastrous setback (like IBM in the late 1980s and early 1990s, or the Chicago Bulls after Michael Jordan).

OBSTACLES: TESTS OF PURPOSE

But few great purposes are accomplished without obstacles or opposition. Nehemiah encountered both. The colonial officials in Jerusalem ridiculed and opposed Nehemiah's efforts to rebuild the wall. Tobiah the Ammonite chortled, "What they are building—if even a fox climbed up on it, he would break down their wall of stones." And Sanballat the Horonite chimed in, "What are those feeble Jews doing? . . . Can they bring the stones back to life from those heaps of rubble—burned as they are?" (Neh. 4:2–3) Which just goes to show you that if your purpose is good and worthwhile, you will probably have some vocal opponents.

Nehemiah knew that he alone could not accomplish his purpose of rebuilding the wall; he needed to strengthen the purpose of the entire team. This he did by reminding them that they were not just rebuilding a wall, they were rebuilding and defending their families and a nation. He posted them by families, with their swords, spears, and bows. "After I looked things over, I stood up and said to . . . the people, 'Don't be afraid of them. Remember the Lord, who is great and awesome, and fight for your brothers, your sons and your daughters, your wives and your homes.' " (Neh. 4:14)

Nehemiah was also willing to forgo the corporate "perks" of his day in order to attain his purpose. Too many of our modern leaders have been sidetracked from their purpose by the lure of corporate jets and exorbitant bonuses; even biblical leaders could be distracted by the lure of increasing their lands or their herds. Not Nehemiah. He stayed "on purpose." Out of reverence for the Lord, he did not lord it over others or acquire large amounts of money, food, or land. "Instead, I devoted myself to the work on this wall. All my men were assembled there for the work; we did not acquire any land." (Neh. 5:16) With the help of a purposeful team, Nehemiah completed the wall in fifty-two days. Not only did he galvanize the Hebrews, his accomplishment of purpose demoralized the competition: "When all our enemies heard about this, all the surrounding nations were afraid and lost their self-confidence. . . ." (Neh. 6:16)

Another "David" who rose to challenge the "Goliaths" in its industry is the world's quirkiest (but probably most "on purpose") ice cream company, Ben & Jerry's. At first, all they wanted to do was have fun and survive (which is extremely difficult when you are selling ice cream in one of the coldest climates in America, you're working out of a converted garage, and you have extremely limited business knowledge).

As they grew, however, they expanded their purpose. In fact, they expanded it too much; the purpose became diffuse. They found that in trying to focus on too many areas, they were diluting their overall purpose. Originally, Ben & Jerry's had four different social agendas: the environment, agriculture, economic opportunities, and children and families. They were literally trying to "save the world." They certainly have not deserted any of these purposes, but they consolidated the mission to focus on the last one, children and families. Of course, they have not lost sight of the overriding business purpose of the company, which is to make a high-quality ice cream with a whimsical aura, and to have fun and make a profit doing it.

ADVERSITY CREATES PURPOSE

In the Bible, no one had harder obstacles to overcome than the prophets and the disciples. The prophets cried out to the larger society when it was wandering from the path of justice, righteousness, and monotheism and moving toward corruption and idol-worship. The disciples were spreading the gospel of a man who had been crucified by the Roman Empire as a traitor and revolutionary, and whose ideas radically challenged the religious orthodoxy in Jerusalem.

For this very reason, the prophets and disciples needed more strength of purpose than the average citizen of Palestine, who just "went with the trends," whether they were monotheism, idol-worship, or obedience (feigned or real) to the higher authorities—be they indigenous or foreign masters. The disciple Paul offers us some stirring examples of that strength of purpose:

> *But one thing I do: Forgetting what is behind and straining toward what is ahead, I press on toward the goal. (Phil. 3:12–14)*
>
> *Therefore we do not lose heart. Though outwardly we are wasting away, yet inwardly we are being renewed day by day. So we fix our eyes not on what is seen, but what is unseen . . . We commend ourselves in troubles, hardships, beatings, and in the good. (2 Cor. 4)*
>
> *No discipline seems pleasant at the time, but painful. Later on, however, it produces a harvest of righteousness and peace for those who have been trained by it. Therefore strengthen your feeble arms and weak knees. (Heb. 12:11–12)*

The modern leader may not be subjected to bodily harm and threat of death, as were the prophets and disciples, but there is no shortage of daunting obstacles for a line manager or CEO. Without a sense of purpose, it is easy to be overcome by these obstacles.

Gordon Bethune took over Continental Airlines when it definitely needed a prophet and a savior. The airline's on-time performance was among the worst in the industry. The organization was "off purpose." Pilots were flying at slower speeds and skimping on air conditioning to save fuel, making the on-time record even worse, and leaving customers "late, hot, and mad."

Bethune quickly re-established purpose. He offered every employee a $65 bonus for better on-time performance each month. This seems like merely a symbolic bonus, but that's what the employees needed—a symbol of purpose, not just "more money." The employees knew what to do to make Continental an "on-time" airline, they just needed the direction to make it happen. Within a few months, Continental had the best on-time record in the industry.

Bethune maintained that it all boiled down to unity of purpose. "There is no autopilot for success. You can't take your eye off the ball. The good news is that it's a pretty simple thing to keep doing just as long as you don't forget about it."[14] It may be "simple," but it isn't always easy. Bethune had to let go a large portion of the management team, overcome a huge amount of negativism and cynicism, and turn the Continental culture around 180 degrees. Continental became a thriving airline with an excellent on-time performance record.

LEADERS WITHOUT PURPOSE

The Bible gives us several examples of "leaders" whose sense of purpose did not extend beyond themselves. A case can be made that despite their talents and strengths, such people are not really leaders at all. Their modern counterparts are those "leaders" whose main "purpose" is pure material gain and personal aggrandizement.

Esau, son of Isaac and Rebecca, is one example of a man whose carnal appetites and lack of purpose disqualified him as a leader and left the field open for his physically weaker but stronger-purposed twin brother, Jacob. Returning from the hunt famished, he traded his birthright as the oldest son for a pot of stew his brother had cagily simmered for him. No amount of rage or revenge could reclaim that birthright.

Samson was a man whose main purpose was pleasure. Here was a person of great physical strength but of total selfishness of purpose. His largest pleasures were sex with various women and his ability to best others in often pointless physical combat. Samson's first action when we meet him in Judges 14 is an act of pure lust (an affliction that has sidetracked many a leader, both biblical and modern). Samson said to his father and mother, "I have seen a Philistine woman in Timnah; now get her for me as my wife." This was not the "nice Jewish girl" Samson's parents had in mind, nor was this to be a union based on mutual respect and love. It was the beginning of a series of affairs that led to Samson's betrayal and death.

Samson was not a leader of his people. The Bible says nothing of his organizational or inspirational abilities. He left no legacy except revenge and destruction. He killed 1,000 men with the jawbone of an ass, and after his betrayal by Delilah and subsequent blinding, he brought down the temple on the heads of thousands of his enemies. Even his last act was one of self-destruction, since he also brought the temple down on himself.

A modern-day Samson is "Chainsaw Al" Dunlap, who specialized in "saving" companies by destroying them. At Sunbeam, Dunlap pursued one purpose and one purpose only: maximization of the bottom line. To do this, he chopped personnel with the same enthusiasm that "Jawbone Samson" had knocked out 1,000 men. Like Samson, Dunlap left no unifying legacy of purpose on which Sunbeam could build and continue, and no team to carry on his work. He simply moved on to the next company to pursue his own individual glory and gain.

Michael Milken is a more complex character than Al Dunlap. Although to many of us the purpose of Drexel Burnham Lambert may have seemed to be based largely on the enrichment of Milken, he was sustained by the belief that he was increasing the wealth of all who bought the stocks he was proffering. And when he was found guilty of insider trading, he paid the financial price and served a prison term, facing the consequences with more grace and contriteness than either Al Dunlap or Samson. And he also developed a broader sense of purpose that went beyond himself. Upon release from prison, Milken set up a foundation to combat prostate cancer and also founded an organization that is dedicated to improving education using the Internet.

THE SEARCH FOR PURPOSE

A great manager motivates others through a sense of purpose. But purpose often takes shape as one progresses on a journey; it's not always entirely visible or self-evident at the start. And often, the individual acts that lead to the accomplishment of purpose are rather mundane.

Remember Nehemiah leading the effort to rebuild the wall around Jerusalem? He wasn't just repairing a wall. He convinced the Israelites that they were reviving a nation, preserving their religion and culture, and protecting the lives and well-being of their families.

We are all familiar with the story of the workmen who were cutting stone and were asked what they were doing. One answered, "I am cutting stone." Another answered, "I am building a cathedral." One manager who constantly reminds his employees that they are building a cathedral and not just cutting stone is William Pollard, CEO of Service-Master, a company whose "lofty" daily activities consist of cleaning toilets, killing bugs, and cleaning carpets.

But Pollard sees these activities in the context of a higher purpose and constantly communicates this purpose to the employees. "People want to contribute to a higher cause, not just earn a living," he notes. "When we create alignment between the mission of the firm and the cause of its people . . . we unleash a creative power that results in quality service . . . and the development of the people who do the serving." ServiceMaster's mission statement? "To honor God in all we do, to help people develop, to pursue excellence and to grow profitably."

That's a pretty lofty mission statement for a group of housekeepers and janitors. But they are making the connection between that mission statement and their daily work. Shirley Nelson, a ServiceMaster housekeeper in a 250-bed hospital, still maintains a sense of purpose after fifteen years on the job because she sees herself not as "mopping floors" but as directly contributing to the health of the patients. "If we don't clean with a quality effort, we can't keep the doctors and nurses in business. We can't serve the patients. This place would be closed if we didn't have housekeeping."[15]

Brad Hill, a senior consultant with the Hay Group, structures incentive programs for the most unlikely of populations: hourly workers. Where does Hill get his sense of purpose? From watching the sufferings of his grandfather, a coal miner who had a nervous breakdown from lack of purpose and who frequently commented, "I'll never be anything but a damned coal miner." "He never had a sense of purpose," observes Hill, "a sense that his work and his life were worth something."

Hill designs gain-sharing plans to measure and reward performance for employees at the lowest level of the organization, people like his grandfather, who formerly were totally isolated from the organization's purpose and who were seldom rewarded when that purpose was accomplished. Brad Hill is accomplishing his purpose of linking *others* to purpose. Says a food safety inspector at one of his client companies, "Now I have the feeling that this is my company too."[16]

Gary Heavin is the CEO of one of the fastest-growing franchises in the United States, Curves for Women, which was ranked as the third best franchise in the January 2002 issue of *Entrepreneur* magazine. This women-only fitness center franchise started out with one location just six years ago, going to 250 the next. "This year [2002], we'll finish with 5,000 units," says Heavin.

Ironically, Heavin says, "I was forty years old before I realized what my purpose was." At age thirteen, Heavin walked into his mother's bedroom one morning to find her dead. She had suffered from high blood pressure and other illnesses that could have been cured by better diet and a program of exercise. Curves for Women was founded so that hundreds of thousands of women can live healthier, longer lives.

Curves for Women has expanded so rapidly that it is now international. "I did an interview in Spain, where we are building a strong franchise network," says Heavin. "I told the reporter, 'Our goal is to catch McDonald's—they export high-fat foods, we're going to export health.' "[17]

None of the leaders discussed in this chapter, whether biblical or corporate, had an "easy" time of it. Purpose is so important because running a business or leading a group of people is fraught with obstacles and difficulties. If the goal is not mapped out in clear, desirable terms, the obstacles frequently blot it from view.

The Bible is full of exhortations to stay "on purpose":

> "We boast about your perseverance and faith in all the persecutions you are enduring . . . So then, brothers, stand firm and hold on to the teachings we passed on to you, whether by word of mouth or by letter." (Paul's letter to the believers in Thessalonica, who were becoming so impatient for Christ's second coming that they had ceased working and were simply waiting, 2 Thess. 1:4)
>
> "Let us run with perseverance the race marked out for us . . ." (Heb. 12:1–3)
>
> "And now, compelled by the Holy spirit . . . I am going to Jerusalem, not knowing what will happen to me . . . I consider my life worth nothing to me . . . if only I may finish the race and complete the task." (Paul, quoted in Acts 20:22–24)

Today's modern business leaders, especially those who have achieved Big Hairy Audacious Goals, all have their own strong sense of purpose, with which they are able to inspire their followers:

> "A Coke within arm's reach of everyone on the planet." (Roberto Goizueta, former CEO, Coca-Cola)
>
> "To become the company most known for changing the worldwide poor quality image of Japanese products." (Sony mission statement)
>
> "A computer on every desk in every home, running Microsoft software." (Bill Gates)
>
> "I feel like every day I'm . . . working to preserve the rainforests." (Maureen Martin, communications coordinator, Ben & Jerry's)

Our best modern experts on management have constantly emphasized the steadying role of purpose (often using terms like *vision* and
mission) in achieving organizational success:

> *"The single defining quality of leaders is their ability to create and
> realize a vision." (Warren Bennis)*
>
> *"All the leaders I know have a strongly defined sense of purpose. And
> when you have an organization where the people are aligned behind a
> clearly defined vision or purpose, you get a powerful organization." (Mar-
> shall Loeb)*
>
> *"Detached from values, money may indeed be the root of all evil.
> Linked to social purpose, it can be the root of opportunity." (Rosabeth
> Moss Kanter)*

When we read quotes like these, we may first think of Bill Gates,
Steve Jobs, Ben Cohen and Jerry Greenfield, and Roberto Goizueta.
The managers of the Bible did not have the benefit of modern manage-
ment consultants and business theorists. But they intuitively knew that
dedication to purpose was the secret of organizational and individual
success. The above quotes could just as easily have been written (in
Aramaic or Hebrew, of course) by Moses, Nehemiah, Queen Esther,
King Hezekiah, or the apostle Paul. Fortunately, their original message
of purpose and mission has been preserved in the pages of the Bible.
You just have to know where to look.

BIBLICAL LESSONS ON PURPOSE

- ∞ Purpose can empower people to reach greater goals than they
  ever thought possible.

- ∞ Great goals are seldom achieved without confronting internal
  obstacles and external opposition.

❧ Adversity can quickly stop a leader who lacks purpose, but it only "fans the flames" of leaders with a strong purpose.

❧ Think big. Even if you fall short, you'll still have accomplished a lot.

❧ Talk about purpose and people will listen, but to get them to follow, you must act with purpose.

❧ Purposeful organizations are exciting, inspiring places to work. Purpose inspires even the most mundane task with meaning.

❧ Constantly communicate your purpose, your dedication to it, and the expected rewards of achieving it.

CHAPTER THREE

Kindness and Compassion

"Did I not cry for those in trouble?"

—Job 29:16

"Oh king, be kind to the oppressed . . . It may be that then your prosperity will continue."

—Dan. 4:27

indness and compassion have not always been considered necessary components of business leadership. Until about a generation ago, the paradigm for American business was "command and control," otherwise known as Theory X, whose assumptions included:

- ❖ People are naturally lazy and need the threat of punishment to make them work.
- ❖ Kindness to employees will too often be interpreted as an invitation to slack off from the achievement of key business results.

The leaders of the Bible, particularly the Old Testament, often seem to subscribe to Theory X. The Bible is full of episodes where misbehavior or inattentiveness to the task resulted in swift punishment, including exile, torture, and death.

But the Bible is also full of examples of Theory Y management. Theory Y posits that people naturally want to achieve (if you can determine and hook into their desired goals), and that leaders who exhibit kindness and compassion will not necessarily be ridiculed and ignored the moment their backs are turned. They may even be admired and emulated, particularly once the employees have tested the compassion and found it to be sincere and lasting. Many modern leaders have been able to permeate their workplaces with kindness and compassion without sacrificing the achievement of business goals.

THE GOLDEN RULE

Cynics believe that Jesus' words, "Do unto others as you would have them do unto you," are an ideal that belongs only in an "ideal environment," such as a Sunday School or monastery. They argue that the real "Golden Rules" of business are "Them that has the gold makes the rules," and "Do unto others before they can do unto you."

No one would pretend that combining compassion and results-orientation is easy to achieve, particularly if short-term results are paramount. But a number of modern business leaders have found that without compassion and kindness to employees, customers, suppliers, and even competitors, short-term results can't be maintained into the long-term. And perhaps more important, without kindness and personal consideration the workplace becomes a mechanistic environment in which employees (and managers) become dispirited. Performance lags, many "retire on the job" or become bitter, and others go off in search of a more "human" environment.

> *"Clothe yourselves with compassion and kindness." (The apostle Paul, Col. 3:12)*
> *"Be kind to one another." (Eph. 4:32)*

A number of businesses and leaders are operating by these simple yet powerful guidelines, some of them for overtly "religious" or "spiritual" reasons, others because it's the right thing to do or because they have seen the negative effects of cruelty and coldness in their business and personal lives. But all seem pleased with the long-term results.

The insurance industry, with its emphasis on bureaucratic procedures, risk ratios, and exclusionary clauses, would not seem to be a likely home for kindness and compassion. But USAA, a large auto and home insurer, believes in the Golden Rule so much that it added a "rider" to it, creating USAA's "Two Golden Rules":

1. Treat each and every person the way you would like to be treated.
2. Treat each and every employee the way USAA expects you to treat the customer.

CEO Robert McDermott adds, "The Golden Rule can only be lived if in fact you first love yourself and then love your neighbor."[1] This love obviously extends to the employees. A few years ago, jobs at USAA were the modern version of building the pyramids, but without the variety. One person spent all day opening envelopes, another sorting the mail, another reviewing a particular type of claim. Today, no one's job is that narrow; jobs have been broadened so that employees feel more like human beings whose collective judgment is important and less like robots performing mindless, repetitive tasks.

With the rapid proliferation of Starbucks, the service and products of this amazingly successful franchise are well known. What is not so well known is the compassion on which Howard Schultz, Starbucks' founder, based the company. This compassion was based on his own experience as a working-class Brooklyn youth whose father rarely experienced anything like the Golden Rule. Schultz's father shuffled between a number of jobs—truck driver, cab driver, factory worker—at which he rarely received benefits and even more rarely felt like a valued member of the organization.

Schultz writes, "I guess I really began to realize that there were many things we did not have access to in terms of privileges. As I got older, I realized there were things about my childhood that gave me . . . the unique view towards wanting to do something for others because we didn't have it ourselves." In a word, Schultz wanted *his* workplace to be more compassionate. "I always wanted to build the kind of company that my father never got to work for."

What kind of company is it? Most of us know Starbucks only from the receiving end: upscale coffees and confections served in pleasant physical surroundings by smiling, motivated young employees. What makes these employees so motivated are the working environment and benefits package Schultz has put together for them. He has made every employee an owner by initiating the "Bean Stock" option plan. He feels his benefits package is "the greatest single advantage we have because of the value and relationship that our people have to the company, to each other, and most important, to our customers and shareholders."[2] One of Schultz's "baristas" (fancy name for counter help who own "Bean Stock") adds, "Because we are treated so well . . . it's reflected in the way we treat our customers."[3]

All of this grew out of Schultz's own version of the Golden Rule: "Do unto your employees what was not done for your father."

Gordon Bethune's leadership of the Continental Airlines turnaround was based largely on focus and purpose. He made the airline run on time. But he didn't do it with cold-hearted efficiency the way that Mussolini made the trains run on time in Fascist Italy. Bethune, despite the large scope of his mission, never lost sight of the value of "being nice."

"Be nice, but how?" he writes in *From Worst to First*. "Simple! You act nice. And you insist that everybody act nice. I treated my direct reports the way I would want to be treated. They treated theirs the same way, and on down the line." What's more, Bethune tied this "niceness" to a very important business variable, compensation. "Everybody knew that part of their compensation . . . would be based on whether the people they worked with said they were pleasant to deal with and whether they were working as a team."[4]

Bethune's industry competitor, Herb Kelleher of Southwest Airlines, has his own version of the Golden Rule: "I know it sounds simple, but I keep saying, follow the golden rule of service. Serve others as you would like to be served." In an industry where people are often referred to as "seats," Kelleher exhorts his troops, "Don't treat people like objects. Do you like to be treated like one? . . . Don't be a hypocrite. Provide the service you yourself would like to receive."[5]

Lest we relegate these biblical leadership principles to two mavericks of the airline industry, how about one of the world's largest power companies? CEO Dennis Bakke of AES founded his company overtly on biblical principles. "The Bible teaches us that each person is holy, special and unique . . . Treat each person with respect and dignity . . . I would love to get the workplace as close to the Garden (of Eden) as possible, knowing we can't. But I shouldn't stop trying."[6] Now there's an ambitious mission statement!

Ben & Jerry's has been called many things: outrageous, irreverent, wacky, hippie-ish. But biblical? Absolutely, particularly in the company's sense of kindness and compassion toward its employees, suppliers, and customers. Notes Jerry Greenfield, whose company is often accused of having "hippie values," "We say, 'It's more like biblical values. Do unto others as you would have them do to you. . . .' Just because the idea that the good you do comes back to you is written in the Bible and not in some business textbook doesn't make it any less valid . . . There is a spiritual aspect to business [although] most companies try to conduct their businesses in a spiritual vacuum."[7]

How does Ben & Jerry's avoid this spiritual vacuum? By taking risks in the name of compassion and kindness. Ben & Jerry's needed to purchase large quantities of brownies for a new flavor of ice cream. Many struggling young ice cream companies would have gone for the most experienced, cheapest, most efficient supplier. Ben & Jerry's went for "none of the above." Instead, they went for the most compassionate choice—Greyston Bakeries, a nonprofit institution that trains and employs the economically disadvantaged. The result? Initially—a disaster! The workers and equipment weren't up to the demands of making 6,000 to 7,000 pounds of brownies a day. But Ben & Jerry's stuck with Greyston through all the technical and personnel difficulties. Today,

Greyston comfortably makes whatever Ben & Jerry's requires and has leftover capacity to sell to other companies.

MATERIAL KINDNESS

Emotional kindness and compassion are felt deeply by the recipient. So is material kindness, particularly when that is what is most needed. When a person is in need of food or shelter, whether temporarily or permanently, it is of little help to tell him of your "strong emotional support" without addressing that need. Jesus knew that the material needs of people had to be satisfied before they would be open to the spiritual message, which is why he was so quick to provide loaves and fishes to 4,000 even when his resources seemed meager (five loaves and two fishes). Perhaps as someone who was born in a humble manger because there was no room at the inn, he could appreciate the material needs of his followers.

One man who would not have turned Jesus and his family away from his inn is J. Willard Marriott, CEO and chairman of Marriott International. Marriott creates an entire culture in which the "stranger" receives a warm bed and, more important, a warm welcome. "They're away from home," he says of his customers. "They're tired. Their feet hurt. And maybe they've lost the deal they came to do . . . By the time they get to our front desk, they're whipped and we've got to take care of them." (Mary and Joseph should have met such an innkeeper!)

But Willard Marriott knows that the waters of compassion can't be drawn from a poisoned well. Kindness begets kindness. Employees who are treated poorly don't treat guests with the warm hospitality that separates the average from the great in this industry: "We have to take care of our employees; otherwise, how can we expect them to take care of our customers?" notes Marriott. "If you've got a grouchy room clerk, or . . . the waitress doesn't say hello, you won't enjoy your stay. And every time I make a speech, and I mean every time, I talk about these things. We want to help people—not only our customers, but the people who take care of our customers."[8]

Marriott is one man who has created a vast hospitality empire based on the compassionate words of Paul in Romans 12:10: "Love each other . . . never be lazy . . . invite guests who need food and lodging."

Noah would have been a poor manager indeed if he had responded with mere "feelings of empathy" when he learned that a flood threatened to wipe out the entire human and animal population of the planet. He immediately organized a work team to respond to the physical need for a floating hotel.

Another manager who responded with practical compassion and kindness to a natural disaster is M. Anthony Burns, CEO of Ryder Systems. When Hurricane Andrew hit Florida, Burns knew he had to do more than keep renting trucks. Instead, he made the lobby of Ryder's corporate headquarters available to the United Way. He donated food and clothing to charitable agencies and loaned out Ryder's trucks to people who needed to transport themselves and possessions to safer, drier places (sort of a fleet of Noah's arks).

Whereas many CEOs are content to "head up" these types of efforts from their desks in corporate dry-dock, Burns went out on the front lines and joined the work crews who were repairing roofs. With Burns's blessing, Ryder employees worked half days at the company and half days in the rescue effort, many of them seven days a week. Burns was elected "Humanitarian of the Year" by the local chapter of the American Red Cross because he had given of himself and his company's resources, not the usual "arms-length" dollar donation. People felt his kindness and compassion firsthand, and that's how he wanted it: "My Mormon grandfather said, 'the best thing you could do was giving service to other people.' And it's good business."[9]

COMPASSION FOR THOSE IN TROUBLE

The Bible has many examples of leaders who advised and/or exercised compassion for those in difficult straits: the prisoner and the oppressed slave; the victims of natural disasters; war refugees; the halt, blind, and the lame (today referred to as the disabled) and even the dead, who, with compassion, might be restored to life. (And many a "dead" corporation has been resurrected by leaders like Lou Gerstner at IBM and Lee Iacocca at Chrysler.)

Daniel courageously prophesied to King Nebuchadnezzar of Babylonia: "Oh king, renounce your sins by doing what is right, and your wickedness by being kind to the oppressed. It may be that then your prosperity will continue." (Dan. 4:27) He was warning a mighty (and decadent) ruler that a nation founded on injustice and lack of compassion contains the seeds of its own destruction.

A number of modern managers (if not all kings) seem to have heard and acted on Daniel's message. Isaac Tigrett, the founder of Hard Rock Cafe, hired some of society's outcasts—street people, bikers, and others who were on the fringes of society and probably would not have fit well into more traditional organizations. He called his organization the "Rainbow Coalition" because of its diverse group of social and ethnic groups. He eliminated "staff meetings," calling them "family meetings" instead. He instituted an equal pay policy and profit sharing.

Says Tigrett, "I didn't care about anything but the people. Just cherish them, look after them, be sensitive to their lives."[10] A hopeless idealist whose business was doomed to financial failure? No, a successful businessman who sold his business a few years later for over $100 million.

Joseph Rebello, the CEO of Citizens Financial Group, is certainly not your typical banker. Although realizing the importance of profits, he also has exercised a considerable amount of compassion and kindness. And like Ryder Systems' Burns, he has been out in the front lines of philanthropy, not just doling out money from his penthouse office. Says Rebello, "If we just make money, we fail."

How has this executive avoided "failure"? First he donated half of his $2 million salary to his alma mater. Then, prior to accepting his CEO job at Citizens Financial Group, he took a leave of absence to work in a shelter for abused children. He encourages his staff to do similar charitable works and has been criticized for having "too much heart" (a criticism leveled at many of the managers and leaders mentioned in this book). He accepts this label gladly and replies, "Ultimately, what matters is the good that we do."[11] This is one banker who has been able to combine compassion and kindness with financial success.

Hal Rosenbluth of Rosenbluth Travel was motivated primarily by compassion, not profit, when he decided to move his data processing and customer service center to Linton, North Dakota. Rosenbluth, from his corporate offices in Philadelphia, had heard that much of the northern Midwest had experienced a severe drought, causing many crop failures and foreclosures on farm mortgages.

Performing further research, Rosenbluth found that Linton was the hardest-hit city in the hardest-hit state. Eschewing any further profitability analysis, he quickly hired about 200 people in the Linton area to perform the data processing and customer service work for his company. This was a tremendous economic and psychological boost to an area whose major source of income—agriculture—had been severely threatened by natural disaster.

Disaster often brings out generosity and compassion. After the September 11 World Trade Center attack, a number of corporate leaders gave economic assistance to the rescue and clean-up effort. The new CEO of GE, Jeffrey Immelt, gave a corporate donation of $10 million, an amount that soon became the corporate standard for a large company.

As a consultant to a major insurance company several years ago, I met a supremely compassionate manager. The company was undertaking a joint venture with another financial services company, and the operations were not merging well. The "partnering" company, located half a continent away, was not familiar with insurance operations and had hired very inexperienced people to process claims. The result was a total backup in the claims process and total demoralization in my client company, which had until then taken great pride in the prompt and knowledgeable response to every claim.

My job as a consultant was to travel to every branch office and speak to the branch director and employees to ascertain exactly what had gone wrong, and to get their suggestions for remedying the situation. I was particularly impressed with the compassion one particular branch manager had for his employees. Before we met with the entire employee group, he insisted on taking me to lunch privately, where he proceeded to brief me not so much on the operational issues but rather on the emotional toll the merged operation had taken on himself and his employees, who had also been threatened with a downsizing. He confided that he was so disheartened that he had difficulty sleeping at night and had asked his doctor for an anti-anxiety medication. This manager's tenderhearted concern for his employees reminds me of the lament of Jeremiah: "Oh that my head were a spring of water. I would weep day and night for the slain of my people." (Jer. 9:1)

The story of King Saul and David, who succeeded him as king, is an example of compassion in the face of hostility. Saul's anger was inextinguishably engendered when he first heard the people singing, "Saul has slain his thousands, and David his ten thousands." From then on, he pursued David with a vengeance, hurling a spear at him in the royal palace and pursuing him throughout the countryside.

Fortunately for David, he had the friendship and compassion of Saul's own son, Jonathan. Jonathan warned David to flee from his father, and David returned this compassion with compassion toward Saul. David was hiding in a cave when Saul entered. David could have killed his vengeful adversary, but instead merely tore off a piece of Saul's robe as a sign that he had the power to kill him, but had not.

David's compassionate sparing of Saul was a major step in his peaceful accession to the throne. He even buried Saul after he was killed in battle. But David's compassion extended even into the next generation.

Shortly after assuming the kingship of all Israel, David asked if there was anyone left of the house of Saul, his former tormentor. There was, a man named Mephibosheth, Saul's grandson and Jonathan's son, who was "crippled in both feet." David summoned Mephibosheth, who understandably, as a member of Saul's household, feared the worst. After all, he was totally incapable of running, and he realized that as the sole surviving member of Saul's household, he could be the target of all of David's revenge.

But David's compassion was greater than his vengefulness. He remembered the kindness of Jonathan and chose to overlook the treacherousness of Saul: "Don't be afraid, for I will surely show you kindness for the sake of your father Jonathan. I will restore to you all the land that belonged to your grandfather Saul, and you will always eat at my table." (2 Sam. 9:7)

SHARING THE WEALTH

In both biblical and modern times, we have had inequities of wealth. Jacob had great numbers of cattle and sheep, while many of the other tribesmen had few. An investment banker may make fifty times as much as the back-office operator who inputs the trades.

It is probably impossible to eliminate all the inequities in any society, be it biblical, feudal, communistic, or capitalistic. But it is highly possible to maintain the attitude (and corresponding actions) that wealth and resources should be shared. John outlines this premise in a very straightforward passage from Luke 3:11: "The man with two tunics should share with him who has none, and the one who has food should do the same."

Our modern world is more complex, but the principles of sharing remain the same. One industry that has never been particularly known for its "sharing" mentality is investment banking. A friend of mine who worked on "The Street" once described his coworkers as "monetary titans and spiritual dwarfs." But an exception (at least in its leadership) is Bear Stearns. Ace Greenberg, the chairman, requires that all 300 of his senior directors give away at least 4 percent of their gross income to charitable causes every year, a sort of corporate tithing. And amazingly (perhaps not so amazingly considering the amount of disposable income these directors have), most of them give much more. Notes Greenberg, "We don't care what they give it to, but we audit them to make sure they do."[12]

Gary Heavin of Curves for Women also believes that the more he gives, the more he gets. "I'm constantly trying to outgive God," he says. "If you give, you'll be given back in multiples." Heavin believes in sharing and tithing so much that he's reversed the equation: 90 percent for others and only 10 percent for himself. Of the $10 million that he earned in 2001, he will pay $3 million in taxes, donate $3 million to charitable organizations, use $3 million to recapitalize the business (much of which goes to launch new franchisees) and keep "only" about a million for himself.

Says Heavin, "When I give, I give a lot; it's because I'm responding to the holy spirit. I operate from a position of gratefulness." And Heavin sees his mission not so much as physical as it is spiritual: "Jesus healed physical infirmities so he could have access to the spiritual. That's what I'm trying to do with Curves; I'm not just creating fit bodies, I'm helping people repair their spirits."[13]

KINDNESS TO THE "STRANGER" AND THE WEAK

Leviticus 19:33 instructs: "When an alien lives with you . . . treat him as one of your native-born." Unfortunately, American business leaders have not always followed this credo. Too often, they have seen immigrant or foreign labor as an easy way to "beat the competition" by paying low wages and providing poor working conditions.

Aaron Feuerstein of Malden Mills, a textile producer in Lawrence, Massachusetts, always exhibited kindness to all his employees, many of whom were recent immigrants who could have been easily abused by a less compassionate and ethical employer. Feuerstein, well known for fair business practices, kept the factory in Lawrence long after many of his competitors had moved South or had begun to use cheap labor from third world countries.

But even the employees who knew him well were amazed at how deep this man's compassion could go. When a fire ripped through the Malden Mills factory in 1995, it was estimated that it would take at least three months to rebuild and get the factory producing again. "Most people would've been happy at their seventieth birthday to take the insurance money and go to Florida," said Feuerstein. Obviously, he wasn't "most people."

Realizing how many people were depending on him for a livelihood, Feuerstein made the decision to pay the company's 2,400 employees their salaries for 90 days and their health care insurance for 180 days. This was an expense of over $10 million when it was unclear whether the factory could regain its production capacity and market position.

Feuerstein's actions were fueled by a strong spiritual belief. In explaining them, he quoted Rabbi Hillel: "Not all who increase their wealth are wise." He also found that when you treated people with compassion, the results were truly miraculous: "Our people became very creative. They were willing to work twenty-five hours a day." Not only was the factory rebuilt and back to nearly full capacity in ninety days, productivity shot up and "off quality" products were reduced from 7 percent before the fire to 2 percent after it.[14]

Most of us are familiar with the biblical story of the "good Samaritan," who stopped to help a man who had been beaten and robbed by thieves. The Samaritan took pity on the victim: "He . . . bandaged his wounds, pouring on oil and wine. Then he put the man on his own donkey, took him to the inn and took care of him. The next day, he took out two silver coins and gave them to the innkeeper. 'Look after him,' he said, 'and when I return, I will reimburse you for any extra expense you may have.' " (Luke 10:34–35)

Aaron Feuerstein also looked after the "strangers" in his care. He risked all he had that he might be able to provide his predominantly immigrant workers with a purpose and a livelihood at a time when they did not know where to turn.

Many times, Jesus raised children and adults from the dead, not out of the need to impress, but out of compassion. In a modern business parallel, Merck spent over $3 million to build the Children's Inn on the campus of the National Institute of Health. These children were undergoing experimental treatment for rare diseases. Merck hoped to raise them from their sickbeds and rescue them from death. Certainly they gained some "political capital" from this largesse, but the prime motivation was helping the children. Roy Vagelos, former CEO of Merck, has stated, "Medicine is for the patients. It is not for the profits. The profits follow, and if we remembered that, they have never failed to appear."[15]

FORGIVENESS

We all know how hard it is to forgive others who we feel have wronged us, and how good it feels to finally forgive. Joseph's brothers sold him into Egyptian slavery and were unaware that he was to become a powerful adviser to the Pharaoh. Joseph could easily have exacted revenge when his brothers came to Egypt to buy grain when their land was afflicted with famine. Instead, Joseph had compassion for his brothers, forgiving them and inviting them to live with him as honored guests in Egypt.

David had mercy on Saul, and was rewarded with a kingship. Paul exhorted the early Christians to "clothe yourself with compassion and kindness. Bear with each other and forgive grievances." (Col. 3:12) What would you do if you were Esau and you and your 400 men came upon the brother, Jacob, who had stolen your birthright and effectively cut you out of your father's will? Would you run him through with your spear, or forgive him? "But Esau ran to meet Jacob and embraced him; he threw his arms around his neck and kissed him. And they wept." (Gen. 33:4)

You might be forgiven yourself if you responded cynically to such melodrama: "This stuff might happen in the Bible, but certainly not in the hard-nosed modern world of business." But think again. Forgiveness and compassion are powerful, boundless forces, and they belong in the world of business as much as they do in familial relationships, whether biblical or modern. They can even be found in such "cut-throat" businesses as advertising.

At the Leo Burnett agency, staffer Jerry Reitman recounted an incident in which he lost an argument with the production chief, Al Lira. "And I didn't lose gracefully. Al sensed it. Finally one day as we were walking toward each other from opposite ends of the hall, he grabbed me in a bear hug, kissed me on the cheek, and walked away. I learned a little humanity from him that day."[16] Jacob and Esau couldn't have had a more poignant reconciliation.

"Love your enemies, do good to them . . . your reward will be great." (Luke 6:35) That command could apply to individuals like Reitman and Lira, but equally to companies like Nissan and Smucker's. Nissan had a union drive in the late 1980s, which the union lost. As soon as the vote was over, Jerry Benefield, the company's president, went on television to preach a message of forgiveness and compassion. "I asked the people who were on the company side not to gloat . . . and I asked the people on the union side to please continue to be good team members and let's not have any animosity whatsoever from either side, and we didn't."[17]

At Smucker's, the union finds it easy to have a forgiving attitude toward management because of the kindness management shows to the employees, largely based on the Amish/Mennonite principles of the company's founders. When an employee lost everything in a fire, the other employees took up a collection for her. But the head of the company, Tim Smucker, also gave her an "extra check on the side." "Six or seven months later they're still saying, 'Do you need anything?' " says the amazed employee.

Is it any wonder that compassion and forgiveness extend to the company's labor relations as well? Smucker's union representative describes them as the company you "hate to hate": "It really is an honor to represent the union against them because they are very easy to work with . . . They really do care about their people."[18]

CARING AND EMPATHY

The leaders of the Bible let their followers know they cared. Jesus was one of the most caring leaders of all time. He wept when he saw Lazarus had died (John 11:25–36), even though he had the power to bring him back to life! At another point in his travels, he "landed and saw a large crowd, he had compassion on them, because they were like sheep without a shepherd." He preached the renewing word to them, and when he found out they were hungry and had nothing to eat, he turned five loaves of bread and two fish into a meal for several thousand. (Mark 6:34–44) Jesus performed feats like this not to impress people with his magical ability to "stretch" resources, but rather out of compassion and kindness. Ben & Jerry's offers "free cone day" in the same spirit of giving and has found that good deeds are often good for company image and profits as well.

In biblical times and in modern corporations, people have enthusiastically followed leaders who cared about them. "They don't care how much you know until they know how much you care" is not an empty cliché. Again and again, it has been shown that true caring creates more employee loyalty and (ironically) better "hard" results than cold exhortations to do more and produce more.

Morgan McCall and Michael Lombardo have done extensive research on "success factors" and "derailers" for managerial success. The two top derailers are:

1. Insensitivity to others, abrasive, intimidating, bullying style
2. Coldness, aloofness, arrogance

Herb Kelleher of Southwest Airlines is famous for his caring, empathic "I'm with you in the trenches" attitude. He loads luggage with the baggage handlers and serves peanuts with the flight attendants. He observes that a true leader needs "a patina of spirituality . . . I feel you have to be with your employees through all their difficulties, that you have to be interested in them personally." It's not uncommon for Kelleher to go out after work with a baggage handler or other staffer and spend many hours listening to them and solving problems. He adds, "We value our employees first . . . If you treat them right, they treat the customers right, and if you treat the customers right, they keep coming back."[19]

Technical professionals are not easy to keep in today's low-loyalty economy. Sandy Weill, Chairman and CEO of Citigroup, has increased his company's retention of this group by putting his money (and his body) where his mouth is. "I think it's the commitment of senior management to this area," he observes. "They need to know that senior management cares. There was many a night I slept on the computer room floor, as they tried to work something out."[20]

Says Dave Komansky, CEO of Merrill Lynch, "It's essential that people know you care about them. That does not mean you pander to them, or that you don't call attention to things that go wrong, or that you're afraid to say no. But they have to know that you care about them as individuals."[21]

Too often, our modern corporate leaders have been too quick to sacrifice a few (or a large number of) individuals for the sake of the "greater good" or perceived corporate survival. The corporate downsizings of recent years have often been justified because "if we don't throw some excess baggage off this boat, we're all going to sink" (sounds a little like the story of Jonah, who was "outplaced" in very dramatic fashion when the sailors threw him overboard).

The more compassionate leaders have at least given their outplaced employees life preservers. For example, Randall Tobias of Eli Lilly decided to offer a select group of employees early retirement with one year's pay rather than engage in wholesale dismissals with smaller packages for each employee. The compassionate leader realizes that when any employee is treated poorly or his needs are ignored, all will notice, and the leadership is tarnished.

Jesus believed in compassion for all his flock of actual and potential followers: "If a man owns a hundred sheep, and one of them wanders away, will he not leave the ninety-nine on the hills and go to look for the one that wandered off? And if he finds it . . . he is happier about that one sheep than about the ninety-nine that did not wander off." (Matthew 18:12–13)

For Gary Heavin of Curves for Women, this concern for all the "sheep" extends to not just employees, but customers too. He notes, "Any franchisee can call me, and I have over 3,000. I had a franchisee call me about one member (and I have over a half million members). She had lost weight but had dropped out of the program. I took the time to write to her and send her an autographed copy of my book."[22] Now there's a leader who looks out for every sheep.

Morrison and Forster is a law firm with a strange sense of priorities— they claim to care more about their employees than they do about billable hours or the bottom line. Says a recruiter for the firm, "We do not tolerate abuse of our employees by partners, no matter how senior or

'important.' " She makes it plain to incoming law graduates and interns
that "our staff is like gold to us and are not to be treated any less pre-
ciously . . . Anyone who is found to be speaking down to somebody or
mistreating them verbally . . . is really out on their ear."[23]

At Fel-Pro, a manufacturer in Skokie, Illinois, caring is a way of life.
Every employee receives an extensive benefits package, an extra day's
pay on his or her birthday (and a free lunch), a free turkey at Christmas,
and a box of chocolates on Valentine's Day. Perhaps more important is
the sentiment behind these gestures. "You give more naturally, not because you feel obligated to . . . You feel that they care for you, so you
have to care for them too," notes an employee.

At many companies, those who put in sixty-hour weeks are "encouraged" until they burn out. An employee at Fel-Pro was amazed when
her boss took her aside and told her, "You are working too many hours.
We value you too much. You are getting burned out. You can take no
work home this weekend." "And," she adds, "they were serious!"[24]

LOVE

Love certainly has a prominent place in the Bible. Without love to
sustain them, the Hebrews could never have survived their many exiles
and sustained their commitment to their God, their land, and each
other. Without love as the cement, the disciples would have been a
group with poor "cohesion" and a diluted sense of mission. Indeed,
that love could help them transcend the apparent death of their leader
through the treacherous behavior of one of their own inner circle, Judas
Iscariot.

What does the Bible have to say about love?

> "Love is patient, love is kind, never glad about injustice. Love never
> gives up . . . never loses faith." (1 Cor. 13:4)
> "We could have been a burden to you, but we were gentle among you,
> like a mother caring for her children. We loved you so much that we were

delighted to share with you not only the Gospel of God but our lives as well." (1 Thess. 2:7–9)

"Clothe yourselves with compassion, kindness, humility, gentleness and patience . . . And over all these virtues put on love, which binds them all together in perfect unity." (Col. 3:12–14)

"If I speak in the tongues of men and angels, but have not love, I am only a resounding gong or a clanging cymbal . . . If I have the gift of prophesy and can fathom all mysteries . . . and if I have a faith that can move mountains, but have not love, I am nothing. If I give all my possessions to the poor and surrender my body to the flames, but have not love, I gain nothing." (1 Cor. 13:1–3)

These are noble, transcendent sentiments that certainly belong in a holy book or place of worship. But does love really belong in the hard-nosed, self-interested, money-changing world of business? Or have we all become Pharisees again? Let's ask some of today's most successful managers and executives.

Herb Kelleher of Southwest Airlines is perhaps the most evangelistic CEO in the cause of love. He states bluntly, "We'd rather have a company run by love, not by fear," paraphrasing, either consciously or unconsciously, 1 John 4:18: "Perfect love drives out fear." The airline flies out of Dallas' Love Field, its stock exchange symbol is "Luv," the company paper is called Luv Line, and its twentieth anniversary slogan was "Twenty Years of Loving You."

Empty rhetoric? Merely the hollow sounds of a resounding gong and a clanging cymbal? Ask the employees. Says one, "Herb loves us. We love Herb. We love one another. We love the company [sounds like the airline version of the Woodstock festival, only with a lot more profit added]. One of the primary beneficiaries of our collective caring is the passengers."[25]

Another example is Gore-Tex, the "miracle fabric" company, which was founded on love as surely as it was on scientific innovation. Says the CFO, Shanti Mehta, "Bill Gore never called me into his office. He always came to my desk, sat on my desk . . . He was a real wellspring from which love [there's that nontechnical word again] flowed throughout the organization . . . After his death, the responsibility of doing this has fallen squarely on the shoulders of all of us."[26]

Ben Cohen of Ben & Jerry's feels love is as important an ingredient in his ice cream as heavy cream or chocolate fudge brownies: "When you give love, you receive love . . . there is a spiritual dimension to business just as there is to the lives of individuals."[27]

Pamela Coker, the CEO of Acucobol, a successful software company, is another proponent of universal love: "Love your customers, employees, shareholders, vendors and community . . . and the profits will follow." A company representative calls every customer once a month, and twice a year the customer receives a gift. Family and friends, not just employees, are invited to all company events. Says Coker, "I am committed to helping every Acucobol employee attain his or her dreams."[28]

The telecommunications industry has not always been known as a hotbed of love and compassion. But listen to two of its titans talk about the necessity for these traits:

> "If we face a recession, we should not lay off employees; the company should sacrifice a profit. It's management's risk and responsibility. Employees are not guilty; why should they suffer?" (Akio Morita, CEO of Sony)
>
> "My philosophy of business? Five words: to love and to achieve. And the second will never happen without the first." (Robert Galvin, former CEO of Motorola, addressing his successor and son, Chris, who will try to put these principles into action in the next generation)

Compassion. Mercy. Forgiveness. Love. These timeless qualities are gradually returning to our boardrooms, our offices, our factories, and hopefully our homes, which are so often influenced by the climate at the workplace. The progress may be uneven at times, but as a general trend, these words from Ezekiel 11:19 are being manifested more often and with more conviction and intensity: "I will take away their hearts of stone and give them tender hearts instead."

BIBLICAL LESSONS ON KINDNESS AND COMPASSION

- Following the Golden Rule doesn't just make people "feel better." It also builds the bottom line by increasing employee loyalty and productivity.

- Reward acts of kindness with monetary incentives and nonmonetary recognition.

- You can't expect employees to treat each other and customers with consideration if their leaders are treating them poorly.

- "Sharing the wealth" usually pays off in terms of increased commitment and the creation of a "larger pie."

- Forgiveness is one of the most powerful actions a leader can take.

- In the push to achieve group goals, don't overlook the emotional needs of individuals; watch over each sheep, not just "the flock."

- Holding people to high standards and showing them that you care are not mutually exclusive; they can actually be mutually reinforcing.

CHAPTER FOUR

Humility

It is not good to eat too much honey, nor is it honorable to seek one's own honor.

—PROV. 25:17

Haughtiness goes before destruction; humility precedes honor.

—PROV. 18:12

ickles and ice cream. Humility and leadership. Some things don't seem to fit together very well initially. I once heard an experienced secretary in a large accounting firm comment on a young accountant's self-effacing personal style, at first in an approving way because it made him so "easy to work with," but then adding in a whisper, "But he'll never make partner unless he loses some of that humility and puts on some arrogance."

The whole issue of "pride versus humility" is an ongoing paradox for leaders in all types of organizations and at all levels. How do you get to a position of leadership, especially in highly competitive organizations, if you don't have some personal ambition? How can truly humble persons advance to a position of influence and authority? And what will happen when they get there? The meek may inherit the earth, but can we be sure they will stay meek when they get it? Are leaders "just like the rest of us" or are they "better" or more valuable in some indefinable way?

Management consultant Patrick Lencioni addresses this seeming paradox: "I have defined humility as the realization that a leader is inherently no better than the people he or she leads, and charisma as the realization that the leader's *actions* are more important than those of the people he or she leads. As leaders, we must strive to embrace humility and charisma."[1]

For examples of leaders who combined the power of humility and charisma, we need look no further than the Bible. Moses was one of the most influential and powerful leaders who ever lived. He overcame the resistance of the most powerful ruler of his era, Pharaoh, to secure the freedom of his people. He led them through the Red Sea and the desert, and smashed the tablets bearing the Ten Commandments when he found the people worshiping a golden calf.

These are the kinds of actions that could "go to one's head." After all his accomplishments, it would have been very easy for Moses to say, "We'll do it because I'm the CEO, and I said so! Without me, none of this could ever have happened. If you want to talk to me, make an appointment through my assistant, Aaron. And if you're one of those who opposed me at any point, forget the appointment!"

Amazingly, the Bible tells us just the opposite: "Now Moses was a very humble man, more humble than anyone." (Num. 12:3) At various times in the Old Testament, Moses falls face down and protests that he is "not worthy to lead." But each time, he receives a call to action.

Moses is not the only reluctant leader in the Bible. It takes a great leader to put his own stature and the size of the task in proper relationship, and these "humble leaders" abound. You could even say that just when a great leader was needed, a person of great humility appeared:

"Who am I . . . and what is my family, that I should become the king's son-in-law? . . . I'm only a poor man and little known." (David, soon to become one of Israel's greatest kings, upon marrying the daughter of Saul, 1 Sam. 18)

"But I am only a little child . . . For who is able to govern this great

*people of yours?'' (Solomon, David's son, upon ascending to the throne,
1 Kings 3:7–9)*

*"Therefore anyone who becomes as humble as this little child is the
greatest in the kingdom of heaven." (Jesus, Matt. 18:4)*

These are wonderfully inspiring sentiments. But do they have any
application in the modern business world? Some of the most successful,
hard-hitting, goal-oriented, and ambitious executives have tempered
those traits with humility. Their leadership styles may not be exact cop-
ies of those of Moses or Jesus (whose is?), but they are exhibiting humility nonetheless.

A HUMBLE PERSPECTIVE

Jamie Bonini knew enough to be humble when he was named manager
of a large Chrysler plant near Windsor, Ontario. He had more years in
academia than he did in manufacturing, and rather than pretending to
"know it all," he admitted his weak spots and asked for help. He did
something that no previous plant director had done—he made frequent
visits to the manufacturing floor. When things went wrong, he blamed
the process, not the workers, and he asked for help from those workers
to fix the process.[2]

Bonini's humble management style was much like that of King
David. In the heat of a battle, David developed a strong thirst. Some of
his "mighty men," imbued with the loyalty that can only be inspired
by a leader like David, offered to go across enemy lines, risking their
lives to bring their leader a drink! David refused to let them make this
sacrifice. He believed in being on the front lines with his men and
didn't feel that any man should sacrifice his life to make the leader a
little more comfortable.

Former CEO Don Tyson of Tyson Foods was another leader whose
humility increased his effectiveness and the loyalty he got from "the

troops." Every day, the head of this huge food manufacturer showed up in a brown uniform with "Don" embroidered on the shirt pocket.[3] And then there is the example of Andy Grove of Intel working in a small, open cubicle virtually indistinguishable from that of an administrative assistant.

Athletics is often considered an area where "only the arrogant survive." Today, with more and more athletes making millions of dollars and exhibiting strong "in your face" attitudes, many coaches have had to develop even more aggressive attitudes. There has been a lot of teeth-baring and aggressive posing, as middle-aged coaches try to get their overpaid young charges to fall into line, exercise discipline on and off the field, and put team goals before their own personal glory.

At times, these clashes of ego have resulted in violence. Bobby Knight, former basketball coach at Indiana University, was well known for browbeating and insulting his players and was finally removed after physically assaulting a student. On the players' side, Latrell Sprewell of the National Basketball Association had to change teams after he physically assaulted his coach.

The arrogance and aggression of both coaches and players were tolerated for years because their teams were winning. But probably the most successful college basketball coach of all time, John Wooden of UCLA, compiled his record number of NCAA championships based on humility, not on ego, aggression, or greed.

"Wooden's faith in God was complete," writes Brian De Biro, his biographer. "This enabled him to balance genuine humility with solid belief in himself." (We've never heard Wooden referred to as the Moses of his athletic program, but the comparison would be apt.) "He never chased perfection because he believed it to be the sole domain of God." (Now that's true humility.) "He never lost sight of his own fallibility and consequently was able to see mistakes as temporary errors in judgment, not permanent flaws in character."[4]

One Bible figure who never lost sight of his own fallibility was the disciple Peter. Once he was approached by the Roman centurion, Cornelius, who was so anxious to hear about the word of Christ that he fell at Peter's feet in reverence. This would have been the perfect time for a less humble man to "Lord it over" Cornelius and pose as a "great man" or representative of God himself. Peter's response was one of total humility: "But Peter made him get up. 'Stand up,' he said. I am only a man myself."(Acts 10:25–26)

A modern-day example of humility is Larry Bossidy, former CEO of Allied Signal, who is well aware of the negative potential of CEO-glorification, our modern-day version of idol worship. "Being the CEO used to mean you knew everything," he notes. "But these are humbling jobs. And the more you search, the more you recognize every reason you have to be humble, because there's an awful lot more to do all the time."[5]

I used to work for a consulting firm whose leader possessed a lot of "charisma." To the more cynical staff, that sometimes meant that we did all the work, while he got all the glory, such as appearances on network television, lucrative book contracts, and frequently being interviewed and quoted by the national press. The chairman was not generally known for his humility or his tendency to give credit to the troops.

That's why his presentation at one of our annual meetings had such impact. This was in the early days of PowerPoint. The chairman gave a rousing speech in which he outlined tremendous revenue and service goals for the firm. "And you know who is going to achieve this, don't you?" he asked the assembled staff. Immediately, the now-famous "PowerPoint finger" pointed out at us from the giant screen. There were a few muffled groans. Once again, we were going to do all the work and the chairman was going to get all the glory.

But then the chairman added, "Oh, I forgot who else was going to achieve these goals." The "finger" turned to point directly at him. Laughter convulsed the audience. Perhaps it was only a symbolic statement, but our fearless leader was saying that he was ready to confront what some of us considered to be his worst fear: getting down into the trenches with the humble troops and sweating the small stuff with us, not just reaping the glory, fame, and big rewards. Although none of us at the time said this was reminiscent of King David going into the battle lines with his "mighty men," it was definitely a humble side of our leader that we had not seen before.

For true humility and lack of ego, though, few moderns can match the disciples of Jesus. They believed in their message so deeply that advancing themselves became a nonissue. These men could have used their status as part of the "inner circle" to advance their own reputations. Instead, they subordinated their egos in the service of the word of the man whom they considered to be their lord and savior. John the Baptist was probably the most eloquent in his subordination of ego:

> *"I am the bridegroom's friend and am filled with joy at his success."*
> *(John, referring to Jesus, John 3:30)*
> *"After me will come one who is more powerful than I, whose sandals I am not fit to carry." (Luke 3:15)*
> *"I am not the Christ or Elijah, but am sent ahead of him . . . He must become greater; I must become less." (John 3:28)*

Of course, what inspired such humility in the disciples was the extraordinary humility of the "CEO"—Jesus himself. He was a master at humbling himself and giving credit to his "team." When they tried to wash his feet, he also insisted on washing theirs. There are a number of modern leaders who also realize that without their followers, their achievements would have been very humble indeed.

HUMILITY AND TEAMWORK

The business leaders of another era (the Rockefellers and the Goulds) were not known for their spirit of humility and teamwork. But more recent leaders have begun to realize that no one person—no matter how innovative, knowledgeable, or wealthy—can be totally responsible for the success of an entire company. Humility is making some headway in executive row.

For instance, Bill Flanagan, vice president of operations for Amdahl

Corporation, was asked by researchers Kouzes and Posner to describe his personal best. "After a few moments, Flanagan said he couldn't do it. Startled, we asked him why. 'Because it wasn't *my* personal best. It wasn't *me*. It was *us*.' "6

Walter Shipley of Citibank says, "We have 68,000 employees. With a company this size, I'm not 'running the business' . . . My job is to create the environment that enables people to leverage each other beyond their own individual capabilities . . . I get credit for providing the leadership that got us there. But our people did it."7

Bob Tillman, CEO of Lowe's companies, a retailer of home improvement products, does not even like to give "personal" interviews, because he doesn't feel that the success of his company is "personal." "I would not have done this (interview) if our PR folks had not pressured me. And the reason for that is . . . I don't agree with singling out our leadership when . . . talking about our success. One person neither builds nor manages a business . . . the more you highlight one person, the more you detract from the team itself."8

Ray Gilmartin, CEO of Merck, takes this a step further: "If I were to put someone on the front cover of *Business Week* or *Fortune*, it would be . . . the person who heads up our research organization, not me. Or I would put a team of people on the cover."9

Lou Gerstner is known for his tough, goal-oriented, hard-hitting management style, not his humility. But even Gerstner, when pushed to the wall, can become humble: "I haven't done this," he says, referring to IBM's amazing turnaround since he became CEO. "It's been 280,000 people who have done it. We took a change in focus, a change in preoccupation, and a great talented group of people . . . and changed the company."10

Says Dan Tully of Merrill Lynch, "It's amazing what you can do when you don't seek all the credit. I find nothing is really one person's idea."11

Bernie Ebbers, CEO of MCI WorldCom, sees himself not as the boss but rather as the "steward." "I look at my stewardship of this company as an opportunity that the Lord has given to me. And that the fundamental principle in my life is to serve Him and to serve people through the opportunities he has given me . . . We forget it's the people that are working with us that really make us what we are."[12]

The Bible reminds us that all parts of the body, however exalted or humble, are equally important to its functioning. "The eye cannot say to the hand, 'I don't need you!' And the head cannot say to the feet, 'I don't need you!' On the contrary, those parts of the body that seem to be weaker are indispensable, and the parts that we think are less honorable we treat with special honor . . . there should be no division in the body, but that its parts should have equal concern for each other." (1 Cor. 12:21–26)

The message behind this analogy? All people have gifts, all people can contribute to a mission, and it is part of the leader's job to make sure that each "body part" is valued and has input. The "head," or the executive suite, cannot exist without the "heart" (human resources or customer service) or the "feet" (the messenger service, truck fleet, or the mail room). And the humble leader realizes that no one part should be exalted above the rest, since it cannot exist without the rest.

A team functions best when all the members (even the leaders) exhibit appropriate humility toward one another. This is expressed beautifully in 1 Peter 5:5: "All of you, clothe yourselves with humility toward one another, because God opposes the proud but gives grace to the humble."

HUMILITY IN THE FACE OF MISTAKES

One thing that makes leadership so difficult is that as you go higher in the organization, your mistakes become more visible and they impact increasing numbers of people. That's why those at the highest levels often spend considerable time covering up, whitewashing, or justifying their mistakes to the press and to those affected by the mistakes.

Great leaders have the ability to be humble in failure and error, if not as a matter of habit, at least some of the time. Ironically, this ability, rather than destroying their image, credibility, and power, often strengthens them.

Job had many strengths. However, he was also strong enough to admit his imperfection: "I am unworthy—how can I reply to you? I put my hand over my mouth . . . Therefore I despise myself and repent in dust and ashes." (Job 40:4, 42:6) This act of humility did not end Job's prosperity; it only increased it. He emerged from ruin to acquire fourteen thousand sheep, six hundred camels, a thousand yoke of oxen and a thousand donkeys. Moreover, he was blessed with ten more children and lived 140 years so that he could enjoy his children and his children's children.

Jack Welch, the recently retired chairman of General Electric, was one of the most successful businessmen of all time, multiplying the company's assets, profits, and stock price many times over during his tenure. But Welch was also capable of making mistakes. Any CEO of a multibillion-dollar company is bound to make some, even if they represent "only" one of those billions.

For example, Welch had engineered GE's disastrous purchase of 80 percent of Kidder Peabody for $600 million; the whole failed deal cost GE $1.2 billion. Welch didn't seek to minimize this mistake, nor did he look around for other heads to blame and lop off. "I've rewarded failures by giving out awards to people when they've failed . . . I always say, if the chairman can buy Kidder Peabody and mess it up, you can do just about anything . . . Now if the chairman can do that and still survive, you ought to be able to take swings everywhere."[13]

Welch's humble approach in accepting responsibility for his error undoubtedly encouraged others at GE (and the many other companies who study and benchmark GE) to take risks and to exhibit humility when those risks didn't always pay off.

Remember Ahab, the husband of Jezebel? He had many vices, including violent seizure of property (the killing of Naboth for his orchard) and idol worship. But he did have one saving grace—humility. When Ahab realized how craven his behavior had been, he tore his clothes, put on sackcloth, and fasted. He adjusted his behavior to meekness and kindness, causing Elijah the prophet to comment, "Have you noticed how Ahab has humbled himself . . . ? Because he has humbled himself, I will not bring disaster in his day . . ." (1 Kings 21:29). Of course, many of Ahab's sins were visited upon his son, but at least dogs did not lap up *his* blood.

In modern times, Procter & Gamble behaved initially in an arrogant and vindictive manner when sensitive information about the company was leaked to the *Wall Street Journal* in 1991. They initiated a police search of over 800,000 telephone lines in the Cincinnati area in an attempt to locate the informant. Soon afterward, they realized that their attempts to solve the problem had only aggravated it instead. There were strong protests by lawyers, the press, and even by Procter & Gamble's own employees.

A truly arrogant company would have stood by their initial misinformed reaction. In fact, they probably would have stiffened their stand the more they were attacked. But Procter & Gamble realized they had made a serious error and that it was time for some humility. The company's CEO wrote a letter to employees apologizing for his "error of judgment," which "created a problem that was larger than the one we were trying to solve."[14]

This episode, rather than weakening the company, strengthened it. By admitting its error quickly and moving on to more important matters, Procter & Gamble avoided the sin of excessive pride, which often damages or destroys people and companies. They avoided the frequent fate of those who are unable to be humble in the face of mistakes, which is set down so succinctly in Jeremiah 8:12: "Are they ashamed of their loathsome conduct? No, they have no shame at all; they do not even know how to blush. So they will fall among the fallen; they will be brought down when they are punished."

Procter & Gamble knew how to blush. This critical leadership competency saved them from landing amid the fallen, perhaps permanently.

One biblical king who also knew how to blush was Rehoboam. He had united the kingdom behind him, but had neglected God's commandments. Therefore, God abandoned him to his enemies as a logical consequence of this disloyalty. In the face of this consequence, Rehoboam could have become more arrogant, rejecting his religion, and straying further into idol worship. However, "the leaders of Israel and the king humbled themselves and said, 'The Lord is just.' " The Lord's response? "Since they have humbled themselves, I will not destroy them, but will soon give them deliverance." (2 Chron. 12: 6–7)

Perhaps the most humble political leader of the twentieth century was Mahatma Gandhi. Like Moses, he totally subordinated his ego and comfort needs to his overriding mission, the deliverance of his people from bondage. Gandhi always dressed simply, lived frugally, and eschewed the emblems of power and prestige.

Gandhi's humility transcended the large political and social forces that he was trying to harness for the liberation of his people; it extended to the personal. On one occasion, a mother brought her child to "the great Mahatma." "He insists on eating candy, which is bad for him," she complained. Surely the great man could influence her son to stop. Amazingly, Gandhi sent her away and asked her to come back in a month. When she returned, he immediately instructed the son to stop eating candy.

"And why could you not tell my son this when we came to see you a month ago?" asked the woman. "Because I myself had not stopped eating candy at that time," answered the great statesman. That's the kind of humility that can move one person or a million.

Chairman Roger Sant and CEO Dennis Bakke of AES are two leaders who readily forgive the honest mistakes of their employees. Why do they have such a tolerant attitude? "Maybe because of the humility that says, 'We've been on the front lines and made big decisions and big mistakes . . . On our first two or three projects, [we] really screwed up . . . We should have been hung out to dry.' "

Sant and Bakke's first power plant lost $20 million per year for six years. They bought an oil field that lost another $20 million. They bought prototype turbines that cracked.

"That whole investment lost dollars for years, until people at the plant figured out how to fix it. Now it's doing very well, very little thanks to us," note these top executives who have learned humility from difficult experience. "The good news about owning up to your mistakes right away is that it is so much easier to move quickly and find a creative solution. You don't sit around wasting time trying to figure out whom to blame."[15]

HUMILITY "PAYS"

Yet another ridiculous oxymoron? Ironically, from ancient times to modern, humility has paid off in practical terms. It's not an easy process to trust, but it often works.

King Solomon was put to the "humility test" when God came to him in a dream and said, "Ask for whatever you want me to give you." Solomon could have been like King Midas and asked that all he touched be turned to gold. But instead, he humbly asked for wisdom: "I am only a little child and do not know how to carry out my duties. So give your servant a discerning heart . . . For who is able to govern this great people of yours?"

God's answer to this humble request was to grant Solomon everything else he might have wished for: not just a wise and discerning heart, but also riches, honor, and long life. (1 Kings 3:7–14)

Humility has paid off for modern leaders as well as biblical kings. Robert Townsend, when he became CEO of Avis in the 1970s, turned the corporate world on its head when he eliminated executive dining rooms, parking spaces, and other emblems of corporate royalty. Taking humility a step further, Townsend showed seemingly great vulnerability when he admitted his mistakes far more forthrightly than was customary for CEOs at the time.

"Admit your mistakes openly, maybe even joyfully," he wrote in the aptly titled *Up the Organization*. "Encourage your associates to do likewise by commiserating with them." Townsend admitted that his "batting average" was probably no better than .333. "But my mistakes were discussed openly and most of them corrected with a little help from my friends."[16] He and King Solomon would have done well together in an executive support group.

Another suitable addition to this "humility support group" would be Steve Chaddick, SVP of systems and technology for Ciena Corporation. His company's acquisition of Omnia Communications promised to help it offer increased bandwidth to businesses and homes. It was a bold move, but in the end, the architecture turned out to be flawed and had to be shelved. The stock price dropped from $51 to $8 in a few months. But at least Ciena could admit it had made a mistake, allowing it to change direction rather than maintain the same disastrous course. Notes Chaddick, "Most business cultures are incapable of accepting error. We teach from the top down that sometimes we will be wrong."[17]

Jack Stack of Springfield Re also found that humility paid. Many leaders, when confronted with a unionization battle, immediately assume that the arrogant, aggressive route is the strategy of choice. Stack chose another method, one that perhaps came more naturally to him since he had started out as a humble mailroom clerk. "We got down on our hands and knees and begged them to trust us. We groveled." Perhaps it was his sincerity, perhaps his humility, but Stack's efforts resulted in a three to one vote against the union.

Pharmaceutical giant Pfizer could (and sometimes does) throw its multibillion-dollar weight around with its suppliers, competitors, and employees. But CEO William Steere wants it to stop short of downright arrogance. "I detest arrogance," declares Steere. "When I find it in a product manager or in a research scientist, I speak out against it . . . Arrogance is the beginning of the end in remaining agile. Arrogant companies—and leaders—fail to see or react to threats. They also miss opportunities to partner with others, because they want to do it all themselves."[18]

Just think if Pharaoh had been more agile and suggested an *alliance of equals* with the Hebrews, or if Haman had teamed with Mordechai to create an interreligious kingdom in ancient Persia. Too often, lack of humility blinds leaders to the tremendous power of alliances and to the destructive effects of arrogant ambition.

If only these failed leaders of biblical times (and those of modern times) had paid more attention to warnings like these:

> *"The Lord has a day in store for the proud and mighty, for they will be humbled." (Isa. 2:12)*
>
> *"Because you think you are wise as a god, you will be brought down." (Ezekiel to the King of Tyre, Ezek. 28:3)*
>
> *"To those who say, 'I am too sacred for you'—Such people are a stench in my nostrils." (Isa. 65:5)*

THE LEADER AS SERVANT

In the past few years, much has been written about the "servant leader" who inspires others and achieves great goals not by "lording it over others" but rather by serving them. But the "servant leader" is not a new phenomenon; its origins date back to Bible.

While Jesus is the best-known servant leader, the concept predates him by almost 1,000 years. In 1 Kings 12, King Rehoboam, who has just ascended to the throne of Israel, is faced with a dilemma—how to motivate the people of Israel to follow him so that he can continue the great legacy of achievement accomplished by his father, Solomon. His followers petition him: "Your father put a heavy yoke on us, but now lighten the harsh labor and the heavy yoke he put on us, and we will serve you."

Like any wise executive, Rehoboam enlists the aid of a consulting team: He asks the elders who had served his father how he should answer the petition. Their advice: "If today you will be a servant to these people and serve them . . . they will always be your servants."

In his arrogance, Rehoboam decides to ignore this advice. Instead, he replies, "My father made your yoke heavy; I will make it even heavier. My father scourged you with whips; I will scourge you with scorpions." Rehoboam's stubborn pride and cruelty made him the ultimate "Theory X" manager, even for biblical times. His "results"? The people of Israel stoned to death the manager whom Rehoboam had appointed to supervise their forced labor, and Rehoboam himself had to flee from Jerusalem in his chariot to escape death. The people repudiated him and made his rival, Jereboam, the king over all Israel.

Perhaps it takes someone not born into royalty to fully embrace servant leadership. Such a man was Jesus, who was born in a manger and whose only crown was the crown of thorns. Such a man could not only preach servant leadership, he could practice it, and his practice inspired his followers to do likewise.

For example, the mother of two of Jesus' disciples came to him and asked that they be given a "privileged place" at his table: "Grant that one of these two sons of mine may sit at your right and the other at your left." Needless to say, this caused some consternation and jealousy among the other disciples. Jesus quickly set the priorities straight: What was most important was not the trappings of power (the place at the table) but rather the service of others: "You know that the rulers of the gentiles lord it over them . . . Not so with you. Instead, whoever wants to become great among you must be your servant . . . just as the Son of Man did not come to be served, but to serve." (Matt. 20:20–28)

Jesus "made himself nothing, taking the very nature of a servant" (Phil. 2:7), and in so doing probably affected the lives of more people than anyone else who ever lived. The most dramatic example of Jesus' humility was his washing of his disciples' feet. It is difficult to imagine a modern leader acting so humbly; it was Jesus' great gift that he never lost his power to inspire, even in the most humble act.

"He poured water into a basin and began to wash his disciples' feet, drying them with the towel that was wrapped around him . . . He came to Simon Peter . . . 'No,' said Peter, 'you shall never wash my feet.' Jesus answered, 'Unless I wash you, you have no part with me.' 'Then Lord,' Simon Peter replied, 'not just my feet but my hands and my head as well!' " (John 13:3–9)

Herb Kelleher of Southwest Airlines was a true believer in servant leadership. "I'd describe leadership as servanthood . . . The best leaders . . . have to be good followers as well. You have to be willing to subject your own ego to the needs of your business." As we've noted, this was not just empty rhetoric. Kelleher literally "served the servers," helping the baggage handlers lift the bags and the flight attendants serve the peanuts.[19]

What made this all "work" was the sincerity of his humility. If humility isn't a strong trait for you, or it just isn't your style, don't try to put on a "Herb Kelleher costume." There's got to be some true humility in you to work with and develop; most employees easily see through false humility. If, after washing his disciples' feet, Jesus had gone out for a lavish dinner with the local dignitaries at which he claimed all the credit for the success of "his" organization, his foot-washing would have been reduced to a meaningless and hypocritical ritual.

Humility means admitting that even the most powerful leader is not totally in control, and that what ultimately makes leaders powerful is not their personal charisma, but something deeper. As Steven Covey writes:

> *Humility says, "I am not in control; principles ultimately govern and control." That takes humility because the traditional mind-set is "I am in control" . . . This mind-set leads to arrogance—the sort of pride that comes before the fall. [One is reminded of characters like King Saul, Samson, and Haman here.] People are supposed to serve. Life is a mission, not a career.*[20]

The great leaders of the Bible like Moses and Jesus realized that their mission on earth was to serve a cause that was far greater than any one leader or person. As a modern example, Gary Heavin of Curves for Women feels a "call to greatness" is at the heart of his success. Ironically, that greatness can be achieved only with humility. "If you really want to be a great leader, you must be a servant leader," he says. "Our company is an upside-down pyramid; I'm at the bottom—it's my job to serve." Heavin has "served his way" into becoming the third fastest growing franchise in the world.[21]

ServiceMaster is a company literally founded on servant leadership. Its 200,000 employees are in the business of serving others (mopping and waxing floors, removing trash), and its leadership is in the business of serving the employees. Charles Pollard, long-time CEO, cites servanthood as the linchpin of his leadership: "Too often, leaders sit in large offices . . . and think they know and understand the people they lead . . . Servant leaders listen and learn from those they lead. They . . . avoid the trap that so many so-called successful leaders experience—the arrogance of ignorance."[22]

There is no scarcity of feet to wash. The towels and water are available. The limitation, if there is one, is our ability to get on our hands and knees and be prepared to do what we ask others to do.

BIBLICAL LESSONS ON HUMILITY

- ❧ A leader is no more intrinsically important than his people, but his actions are.

- ❧ No matter how much you achieve or how much acclaim you are given, you are still human and not a god.

- ❧ Express sincere (not phony) appreciation for your followers. Where and who would you be without them?

- ❧ Recognize the interdependence of yourself and all your followers; the head is useless without the arms or the feet.

- ❧ Honor the unique gifts of each member of your team.

- ❧ As you rise higher, your mistakes have more impact and your need for a humble perspective actually increases.

- ❧ Don't hold people to standards you are not meeting yourself.

- ❧ To humble oneself is risky, but it usually pays off in increased credibility.

- ❧ A leader is "greater" than others only insofar as he serves them.

CHAPTER FIVE

Communication

"Does not the ear test words as the tongue tastes food?"

—Prov. 18:13

"Like cutting off one's feet or drinking violence is the sending of a message by the hand of a fool."

—Prov. 26:6

leader who cannot communicate clearly, powerfully, and succinctly barely qualifies as a leader. The best ideas are useless if not communicated in a compelling way.

The leaders of the Bible did not have e-mail, fax machines, telephones, or even microphones. The printing press did not exist during the times of either the Old or New Testaments, forcing them to rely on handwritten scrolls that also had to be duplicated by hand. Perhaps because they lacked sophisticated technologies to lean on, they became masters of the written and spoken word, taking great care to ensure that their messages were communicated accurately from time to time and place to place. Consider the following examples of communication described in the Bible:

❖ The Sermon on the Mount
❖ The protests of the prophets against idol-worship and the corruption of their own rulers and foreign rulers

❖ Moses' exhortations to the Israelites as he led them out of Egypt and through the desert
❖ The delivery of the Ten Commandments

These communications rank as some of the most powerful, effective, long-lasting messages ever communicated in the history of humankind. No one could ever dismiss them as "last week's memo" or the "usual platform speech." They were impassioned, inspired, and uniquely memorable.

And despite the lack of sophisticated telecommunications equipment, the leaders of the Bible made sure that there was plenty of two-way communication as well. Moses, Jesus, and David were masters of managing group meetings and group process (with some of the groups reaching into the thousands). Particularly during the time of Jesus, letters (epistles) went back and forth across the Middle East, Greece, and Rome and were the primary method of communication and coordination among those who were attempting to spread the gospel in an often-hostile environment.

Today's leaders, with modern media at their disposal, are able to reach many more people instantaneously. But the principles of communication remain the same. Ironically, because of the "overkill" of electronic communication (many of us receive several dozen e-mails a day, most of them from people just down the corridor!), face-to-face communication has taken on added importance and impact. Today's smart leaders complement "high-tech" communication approaches with "low-tech," face-to-face contact to preserve the personal power of communication.

THE IMPORTANCE OF COMMUNICATION

Without frequent and appropriate communication of overarching ideas, mission, and vision, Judaism or Christianity would not exist today. The leaders and prophets of the Bible took great care to ensure that their ideas were communicated powerfully and accurately so the meaning was not diluted or changed. The people did not always get the message, sometimes they didn't like it, and sometimes they failed to follow it, degenerating periodically into idol worship and deviation from the moral path. But a "great communicator" always arose to revive the message and put the people back on the path.

When Samuel anointed Saul as the first king to rule over all Israel, he was well aware of the potential for abuse of power, and he took great pains to ensure that the people understood this potential as well as the great potential for good that having a strong monarch promised. He also made sure that the entire nation of Israel was present when he delivered his message.

"Samuel said to all the people: 'Do you see the man the Lord has chosen? There is no one like him among all the people.' Then the people shouted, 'Long live the king!' " This could have been a perfect time for Samuel to inflate himself and the new king by stirring up the crowd even further. But instead, he communicated the need for moderation and caution. Power would have to be balanced by responsibility and controls: "Samuel explained to the people the regulations of the kingship. He wrote them down on a scroll . . . Then Samuel dismissed the people, each to his own home." (1 Sam. 10)

A skilled communicator is comfortable in a variety of communication forums. Jesus utilized small task force meetings with his disciples, speeches to the general public, and confrontations with the ruling religious and secular authorities. Each was handled in a different way. Similarly, Moses met one-on-one with Pharaoh, in small groups with his chief lieutenants, and in large groups with the entire nation of Israel.

Today's best leaders need to be comfortable with groups of all sizes and communication methods of many types as well. There is a different kind of power in communicating with people individually, in small groups, and in large groups, and the wise leader develops a comfort level with each, mixing and matching these methods into an effective communication effort that drives the organization toward its goals.

INDIVIDUAL COMMUNICATION

The wisest leaders, from Franklin Delano Roosevelt with his "fireside chats" to Hal Rosenbluth of Rosenbluth Travel with his "Hal Hotline," know that it is important to make each person feel that he has direct connection to and communication with the leader. FDR's radio "chats" made each listener feel that he was addressing him individually.

Rosenbluth created a voice mail link where any associate (employee) at any level can leave a message, and he responds personally to every message. "It's an avenue for me to keep my finger on the pulse of the company, which is really the pulse of thousands of people," he notes. (Rosenbluth does not ignore the need for group forums, however. He frequently has two-day focus groups with a cross-section of employees, where he asks them to draw pictures depicting their feelings about the company and probes for areas of frustration and satisfaction.[1] Like former New York City mayor Ed Koch, he also asks his followers for candid feedback on "How'm I doing?")

Martha Ingram of Ingram Industries did not neglect personal communications when she took over this huge video wholesaler and book distribution company after her husband died suddenly. Realizing the power of individual connection—particularly at a time of leadership transition—she installed a toll-free hotline that rings in her office. Any employee who has a problem and feels she can't go through normal channels can call the CEO directly. The hotline is not used as often as you might think (people still think twice before calling a CEO), but its very existence serves as a humanizing and galvanizing force.[2]

The leaders of the Bible also understood the importance of individual communication. Moses had frequent meetings with his young aide and successor, Joshua. Jesus gave individual attention to each of his disciples. One-to-one communication was particularly important between Queen Esther, who was inside the seat of power, and her cousin Mordechai, who could communicate her messages and suggested actions to the endangered Jews, who were anxiously awaiting her every dispatch.

GROUP COMMUNICATION

Wise leaders leverage the power of individual communication with the added power of group communication. Andy Grove of Intel had six "open forums" a year with groups of employees. Like many CEOs, Grove spent much of his time communicating with the modern equivalent of the king's court and the high priests of his industry.

But like David convening with his "mighty men," Grove cherished the opportunity to speak with and rally his troops. "I find these open forums far more stimulating, in terms of the variety and incisiveness of the questions, than meetings with security analysts," says Grove.[3] And by engaging in honest two-way communication with his charges, Grove gained even more than "stimulation." He gained increased loyalty and the increased flow of ideas that are created in a nonthreatening environment.

Lands' End, the mail-order apparel company based in Wisconsin, also knows the power of group communication. Top executives of the company meet regularly with seven lower-level employees (packers, inseamers, monogrammers, sales and service people) for a "working lunch." Because these people are so close to the action, they come up with some of the best ideas for improving the operation. No doubt employee loyalty, performance, and retention are also reinforced by this frequent communication.[4]

Another group reminiscent of David's "mighty men" is OpenAir com, a Boston-based provider of business services software. At 9:30 each day, they convene a "Morning Huddle," which is held by the water cooler. Says CEO Bill O'Farrell, "We're standing up (it's unlikely that David's "mighty men" had time to sit in the heat of battle), we do it quickly, and it's not a bureaucratic exercise . . . It's reemphasized that our company is built on collaboration." There are no chairs allowed at this meeting (a strong nonverbal reminder that this is an action-oriented company and meeting), and everyone is expected to contribute.[5]

Joshua was a leader who understood the power of group communication and the use of it to maintain credibility and purpose. Since he had just succeeded Moses, the most powerful of Jewish leaders to that time, it was important that he communicate consistency of message and also invoke the power of his predecessor. He did this with a masterly combination of verbal and nonverbal techniques.

First, Joshua "set the stage" dramatically by building an altar on a mountaintop exactly as Moses had commanded. He also repeated Moses' message exactly, which further reminded his followers of his direct acquisition of power from Moses, and he arranged the people exactly as Moses had commanded. "There, in the presence of the Israelites, Joshua copied on the stones the law of Moses . . . All Israel . . . were standing on both sides of the ark . . . as Moses, the servant of the Lord had formerly commanded . . . Afterward, Joshua read all the words of the law—the blessings and the curses—just as it is written in the book of the Law. There was not a word that Moses had commanded that Joshua did not read." (Josh. 8:32–35)

Another biblical master communicator was Ezra. Ezra understood the power of verbal communication, supporting nonverbal dramatics, and repetition, particularly when these were reinforced by the power of group communication.

> *Ezra the priest brought the Law before the assembly . . . He read aloud from daybreak until noon . . . And all the people listened attentively . . . Ezra . . . stood on a high wooden platform built for the occasion . . . Ezra opened the book. All the people could see him because he was standing above them, and as he opened it, the people stood up. (Neh. 8:2–8:5)*

What CEO or political leader wouldn't envy the communicative power that Ezra possessed? Moreover, this was not just a one-time event, it was an ongoing campaign. "Day after day, from the first day to the last, Ezra read from the book." (Neh. 8:18)

A modern leader who appreciates the negative or positive power of communication is Eric Schmidt, CEO of Novell, who noted that the company he had taken over frequently exhibited dysfunctional communication patterns. He observes that in a culture of fear, people often suppress their feelings. They don't complain to their bosses for fear of being disciplined or fired, but they will complain vociferously to their peers, resulting in a culture of "cynicism and pervasive bellyaching."

Schmidt writes about the "Novell nod," in which all present at a meeting would publicly agree on an issue. As soon as the meeting broke up, however, people would say to those with whom they felt comfortable, "That was the stupidest thing I ever heard." Schmidt realized the danger of this type of communication pattern, so he consciously acted to reverse it. He created an early warning system. "I've told my staff to sit down every day with everyone who reports to them and ask overtly how they're doing and if they're happy. . . . Most of them will be honest with you if you give them the opportunity."

Ironically for a high-tech executive, Schmidt is also a strong advocate of face-to-face communication: "Politicians use the handclasp, and so do the best industry leaders . . . Since I've been here, I've spent way too much time on the corporate jet. I routinely hit five cities a day. That lifestyle is grueling but utterly necessary."[6]

A biblical leader who embraced a grueling but utterly necessary travel pattern for the sake of improved communication was the apostle Paul. He had a message to communicate, and nothing was going to keep him from communicating it! Not rough seas or hostile crowds, Paul crisscrossed the Middle East, Rome, and Greece numerous times as he set up churches and spread the message of Jesus Christ. Wisely, Paul supplemented these travels with letters to key peers and subordinates when he could not be physically present. He also used his trusted lieutenants to help him communicate. In a letter sent from Rome to followers in Colosse, he writes, "Tychicus will tell you all the news about me. He is a dear brother . . . I am sending him to you . . . that you may know about our circumstances and that he may encourage your hearts." (Col. 4:7–8)

Reminiscent in his travels of Paul is Peter Brabeck-Letmathe, CEO of Nestle. Although no doubt he has a few lieutenants (like Tychicus) whom he can send out, he personally visits almost 4,000 employees a year. "I go out in the field all the time . . . I am seldom in Vevey (company headquarters)—maybe one week a month. Otherwise I travel to our facilities and gather local management around me. We talk and talk; I explain to them what we are doing and they question me."[7]

In the early days of the business, Sam Walton of retailing giant Wal-Mart established Saturday morning meetings of key executives. This type of focused communication became even more essential as the company grew (as it no doubt did as the children of Israel grew from a tiny band to a conglomeration of twelve large tribes).

"The Saturday morning meeting is where we discuss and debate much of our philosophy and our management strategy," writes Walton in his autobiography, *Made in America*. Like Joshua and Ezra with their elaborately staged presentations, Walton was a master at making communication more dramatic. The Saturday morning meeting was rarely just a straightforward business discussion. Like the ancient Hebrews and the modern Japanese, Walton often encouraged his executives to sing in these meetings. He would also bring in an executive from another company, an athlete, or even an entertainer or comedian. He reasoned that the more forms in which a message is communicated, the more powerful it becomes.[8]

COMMUNICATING THE MESSAGE

It is one thing to understand the importance of communication. It is another to communicate a message effectively. A message must be communicated in language the audience understands. The audience must be made to believe that they can achieve whatever goals are being communicated. The message needs to be repeated, but not in the same exact words every time, and not so often that it gets tiresome rather than motivating. And often, the most powerful messages are communicated indirectly, using allegory, symbols, and stories.

But no matter how carefully crafted, the message will not be believed if the source lacks credibility. This was true in the time of Pharaoh and it continues to be true in modern business, politics, or civic affairs.

OPEN COMMUNICATION

Recently, there has been much talk about "open book management," "full disclosure," and other terms that indicate a more thorough sharing of information throughout the ranks of employees (often referred to now as partners or associates). In practice, this openness is practiced to different degrees depending on the industry and the organizational culture.

But there are companies in which the commitment to free flows of information between employees and management is more the rule than the exception. Knowingly or not, these companies continue in the heritage of biblical leaders like Luke, who prefaced the Book of Luke with a statement that "since I myself have carefully investigated everything from the beginning, it seemed good also to write an orderly account for you . . . so that you may know the certainty of the things you have been taught." (Luke 1:3–4) Or in modern terms, "This is the truth, the whole truth, which I am communicating to you because I trust you to use it wisely."

Hewitt Associates is a benefits consulting firm that has been frequently cited as one of the best companies to work for in America. One reason for this is the openness of communication that is a linchpin of their culture. Notes one employee, "Because the firm tells everyone what is going on and will answer, literally, any question openly and honestly . . . people don't have to spend time tuning in to the rumor mill, they simply ask."[9] A simple model, but one seldom implemented.

Jack Stack of Springfield Re, a division of International Harvester, practically "wrote the book" on open book management. He instituted it because he literally felt he had no choice. The company was in dire financial and operational straits and had essentially been "cut loose" by its parent. Stack could not look to "corporate" to get Springfield out of the desert. Instead, he decided to trust his employees with key financial and operating information, which they had never had access to before and which many observers doubted they could understand, let alone act on.

"There was too much on the line for management not to give employees the truth," observes Stack. At workstations throughout the plant, grease boards showed the numerical goals and a running record of actual performance. It was a communication strategy of total trust, which easily could have backfired due to lack of commitment from a workforce that had every reason to be discouraged.

The result? Springfield Re not only met and exceeded most of its production goals, it also became a model for other companies on how to communicate openly and enlist employees in production goals. Springfield Re even developed an additional source of revenue: They charge a fee to visitors from other companies who want to "borrow" and learn from their communication and production methods![10]

Another company that values the free and frequent flow of information is AES. Says its top executive, Dennis Bakke: "We have very few secrets here at AES. . . . Besides compensation levels, all financial and market information is widely circulated . . . Some people are worried about how public we are with our information; they're concerned it's going to get leaked to competitors. But we think it's a risk worth taking because otherwise, how would our people become business people?"[11]

TARGETING THE MESSAGE

Another key to effective communication is aiming the communication directly at the needs and wants of the audience, speaking a language that they understand and with which they "resonate" on an emotional as well as cognitive level.

Often, targeting involves use of metaphors, analogy, myths, and stories, because direct communication (facts, figures) is not always the most inspiring way to get people to see the urgency or applicability of a message or course of action.

Jesus, for example, knew that his target audience was extremely familiar with the analogy of a shepherd and sheep to symbolize a leader and the led. In John 10, he puts his efforts to proselytize into this framework, making his message more accessible to potential converts and less objectionable to his enemies than if he had communicated it directly:

> *I am the good shepherd. The good shepherd lays down his life for the sheep . . . I have other sheep that are not of this sheep pen. I must bring them in also. They too will listen to my voice, and there will be one flock and one shepherd. This command I received from my Father.*

This was a lot more palatable than his directly saying that he planned to lead his Jewish followers away from traditional Judaism, would recruit additional followers from the gentiles, would die on a cross in pursuit of that effort, and that he was the son of God.

It might seem incongruous that the maverick leader of a women's cosmetics company would lean on biblical allegory to communicate her mission to her vast female army of sales representatives, but Mary Kay Ash was neither an ordinary leader nor a typical communicator. Speaking at a sales convention, she roused the troops by pointing out that the ancient Romans had conquered the world but had never been able to totally conquer "the followers of the great teacher from Bethlehem." The reason? The followers of Jesus met together weekly and shared their difficulties with each other.

"Does this remind you of something?" asked Ash. "The way we stand side by side and share our knowledge and difficulties with each other in our weekly unit meetings?"[12] With a simple, stirring comparison, Ash challenges her followers to duplicate the heroics of the biblical heroes and heroines, compares them to people who have overcome great odds to attain success, and inspires them to attain their own heroic mission.

Compare that type of communication with the brief memo or e-mail that might emanate from the leaders of a less inspired company (my apologies if this too closely resembles the communications at your company):

❖ Weekly unit meetings are mandatory for all staff.
❖ Please bring all sales reports and spreadsheets.
❖ The agenda is attached; please submit your discussion items at least three days in advance of the meeting.

❖ If anyone fails to attend the meeting, your supervisor will be contacted.

Robert Marcell, head of Chrysler's small-car design team in the early 1990s, was faced with a serious communication and morale problem. He felt that despite the increasing Japanese domination of the small car market, Chrysler had the ability to manufacture and market a domestically made small car. His problem? Many others within Chrysler, including his own team, doubted Chrysler's ability to do this alone and wanted to partner with a foreign manufacturer.

Marcell could have done a statistical study or issued a dry report on trends in the domestic and international small-car market. Instead, he decided to take a more daring and hard-hitting communication approach. Reasoning that he had to hit people "where they lived" (emotionally and geographically), he prepared a fifteen-minute slide show that showed pictures of his hometown, a Michigan mining community devastated by competition from foreign companies.

After each slide of boarded-up schools, the ruins of the town's ironworks, and closed churches, Marcell solemnly and simply announced, "We couldn't compete." He then observed that the same thing could happen to Detroit unless at least one car company was willing to reenter the subcompact market. He then challenged the group to develop an American subcompact and went directly to CEO Lee Iacocca to make a similar emotional appeal: "If we dare to be different, we could be the reason the U.S. auto industry survives. We could be the reason our kids and grandkids don't end up working at fast-food chains."[13]

Iacocca also responded on a gut level (backed up by statistics, of course) to Marcell's impassioned appeal. He gave the OK to begin designing and manufacturing the Dodge Neon.

Centuries earlier, Paul was a master at targeting the needs of his audience; he had to be, since he was so frequently fleeing a city or desperately defending himself from death in the courts. In Acts 22, he finds himself arrested and surrounded by an angry Jerusalem mob that demands that the soldiers do away with him because he is challenging the religious orthodoxy prevailing in the city.

A lesser man might have been rendered speechless, but Paul quickly sized up his audience. First, he addressed them in their own language, Aramaic, and implored them: "Brothers and fathers, listen now to my defense." When they heard him speak to them in Aramaic, they became very quiet. Paul then established his credentials as one of the crowd, a Jew, albeit one who had been through a very strange and exciting spiritual experience. He challenged the commander's right to flog him, since he (Paul) was a Roman citizen. Amazingly, the commander became flustered, not knowing what to do.

Paul was released and given his "day in court." Addressing the Sanhedrin, he followed the cardinal rule of good presentations: He established eye contact. "Paul looked straight at the Sanhedrin and said, 'My brothers, I have fulfilled my duty to God in all good conscience to this day.'" (Tony Burns, CEO of Ryder Systems, says, "You look someone in the eyes. You can tell by the look in his eyes or the inflection in his voice what the real problem or question or answer is.")[14]

And because Paul knew his audience, he also knew how to divide them. "My brothers, I am a Pharisee, the son of a Pharisee. I stand on trial because of my hope in the resurrection of the dead." The Sadducees did not believe in resurrection, spirits, or angels, but the Pharisees did. Paul created such an argument between these two sides of the court that his case was transferred to the court in Rome, where he was tried in a succession of courts, each time defending himself eloquently and successfully. Using his great communications skills in each court, he even tried to convert his captors to Christianity! Everywhere Paul went, he unflinchingly communicated his message.

REPETITION

The Bible and the heroes who speak its words are notoriously repetitious. Artless repetition is boring, uninspiring, and ineffective. Ideas repeated in different ways and words, at just the right intervals, constitute effective communication. This is particularly true if the ideas are new or if they represent a new paradigm that the audience finds difficult to understand or that represents radical change.

Paul, who truly represented a new and "foreign" paradigm (Christianity), addressed the synagogue in Thessalonica not just for a brief "guest sermon" but for three successive Sabbath days. Even though he made some converts, many who heard him stuck with their old beliefs. He needed to repeat his message many more times and in many different ways before he would recruit large numbers of converts.

Modern business leaders, particularly those who are also introducing or explaining new paradigms, also need to use the technique of repetition. Writing in *Fast Company*, Tom Peters observed:

> *Leadership takes an almost bottomless supply of verbal energy: working the phones, staying focused on your message, repeating the same mantra until you can't stand the sound of your own voice—and then repeating it some more, because just when you start to become bored witless with the message, it's probably starting to seep into the organization.*[15]

We do not know whether leaders like Jan Carlzon of Scandinavian Airlines and Percy Barnevik of Asa Boveri Brown ever became "bored" with their message. Certainly we know they had to repeat it many times in many forums; if they did not become bored that is a testimony to the strength of their dedication and vision.

Although the Bible is highly repetitious, and the leaders in it had to repeat themselves frequently, a search for the words *bored* or *boredom* in the Concordance of most Bibles yields few or no references. Paul's instructions to his young subordinate Timothy show large amounts of perseverance and no presence of ennui: "I give you this charge: Preach the word; be prepared in season and out of season; correct, rebuke, and encourage—with great patience and careful instruction." (2 Tim. 4:2–3)

The inspired leaders, biblical or modern, find repetition an indispensable communication tool, and may even come to find this repetition part of their inspiration, because it fuels progress toward the targeted goal. And exaggeration, as long as it is not overdone, frequently works well in tandem with repetition. Jack Welch of General Electric observed:

> *In leadership, you've got to exaggerate every statement you make. You've got to repeat it a thousand times and exaggerate it. So I'll say things like, "No one can get promoted if they're not a Green Belt in Six Sigma." Such statements are needed to move a large organization. And then you must back them up with personnel moves to show people you're serious.*[16]

LISTENING SKILLS

Will the led truly listen and respond to the exhortations of the leaders, even when these seem unrealistic, daunting, and/or repetitive? The answer to this partly depends on the answer to another question: How well is the leader listening to the followers? Does the leader want to hear only good news, brushing off or ignoring attempts to point out tacks in the road (or scorpions in the desert)? Or is the leader truly willing to listen to constructive criticism or ways that the operation can be improved? When the followers look at the leader, do they see a pair of ears in front of them, or only a large, ever-moving mouth?

The Bible is full of leaders who failed to listen. Lot's wife didn't listen to the warning not to look back at the burning cities of Sodom and Gomorrah, and wound up as a pillar of salt. Pharaoh did not listen to Moses, not even after his nation was hit with ten catastrophic plagues.

Noah, on the other hand, was a man who saw and understood the value of listening. Seeing the corrupt state of the world around him, he had no reason to doubt that God ("top management") was about to destroy it by flood and start over. As someone who had never built a boat, he was ready to listen and comply when God gave him the exact measurements (450 feet long, 75 feet wide, and 45 feet high). He even listened when God told him that he could fit his entire extended family on this ark, along with two of every type of animal on the face of the earth.

A modern example of someone with exceptional listening skills is J. Kermit Campbell, the CEO of Herman Miller, a furniture company with over 5,000 employees. Campbell vowed to meet every single one of them one to one and listen to their individual concerns. He accomplished this (while still being able to run the company!) by going directly to each employee's workstation, making round-the-clock visits to all shifts.[17]

Another great listener was Sam Walton of Wal-Mart. He set up a hotline through which any employee could call headquarters in Bentonville, Arkansas, if they were not happy with the inventory they were receiving or with what was going on in the store. Walton was also not one to keep his leaders "in their tents" at corporate headquarters. Instead, every Monday through Thursday, he sent his top executives out into the field, flying from store to store. What was the mission of these highly paid executives? To listen to employees who were often making minimum wage.

Regional vice president Andy Wilson relished these trips because "all the best ideas" came from these front-line employees, keeping Wal-Mart agile and responsive to its customers.[18] As Proverbs 18:13 notes, "He who answers before listening—that is his folly and his shame." Sam Walton knew that any response from corporate without listening to the troops in the stores was bound to result in the retail version of folly and shame—poor service and lost revenues.

Richard Teer Link of Harley-Davidson was a leader who was forced to listen. Sales of the famous motorcycle were going down, and he didn't have a clue why. His response was to listen not just to employees, but (glory be!) the customers. He organized Harley Owners' Groups (HOGs) and asked probing questions to determine the underlying need that made a person buy his motorcycles. By listening carefully, he found that customers were not just buying a mode of transportation, or even a beautiful machine. They were buying freedom, independence, and escape from the stress and routine of their everyday lives. This resulted in an entirely different marketing approach. Sales soared, as did membership in the Harley Owners' Groups that Teer Link had started as a sounding board for customers.

Pitney Bowes holds annual jobholders' meetings, where management listens to literally every concern an employee wants to bring up. One employee's complaint that there was too much oil in the salad bar was given as much consideration (if perhaps not as much time) as concerns with working conditions, staff morale, and global strategy.[19]

Of course, it is relatively easy to listen when things are going fairly well. It takes a real leader to listen carefully and politely when employees are angrily pointing out serious management errors or taking issue with the basic strategy of the company. James, Jesus' disciple and half-brother, gave excellent management consultation when he wrote, "Everyone should be quick to listen, slow to speak, and slow to become angry." (James 1:19)

This is not always easy, but some leaders are able to listen to both the good and the bad without getting defensive about what they have done or feeling personally attacked. Those who are able to do this usually emerge with a better relationship with their critics and with a more profitable operation, because they uncovered a flaw that needed correction.

Andy Grove of Intel understood that there were Strategic Inflection Points, events that are so significant that they may change your entire business strategy. He courageously stated, "It is important at such times to listen to people who bring you bad news, and to know these people are often in the lower ranks of the organization. Unless you welcome their contrarian views—and learn to live with the fear that such views can bring—you will never learn from these useful Cassandras."[20]

Gordon Bethune, CEO of Continental Airlines, also sees the value of listening to those who are critical of the operation. Indeed, he was called on board to clean up the damage that a former regime of "yes-men" and "yes-women" had fomented by their inaction and inability to challenge a host of unproductive management practices. Bethune urges:

> *Make sure you only hire people who will be willing to kick the door open if you lose direction and close it. You may be able to ignore some-*

body's opinion if you don't like it, but if the person has the data to back it up, your intellect should be able to overwhelm your vanity.[21]

The Bible tells us that we should be alert to messages from *any* source that warn us that we may be going down the wrong path. Balaam was a man who didn't know how to listen or to whom to listen. Balak, the king of Moab, tried to hire him to pronounce a curse against the people of Israel. Balaam initially balked because he feared God, but his greed got the better of him, and he set off to visit Balak and to put a curse on his own country once more.

Balaam's donkey must have had clearer vision than her owner (after all, he was blinded by greed), for she could see the angel of the Lord standing in the middle of the road to thwart this immoral journey. The donkey first veered off the road, then pressed herself against a wall (crushing Balaam's foot) and finally lay down and refused to move. She even spoke to him. Rather than "listening" to the signs that something might be amiss in his strategy, Balaam angrily beat his donkey until he saw the angel, sword in hand, standing in the road. The angel informed him that if the donkey had not turned away from the journey three times, Balaam would have already been killed!

Situations in which it's appropriate to listen to donkeys are mercifully very rare. But often, leaders must listen to many differing human points of view. William Steere, CEO of Pfizer, notes: "Remaining open to conflicting or even painful information keeps you from being complacent and insular . . . success is achieved when you have very smart people advancing different points of view . . . Our goal is for everyone to be heard and every point of view examined."[22]

The prophets were often considered to be the "bringers of bad news" because they were quick to point out when the leaders and people of Israel had gone astray from their mission, had become corrupted, or were being threatened by an outside enemy. They were therefore frequently rejected or imprisoned by the very leaders who could have benefited from their advice and warnings.

Jeremiah was such a prophet, who risked his own life to send a warning to the king of Judah. Jeremiah had received a prophesy of all the disasters that would befall Judah, so he dictated the information and saw that the scroll was brought to the king. The king's response? Whenever his servant had read three or four columns of the scroll, "the king cut them off with a scribe's knife and threw them into the firepot until the entire scroll was burned in the fire . . . The king and all his attendants who heard all these words showed no fear, nor did they tear their clothes." (Jer. 36:23–24)

Here was a leader who ignored well-intentioned advice that could have saved his country and people tremendous suffering if he had only listened to it (not to mention, the advice was free). By contrast, John Gigerich, chief information officer of Union Carbide, actually sought out discomfort and bad news within the organization. He knew there were serious conflicts about the use of technology and the firm's strategic direction, and he reasoned that these festering sores would only become more infected without attention. Gigerich's vaccine? Large doses of communication, particularly listening. He surfaced the issues, responded to the resistance he encountered, and spent months discussing, explaining, and responding to employee concerns before he determined and instituted the proper changes in each department.

Roya Zamanzadeh is CEO of Pear Transmedia, a thirteen-person Web design and development company, whose clients include Bugle Boy and Mattel. When asked what made her "ripe for the job," she doesn't mention a thing about technical or marketing expertise. Instead, she focuses on her listening skills. "I've spent years working in traditional corporations, and I've learned that it's imperative that the needs of employees be answered . . . A good ear is important."[23]

It takes a strong leader to listen to the concerns of a line employee, particularly when the employee has a strong point of view and personality herself. When Elaine Frankowski, a biochemist at Cray Research, once was criticized by John Rollwagen, the CEO, she responded by saying, "Don't whine at me, it's not my fault." To her amazement, "two days later, he talked to a group of people, and he had actually heard what I said." The altercation had been uncomfortable, but the communication had been frank and the results fruitful. In Frankowski's former company, no one from top management would probably have even taken the trouble to speak to her: "If you're not in management (at that company), you're no one," she observes.[24]

COMMUNICATION SKILLS—
INNATE OR LEARNED?

There is a wide-ranging debate about the innateness or "learnability" of effective communication skills and the nature of "charisma." Can communication skills be learned and improved, or does a leader have to be naturally charismatic to communicate effectively and gain the enthusiastic support of others?

To help answer this question, we can turn first to the Bible and next to a couple of modern leaders. Moses was an extremely effective leader, but not a particularly dynamic speaker. When asked to make a key "presentation" on behalf of his people to the Egyptians, Moses protested: "Oh Lord, I have never been eloquent, neither in the past nor since you have spoken to your servant. I am slow of speech and tongue." Most biblical scholars interpret this to mean that Moses had a speech impediment, or, in modern terms, a "communication disorder," which today would land him in special education class.

God's suggestion to Moses was to team him with his brother Aaron, who was a better speaker. But it was Moses, not Aaron, who spoke to Pharaoh and led his people out of Egypt. What he lacked in speaking ability, Moses possessed in conviction, courage, and compassion for his people. These traits were communicated unmistakably to all who were exposed to him, both follower and foe.

Another leader who had a speech impediment, a childhood stutter, was Jack Welch. Welch recounts how his mother refused even to acknowledge his stutter. He and his mother would drive to the train station at night to pick up his father from his job as a conductor. They would sit in the dark and talk, and eventually Welch stopped stuttering. He became an excellent speaker, particularly when addressing General Electric managers at the company's famed Management Development Center in Crotonville, New York.[25]

Although natural charisma and communication training can certainly help a leader communicate more effectively, these are not the key ingredients to success in this area. Most people respond to sincerity and knowledge, which cannot be readily rehearsed or "canned." Herb Kelleher has stated that the best communication comes directly from the heart. The Bible supports him wholeheartedly:

> *"I do not think I am in the least inferior to those 'super-apostles.' I may not be a trained speaker, but I do have knowledge." (Paul, in 2 Cor. 11:5–6)*
>
> *"The lips of the righteous know what is fitting." (Prov. 10:32)*

BIBLICAL LESSONS ON COMMUNICATION

- ❧ To motivate others to reach your goals, you must constantly communicate your message.

- ❧ Use a variety of communication methods. Don't neglect the power of face-to-face communication; it's a time-honored method often missing in today's barrage of impersonal electronic messages.

- ❧ Effective leaders are equally comfortable communicating to individuals, small groups, and large gatherings, customizing their approaches for each audience.

- ❧ Repetition is an important tool, but use varying words and media so your message doesn't become stale.

- ❧ Share information; people will probably find out anyway, but from a less desirable source.

- ❧ Use language, images, and metaphors that hit your audience at "gut level."

∞ Listen carefully to people and show them you've heard them by responding verbally or taking action.

∞ Acknowledge bad news and thank those "prophets" who have had the courage to deliver it to you.

∞ You do not have to be a naturally gifted speaker. Communication skills can be learned.

∞ Jack Welch stuttered as a child, and Moses was "slow of tongue."

CHAPTER SIX

Performance
Management

"He who heeds discipline shows the way to life . . . but whomever ignores correction leads others astray."

—Prov. 12:1

"I have not hesitated to preach anything that might be helpful to you."

—Acts 20:18

f you had mentioned the phrase "performance management" to anyone in the Bible (even if you tried to translate
it into Hebrew or Aramaic), you probably would have been
accused of speaking in tongues. Actually, you might have
been accused of speaking in tongues if you'd used these words in an
American corporation a decade or two ago.

Performance management includes the following three stages: one,
goal setting and motivation (usually done "in the beginning," before
much action has taken place); two, encouragement (applied while the
task is being accomplished); and three, rewards and consequences
(applied after the task has been completed). When correctly applied,
performance management spurs people on to even greater accomplish-

ments in their next task or project, simultaneously developing their skills and increasing their desire.

Although the term "performance management" will not be found in the Bible, the elements of this technique are found in almost every one of its chapters. Adam and Eve's expulsion from the most pleasant environment ever designed, the Garden of Eden, was a result of their failure to act according to the performance guidelines their superior had communicated to them. (It also might have been helpful if they had had some prior experience with forked-tongued consultants and "forbidden fruit.")

Noah, on the other hand, responded positively to his leader's encouragement to reach seemingly unattainable performance goals. Realizing the consequences of nonperformance, he paid close attention to the boss's blueprint for both an escape plan and the boat that would carry him through the worst environmental (and moral) crisis the world had ever experienced. While Adam and Eve managed to spoil the world's most ideal environment, Noah managed to survive the most adverse one. Ironically, they had the same boss! Even the best leader needs competent, responsive employees if he is to achieve maximum performance.

The ancient Hebrews and early Christians were not exactly out for a stroll in the park (or even a "brief tour" of the desert). Moses had to constantly encourage his people during the forty years in the desert, when the Promised Land seemed as far away as Pluto might seem to us today. Realizing the daunting scope of building the First Temple, David gave his son Solomon large doses of encouragement. Jesus promised his disciples, who had left good livelihoods as fishermen, that he would make them "fishers of men," which had less immediate, but more long-lasting payback.

Consequences figure heavily in the Bible. In most cases, the "players" are told exactly what will happen to them if they adhere to or deviate from "company policy." Jacob knew that he would have to flee precipitously if he stole his father's birthright from his physically stronger brother, Esau. Christ foretold that Peter would betray him three times; he also wisely let Peter live with the consequences of his actions rather than punish him directly. And positive actions usually result in ultimate reward, whether it is Jacob laboring an extra seven years to win the hand of Rachel or David sparing the life of Saul in the cave and eventually ascending to the throne himself.

Excellent performance management takes the patience of Job, courage of David, wisdom of Solomon, and the compassion of Jesus. But that doesn't mean that today's "merely human" leaders can't aspire to manage performance in ways that rival their biblical precursors. Many of them are doing so already.

MOTIVATION AND GOAL SETTING

The first stage of performance management consists of helping people set ambitious yet realistic goals and motivating them toward the achievement of those goals. In 1 Thessalonians, Paul writes to the converts in Thessalonica that, "as apostles of Christ, we certainly had a right to make some demands of you, but we were gentle among you, like a mother caring for her little children . . . encouraging, comforting, and urging you . . ." Paul was a master of motivation, tailoring his urgency and emotional tone to the readiness of the "employees."

Jack Stack of Springfield Re also tailored his motivational message to the readiness of the "troops" when he took over the Melrose Park factory at International Harvester. He had 500 unionized workers, most of whom operated in a culture of poor quality and low morale. Stack told them, "If you beat your all-time high, I'll buy you all a cup of coffee."

This doesn't sound like high-level motivation (or a high-priced incentive). But keep in mind that production levels were so poor that matching the all-time high was only *worth* a cup of coffee. Anything more would have been overkill, inflated praise for a modest gain.

It was also symbolic motivation. Like Paul, Stack was caring for and feeding his "children." It was probably the most nurturing thing anyone had done for them in years. And Stack succeeded. He "had" to buy everyone in the plant a cup of coffee when they exceeded the previous benchmark.

The second week, Stack upped the ante, offering the workers coffee and rolls if they could beat the previous week's mark. He was increasing the goals gradually while consistently offering more rewards. The following week, he offered the employees a double bonus: not just coffee and rolls, but pizza and beer. Moreover, these would be served in Stack's own home. The employees exceeded their previous benchmark, and Stack served 200 people pizza and beer in his home. "It was the first time that anyone in management had ever . . . actually told them how they were really being evaluated," muses Stack.[1] But goals do not always have to be set low and increased gradually to be motivating. When Charles Heimbold, CEO of Bristol-Meyers Squibb, had his first meeting with his managers in 1994, the company was doing reasonably well. Whereas Stack's biggest danger at Springfield Re was desperation, Heimbold's was complacency. "I brought everyone together and said, 'We're going to have a doubling of our sales and our earnings per share by the end of the year 2000,' " he reminisces. This was a much higher growth rate than had ever been achieved before. "When you repeat these expectations frequently enough, you can get people to understand and buy in. People start to say, 'Yeah, maybe we can do that.' That's the feeling I wanted to create. I wanted our people to believe."[2]

Both the early Hebrews and Christians were struggling sects who were fighting to maintain their very existence. Numerical gains in the membership were small. But both groups motivated themselves with longer-term goals. The Hebrews believed in God's promise that they would some day be as numerous as the stars in the heavens. The apostles believed that some day their tiny "sect" would have more adherents than any religion in the world. The constant repetition of these expectations by a succession of strong leaders explains their long-term success.

But even in the Bible (and certainly corporate America), intrinsic, spiritual rewards are not always enough to motivate for performance. David was a courageous man and great leader, but he was also offered material and other incentives for killing Goliath. "The king will give great wealth to the man who kills him (Goliath). He will also give him his daughter in marriage and will exempt his father's family from taxes in Israel." (1 Sam. 17:25)

The heads of modern corporations do not give away their daughters as performance incentives, nor can they exempt their employees from taxes, but they do use monetary rewards. Bernie Ebbers of MCI World-Com makes certain that everyone in the firm has stock options and so is paid like an owner, much like David increased the sense of ownership in his "mighty men" by making sure that all received a share of the spoils of war. Says Ebbers, "You can't go through the building without seeing charts . . . showing them what those options are worth."[3]

Charles Heimbold, CEO of Clairol, also makes sure everyone in his company has stock options. He reasons that if he gives people ownership, accountability, and knowledge, they'll contribute more to the company's success because they can see the link between their performance and company performance. One example was Clairol's Herbal Essences, a product that was introduced in the 1970s and lagged terribly in the 1980s. Everyone on the Clairol team knew they needed to reposition the product or ditch it. In a company where performance was not as closely linked to reward, it would have been ditched. But Clairol's team saw the product's potential, and they repositioned it for the Generation X and thirty-something market. Sales soared, as did the value of everyone's stock options.

INSPIRATION

People do not respond just to "hard dollars," however. Inspiration by a leader often plays a major role in spurring people on to maximum performance. Moses inspired the Hebrews to traverse a desert in pursuit of the "land of milk and honey." Nehemiah inspired people not with money but with a goal that was larger than money—the reconstruction of the wall around Jerusalem. And Jesus attracted his first disciples with an inspiring new paradigm: "I will make you fishers of men." They were transformed simply by joining his organization, before they performed a stitch of work.

At Novell, Eric Schmidt has an annual dinner as part of the President's Award program to honor unique, substantial individual accomplishment. Spouses are invited, plaques are awarded, and for good measure, so are stock options. "These are simple gestures, but it's amazing what they do for people. Recognition like this makes it much harder for them to leave the company; and it keeps them much more engaged in their work."[4] By inspiring and recognizing people for achievement, Schmidt makes it more likely that this is not the employees' "last supper" with Novell. As with Jesus' disciples, gatherings like these increase group cohesion and motivation and remind all of the inspiring mission of which they are a part. And those who have not yet earned the award are inspired as well.

Ray Gilmartin, CEO of Merck, is quick to point out the necessity of inspiration if a leader (and the company) is to be successful. In choosing his leadership team in 1994, Gilmartin selected people with a balance of skills. Yes, they had to have the right skills. But they also had to be "people who demonstrated the core values of the company, people who would inspire our employees."[5]

One way to inspire is to set large goals. Says Dave Komansky, chairman and CEO of Merrill Lynch, "You've always got to ask more of yourself and your people than either you or they think can be accomplished. If you ask someone to climb a four-foot wall, they're going to climb the four-foot wall and feel great. Chances are, if you had asked them to climb an eight-foot wall, they would have climbed that wall as well, but you never asked them and they didn't think about it."[6]

Joshua had an advantage as he approached the walls of Jericho. His people could *see* the wall and exactly how high it was—impossibly high. The only way to knock it down was through a new method—a new paradigm that had not been tried before. Fortunately, Joshua's motivation was very strong, and he communicated that resolve to the rest of the organization. He also must have recruited some pretty mean trumpet players!

Inspiration is not just needed when major obstacles (like walls, kings, deserts, and famines) loom ahead. Sometimes people are feeling disempowered and demotivated because of mistakes they have made in the past. The best leaders stay committed to the ultimate goal even when they or their followers have committed "missteps" as they strode toward the goal.

When King David instructed his son Solomon to build the temple in

Jerusalem, he warned him, "don't be discouraged by the size of the task." (1 Chron. 28:20) Solomon knew that he was an inexperienced young man and would probably make some mistakes as he proceeded. His father's wise words included the implicit encouragement to be unfazed by errors.

In an undertaking the size of Solomon's temple, errors are inevitable. After all, he had 70,000 carriers, 80,000 stonecutters and 3,600 foremen. He "overlaid the ceiling beams, doorframes, walls and doors of the temple with gold" and the inside of the Most Holy Place with "talents of fine gold. The gold nails weighed fifty shekels . . . he made a pair of sculpted cherubim and overlaid them with gold. The total wingspan of the cherubim was twenty cubits." (2 Chron. 3) What do you think would have been the effect on this project and the team that completed it if Solomon had been preoccupied with errors and "waste" instead of the success of the overall mission?

In the early days of W. L. Gore and Associates, when Gore-Tex was still on the drawing board (and the company had scarce funds for "experimentation"), a group of engineers wasted $1,000 worth of material. "We were just standing there with long faces," mourns one of the engineers, "and Bill Gore walks up and says, 'What's wrong, guys?' and we said, 'Well, we just put $1,000 of scrap on the floor.' And he said, 'Try it again tomorrow. I know you can do it . . . And he walked away.' "[7]

Bill Gore had the foresight to know that some day $1,000 would seem like a small expense in the overall life of his company. He also knew the power of motivation and demotivation. Confronted with $1,000 of wasted material, he could just as easily have screamed, "Don't you know we're working with scarce resources here? We'll never succeed at this rate!" He could have applied negative consequences. But instead, like Solomon and the building of the temple, he kept his eye on the long-term goal, the development of Gore-Tex, and encouraged continued progress toward its achievement.

ENCOURAGEMENT

The critical second stage of performance management is encouragement. Many a lofty project has been launched with great enthusiasm, only to "peter out" for lack of ongoing encouragement. In Hebrews 3:13, the early Christians are urged to "encourage one another daily, as long as it is called Today." Paul made a point of reminding his followers that "I have not hesitated to preach anything that would be helpful to you." (Acts 20:18) The more difficult the task, the more important ongoing encouragement becomes. The wisest biblical leaders knew this instinctively, and the best modern leaders are also masters at encouragement, not just at periodic "rah-rah" sessions, but in their everyday actions.

Dennis Bakke and Roger Sant of AES realize that it would be impossible for them to actually carry out, or even lead, all the tasks necessary to run a huge power company. Their major role? Says Bakke, "We're the chief encouragers. We celebrate AES people. We attend orientations and plant openings. We give the speeches at five-year anniversary parties."

Sant is quick to add that encouragement adds daily meaning to the work. "People always say they don't have time to celebrate because they're too busy, but stopping and remembering is really important. What is work if you don't see the meaning in it? You have to celebrate the meaning in it."[8]

It's one thing to encourage employees when things are going well. It can take even more fortitude for a leader to encourage his people in the face of physical and emotional adversity. When ice storms hit in Quebec, Charles Heimbold of Bristol-Meyers Squibb didn't just cluck his tongue from his comfortable office in the United States. Instead, he was "on the phone right away to find out what happened to our people, and making sure we're getting emergency supplies up there. They can see that I am as committed to my coworkers and to our success as they are."[9] Heimbold was in essence saying to his employees, "You are in need. Whatever you want me to do, I'll do." To manage others' performance, a leader has to perform reliably himself.

Barnabas, one of Jesus' disciples, was originally called Joseph, but he was given this new name, which meant "son of encouragement." A modern-day "daughter of encouragement" is Anita Roddick of The Body Shop. Roddick encourages her employees not just to achieve their daily tasks, but to think in a larger perspective: "It's got to do with the human spirit," she says. "When anything comes from the heart—any energy, any action—it comes with a passion that is unstoppable. My staff does not go home dreaming of moisture creams. They go home absolutely riveted when they come back from a project in Bosnia or Kosovo. The experience has changed their values."[10] Roddick's reference to "the heart" is key here; the word *encouragement* actually comes from the Latin root for *heart*.

Moses encouraged the tribes of Israel by blessing them. Most of us are encouraged when we are blessed and discouraged when we are punished or ignored. Moses' blessing of the tribes was eloquent and genuine. Rather than making the tribes complacent, it encouraged them to achieve even higher goals than they had already: "About Joseph, he said, 'May the Lord bless his land with the precious dew from heaven above and with the deep waters that lie below . . . with the best the sun brings forth and the finest the moon can yield . . . with the choicest gifts of the ancient mountains and the fruitfulness of the everlasting hills . . .' " (Deut. 33:13–14)

Mary Kay Ash encouraged her employees at Mary Kay with a similar attitude of celebration and blessing. She signed hundreds of birthday cards offering free lunch and a free movie. She commemorated employees' "blessed events" such as weddings and babies with personal gifts. She put flowers and white tablecloths in the company cafeteria, and perfume and makeup (Mary Kay brand, of course) in the rest rooms. A sign outside her office read "Department of Sunshine and Rainbows." Her credo was "Appreciation is the oil that makes things run."[11] Ash realized that constant verbal and physical demonstrations of encouragement are necessary for the achievement of ambitious goals and to make employees feel truly valued.

Moses knew the encouraging power of overarching goals. When the desert sands seemed unending, when food became scarce, and when internal dissidents threatened to undermine the organization's purpose ("Let's return to Egypt!"), Moses reminded the Israelites of their goal, a "land of milk and honey" that truly existed, even if they had never seen it.

Joe Liemandt, CEO of Trilogy, a technology firm in Austin, Texas, is also a firm believer in the encouragement that an overarching goal can provide: "So what keeps our people coming to work every day? It's our environment. Employees get energized around a goal—and that energy is contagious."[12] In the fast-moving world of high tech, where goals can shift weekly, it's important to maintain that energy. And the option of "returning to Egypt" might as well not exist, since it's a sure guarantee of technological obsolescence.

The book of Hebrews reminded biblical leaders to "encourage one another daily" (Heb. 3:13) and exhorted the early Christians: "let us encourage one another." (Heb. 10:24) Gordon Bethune of Continental Airlines also knows the value of encouragement. He took an ailing airline with one of the worst customer service and on-time records and put it back near the top of its industry. He did this with words and deeds of encouragement, both large and small, starting with a $65 bonus in each employee's paycheck for better on-time performance.

This was just the first in a long string of encouraging words and deeds. After the successful turnaround, Bethune wrote, "The biggest single criterion for success as a leader is to recognize and openly appreciate your subordinates. They'll kill for you if you do that."[13] If you have any doubts about that, ask the troops who killed for David and Joshua as they pursued their missions.

Another company that realizes the importance of daily encouragement is Weyerhauser. Steve Hill, senior vice president of human resources, notes that it's often the maximum use and encouragement of the human resources of a company that yield the most competitive advantage. "There isn't a lot of difference between our two-by-fours and Georgia Pacific's," he notes. "So we need to be cost conscious and create a great working environment and really encourage people."[14]

King David's men and Joshua's army did not go confidently into battle because they knew they had "superior" weapons. They had confidence because they were better led and more frequently encouraged than the opposition.

Soup would seem like a rather prosaic product that would not inspire employees to knock down walls or cross raging rivers. But at Campbell

Soup, CEO David Johnson has turned encouragement into a religion. Posted throughout company headquarters are scoreboards that compare the company's net profit increases to those of other food companies. And Johnson constantly reminds his executives and employees of the company's "20–20–20" goal: 20 percent earnings growth, 20 percent return on equity, and 20 percent return on invested cash.

These are ambitious goals, and when achieved, they are not taken for granted. When a major target is hit, Johnson hires a brass band and holds a celebration that would rival the celebration after Solomon's building of the temple.

But in monitoring performance, negative results have to be acknowledged and corrected as well. The Bible instructs us that the best way to correct is: "if someone is caught in a sin, you . . . should restore him gently." (Gal. 6:1) Charles Wang, chairman of Computer Associates, believes that a leader who does not correct people is squandering a precious resource,

"I think one of the things leaders forget is that people look to us to tell them the truth in terms of how they are doing." He acknowledges the difficulty of doing this gently and positively, but adds that if correction is not given, "you're worse off because you don't know where you stand . . . As management, we must tell people what we expect. And if they don't meet expectations, we have to tell them, and tell them why, so they can improve . . . If managers don't do it, they are not really taking ownership."[15]

Carol Bartz, CEO of Autodesk, a producer of CAD/CAM software, also believes in the power of gentle correction. "I frequently say, 'what you don't inspect, they don't respect,' " observes Bartz. So she does a lot of inspecting. "I do that with my daughter's homework and I do it at the company." She encourages people to keep their commitments, but she also encourages them to let her know quickly if something may interfere with the keeping of those commitments: "Whatever it is, I expect it to be delivered . . . And I always tell them the bad news better come out real fast. The faster we can figure out that something either has changed or needs to change, the quicker we can reassess and get going again."[16]

We can hopefully assume that both Bartz's daughter and her employees have improved their performance through this gentle yet direct style of correction. While Bartz's daughter's grades remain unpublished, presumably protected information, the company's results are very public: $100 million net income on revenues of $820 million in 1999, the year she was interviewed.

CONSEQUENCES

The third stage of performance management takes place after a task, project, or year is complete. Although formal performance appraisals tend to occur at the end of predetermined periods of time, the best leaders are giving ongoing informal feedback in the form of positive and negative consequences. Performance feedback should be timely, job-relevant, goal-related, and attainable. It should also be communicated in a way that makes the recipient feel motivated to improve, not punished for irrevocably "bad" behavior.

Timely, Fair Consequences

The Bible observed the need for timely correction of misdeeds almost 2,000 years ago: "When the sentence for a crime is not quickly carried out, the hearts of the people are filled with schemes to do wrong." (Eccles. 8:11) Not only are we giving the wrong message when we fail to give quick negative consequences to an employee who has failed to perform, we are also setting a bad example for the rest of the team.

Dan Tully, chairman emeritus of Merrill Lynch and Company, is a strong modern proponent of swift, honest feedback and consequences to match. "You must give people honest, candid feedback," he notes. "You owe it to them so they can reach their full potential, and you owe it to the people around them, the ones above and below them . . . If the guy in the middle is a stiff, and I let him stay there and destroy the people around him, shame on me."[17]

Part of the reason that John Akers's time at the helm of IBM was so rocky was the tradition of nonaccountability and entitlement that had developed in the company. IBM had become a "jobs-for-life" company where mediocre, unaggressive performance had become not just tolerated but often the norm. Performance feedback had become bland and unconnected to future strategic actions the company needed to take. To get discharged by IBM, you literally had to shoot someone or pilfer a valuable piece of equipment in broad daylight.

This lack of consequences was having a severe effect on the company's productivity and morale. In a 1991 interview with *Fortune*, Akers said, "We've been . . . not sufficiently demanding of ourselves regarding those folks who aren't doing the job. We have had a very low level of separations for poor performance. That level will go up—must go up."[18]

Unfortunately, the level of accountability was raised too little and too late. At the time of Akers's interview, IBM had already begun its first-ever series of downsizings. In the process, it lost not just the poor performers it was seeking to eliminate, but also some very good performers who concluded they would be better off in another company where consequences were tied more directly to performance. Those who stayed went through a tough transition period, but under Lou Gerstner, IBM has now become a company where "as you sow, so shall ye reap."

Most employees will accept negative consequences that are administered fairly—in proportion to the offense—and justly, without favoritism or vindictiveness. Jeremiah prayed for God to "correct me, Lord, but only with justice—not in your anger." (Jer. 10:24) This is the earnest wish of so many modern employees who have been disciplined with too little justice and too much anger. Such discipline actually undermines the credibility of the leader.

Most employees wish for leaders who are capable of and willing to carry out the words of Jeremiah 31:20: "I will discipline you, but only with justice."

Two leaders who adhere to this philosophy are Bob Knowling, formerly of US West, and Gordon Bethune of Continental Airlines. Knowling felt that in the phone company as it existed a few years ago, performance was lagging because no one was held accountable and no one's job was ever at risk. "It was demoralizing for the high performers, degrading to the poor performers," he observes. "Yet most poor performers know they're poor performers. If you've been honest in your assessments of them and treated them fairly and respectfully, they usually accept the fact that they have not made the grade."[19]

Gordon Bethune realized that one step in reviving the airline in 1995 was the removal of low-performing or nonperforming staff. This task was understandably approached with some trepidation; if handled poorly, the result would probably be lost productivity rather than the productivity gains that were intended.

Bethune wanted to make sure that the consequences were applied fairly and justly. The lowest performance rating at Continental is "4." Says Bethune: "We simply asked all the 4's to leave . . . Either they weren't doing well enough at their jobs . . . or because they weren't team players . . . And you know what? That final cut didn't cause the smallest amount of unhappiness or fear . . . in the ranks. 'Jeez, they got rid of Harry—that jerk should have been shot twenty years ago and somebody finally did something.' "[20]

The rank and file employees did not quote Ecclesiastes ("When the sentence for a crime is not quickly carried out, the hearts of the people are filled with schemes to do wrong"), but similar thoughts were probably on their minds.

But consequences applied too harshly by leaders can have as demotivating an effect as lack of consequences. Rehoboam, son of Solomon and successor to him on the throne, obviously did not possess his father's wisdom or judgment. This is the man who said, "My father made your yoke heavy; I will make it even heavier. My father scourged you with whips; I will scourge you with scorpions." (2 Chron. 10) The people understandably rebelled against a "CEO" who began his reign with such a declaration of unreasonable harshness.

Another example of harsh consequences is that of three men— Korah, Dathan, and Abiram—who dared to challenge Moses' authority. They felt that Moses had set himself too far above the rest of the people. They also refused to come when Moses summoned them: "We will not come! Isn't it enough that you have brought us up out of a land flowing with milk and honey to kill us in the desert? And now you want to lord it over us? Moreover, you haven't brought us into a land flowing with milk and honey or given us an inheritance of fields and vineyards." (Num. 16:12–14)

The consequence to these three men was swift, sure, and perhaps a little too harsh for our modern tastes: "The ground under them split apart and the earth opened its mouth and swallowed them . . . They went down alive into the grave with everything they owned; the earth closed over them and they perished and were gone from the community." (Num. 16:31–33)

This was definitely an example of Theory X management, Old Testament version. Lou Noto, vice chairman of Exxon Corporation, felt that his company was also the victim of a culture that punished the slightest attempt at innovation or risk. Goals were set artificially low because anyone who didn't meet a major objective was severely punished: "If you couldn't meet it, it was the end of the world," observed Noto. "We want to encourage the right kind of risk. To do that, we have to break this ironclad rule that says if you don't succeed, we're going to put you in front of a firing squad."[21]

Whatever you may feel about the punishment given to Korah, Dathan, and Abiram, it is good to remember that even the most powerful human leader is not God. Who are we to duplicate such severe punishment? Today's modern business leaders have to gauge very carefully how they react to those who dissent or propose innovations to the established order. The person who was "swallowed up" or exiled may be the very person whose ideas could have gotten the organization out of the morass.

In the Bible, some of the strongest negative consequences are actually reserved for leaders who abuse their power and who fail to realize the disastrous effect they have on their followers: "Weep and wail, you shepherds; roll in the dust, you leaders of the flock. For your time to be slaughtered has come; you will fall and be shattered like fine pottery." (Jer. 25:34)

One leader who probably should have read this passage and taken it to heart was Horst Schroeder. Schroeder was a German national who had worked himself up to head of European operations for the Kellogg Corporation. He was brought to the United States as the heir apparent to Bill La Mothe, CEO. He was an effective taskmaster, but his application of consequences was too harsh for the Kellogg culture. He was frequently abrasive and imperious, giving frequent tongue-lashings to subordinates in meetings.

Schroeder was spared the fate of being swallowed up by the ground, but his end was just as humiliating—he was "grounded." He was flying on the corporate jet for a planned business trip and La Mothe, who was still in power, ordered the pilot to land the plane at Kellogg's corporate headquarters, where Schroeder was summarily fired.[22]

Rewards

Too often, consequences are thought of in the negative sense. One of a leader's most important (and often overlooked tasks) is the application of positive consequences for work well done. When "nothing goes wrong," some leaders may simply heave a large sigh of relief and go on to the next task without acknowledging the positive efforts that went into the task just completed.

The leaders of the Bible did not neglect the important role of positive consequences and rewards. Thousands of years before Ken Blanchard, they were catching their employees "doing something right." The wise modern leader "goes and does likewise."

In 1 Corinthians 3:8, Paul states, "The man who plants and the man who waters have one purpose, and each will be rewarded according to his own labor." One organization that takes this to heart is Starbucks, which has instituted the Bravo! recognition program. Under this program, any employee may acknowledge any other employee for resourcefulness in service, sales, or savings. One recipient of the award was a line worker in the Midwest who, upon receiving a last-minute order for $1,300 worth of coffee, found the extra labor, coffee, and bags necessary to fill it rather than turning it down for lack of resources. The general manager of the Encino, California, store was also recognized for providing coffee to Red Cross aid stations after the 1994 Los Angeles earthquake.[23]

Another example of rewarding people according to their labor was Gordon Bethune's $65 bonus for on-time performance at Continental Airlines. Up until that time, such immediate rewards for desired performance had not been part of Continental's reward arsenal. Not only was the effect immediate and positive, it set the stage for more extensive, ongoing rewards for positive performance in a number of other areas. The "domino" effect of these rewards helped Continental turn around to become the profitable, on-time airline it is today.

Rewards figure strongly in the Book of Esther, particularly rewards bestowed directly from the top of the organization. A great deal of thought is given to the question, "What is to be done for the man the king delights to honor?" In that story, Mordechai, the Jew whom the king's minister Haman tried to have executed, is led through the streets by Haman himself, garbed in a magnificent robe and seated on a powerful steed. Moreover, Haman is forced to shout, "This is what is done for the man the king delights to honor."

Modern "kings" have dispensed with robes and horses, but the wise executive knows that rewards given directly from the top can have a large effect on employee actions and productivity. At Custom Research, a marketing company with just over one hundred employees, owners Jeff and Judy Pope took a large chunk of their profits to reward the entire staff when the firm won the coveted Baldrige Award in 1996. Rather than award a robed ride on horseback, they took the entire staff on a five-day, all-expenses-paid trip to London.

An extravagance and an exercise in overkill for a small company? Not at all, says Jeff Pope. "It was money well spent. I'll do it every time. If you share the pie, it gets bigger."

When Midwest Airlines went public in 1995, CEO Tim Hoeksema wanted to give a meaningful and lasting award to the employees who helped them get there. And so, over the objections of his investment bankers, he insisted that $1 million of stock be set aside for employees, even part-timers. This decision echoes King David's decision to divide the spoils of war among all his men, including those who had "merely" provided support behind the battle lines.

Hoeksema's actions also mirror Joshua's generosity toward his fol-

lowers—the Reubenites, the Gadites, and the half-tribe of Manasseh—
all of whom had helped him conquer the neighboring tribes: "You have
done all that Moses . . . commanded, and you have obeyed me in everything I commanded. For a long time now . . . you have not deserted
your brothers, but have carried out the mission . . . Return to your
homes with your great wealth . . . and divide with your brothers
the plunder of your enemies . . ." (Joshua 22) Both Joshua and Tim
Hoeksema realized that this would not be the last time they would be
counting on "the troops" to achieve ambitious goals, and both recognized the power of positive reward in developing employee loyalty and
getting commitment to future performance.

Jack Welch also knew the power of rewards, whether it was a bonus
or an appreciative "call from on high." In his meetings, Welch very
visibly took notes on who was to do what, what the expected results
where, and when the results were expected. He reviewed these expectations at the end of every meeting.

But, unlike many leaders who use expectations only as a threat,
Welch was quick to reward those who met them. He had a staff member phone him every time an agent got a price concession from a vendor. Immediately, the agent would hear the phone ring and the voice
of Chairman Welch trumpeting, "That's wonderful news; you just
knocked a nickel off the price of steel." And a few days later, the agent
would receive a congratulatory note directly from the chairman.[24]

Another company where the "king delights to honor" and reward
excellent performance is UNUM, an insurance company headquartered
in Maine. Anyone in the firm can nominate anyone else for the Chairman's Award, but the recipient must be below the senior vice president
level. Teams of employees review a large pool of nominees, reducing
the pool to twenty-five; the chairman then selects the group of five to
ten final winners.

The recipients each receive $5,000 in stock, a $2,500 travel certifi-
cate, and a Mont Blanc pen and pencil set. In addition, the awardees
are the invited guests of honor at a banquet hosted by the chairman and
attended by the board, senior management, and the awardees' immediate supervisors.[25] The message to those honored, to those who nomi-

nated them, and to the entire rest of the company is the same message conveyed in 2 Timothy 2:6: "The hardworking farmer should be the first to receive a share of the crops." Or to put it more succinctly, "As you sow, so shall ye reap."

Largely out of necessity, Jack Stack of Springfield Re has had to make the business connection between reaping and sowing very plain to all the employees. The division had been cut loose to stand on its own by parent International Harvester, and it was in a highly leveraged debt situation. Stack had to make all employees painfully aware of the effect that their individual productivity (or lack thereof) would have on the company's bottom line and, ultimately, survival.

Notes one Springfield Re line worker, "Every week you sit down with your supervisor and he gives you the numbers. You can see how your own work affects the statements. At first I was not interested and did not think it was of benefit to us . . . But as you learn about it, it becomes more beneficial . . . If you are not working up to standard, it's going to show up on that paper."

Stack has created an environment where employees see the connection between their actions and the bottom line. Everyone right down to the lowest assembly worker can see the positive impact of controlling costs and the negative impact of failing to do so. Employees now realize that bonuses are not arbitrary, but are contingent on lowering costs and maximizing productivity. They almost lost their bonuses when health care payments went $60,000 over budget. Notes Stack, "It was the first time that employees really understood that some insurance company wasn't paying their claims; that it was really coming out of their sweat and equity. People got a sense of ownership that they could in fact control health care costs and could make a difference."[26]

Firm but Fair Practices

The phrase "firm but fair" is one of the biggest clichés in the business world (not to mention education and sports). Everyone wants a boss (or teacher, or coach) who combines structured, exacting behavioral and performance guidelines with kindness and impartiality. This balance is difficult to achieve, but those leaders who are able to do so receive maximum loyalty and productivity from their people.

One example is Phil Myers, the ServiceMaster account manager mentioned earlier who defends his people against insensitive treatment by anyone, even the most powerful executive. But Myers is no touchy-feely "pushover." He demands the same accountability from his employees that he does from the unfortunate executive who dares to mistreat them. Myers is the first to appreciate and reward employees: "Hey, I've been in the ranks. I know what it's like to be a housekeeper." But he also makes it clear that less than excellent work is not acceptable. If there is a person who is not performing adequately or who is undermining the spirit of the team, Myers follows a three-step process:

1. Confront the negative behaviors.
2. Give the employee a chance to change.
3. Terminate if there is no improvement.[27]

It is appropriate that Myers works for a company based on biblical principles, because his disciplinary approach could be traced to three verses:

> *"Stop sinning or something worse may happen to you." (John 5:14)*
> *"Yet now I am happy, because your sorrow led to repentance." (2 Cor. 7:8)*
> *"I will discipline you, but only with justice." (Jer. 31:20)*

BIBLICAL LESSONS ON PERFORMANCE MANAGEMENT

∞ Constantly communicate performance expectations: "before," "during," and "after."

- Set ambitious but realistic ("stretch") goals.

- Encourage goal attainment with the promise of meaningful rewards—extrinsic and intrinsic.

- Be forgiving of honest mistakes made and risks taken in pursuit of performance goals.

- Celebrate your team's efforts and accomplishments, both as you go and when you finish.

- Give positive and negative consequences in a fair and timely manner, based on performance, not partiality.

- Like David and his "mighty men," make team members feel like owners and partners.

- Help employees make the connection between their actions and bottom-line organizational success.

CHAPTER SEVEN

Team Development

"The body is a unit . . . and though its parts are many, they form one body."

—1 COR. 12:12

"As iron sharpens iron, so one man sharpens another."

—PROV. 27:17

uick, can you identify who coined the phrase, "People are our most important asset"? By now, it's irrelevant. Whichever company you work for, you've seen or heard that phrase before. Regardless of who originated it, the quote has become so common that it has become a cliché, as have references to "the team." The extent to which different companies honor these concepts in practice varies, but they all pay devout "lip service" to them.

But the leaders of the Bible, who rarely used the word *team,* were masters of team practice. They had to be. Their technological infrastructure was rudimentary at best and sometimes nonexistent. There were no computer networks, and for the most part no "bricks and mortar." The people of the Bible lived in tents for much of their history, without permanent dwellings. The only thing as permanent as "the people" were the flocks of sheep, goats, and cattle, and the land itself, which they did not always occupy.

But the distinct advantage of both the Hebrews and the Christians was their respect for and use of the "human resource." Unlike the marauding tribes against whom they often defended themselves, they valued individuals highly. And they were able to galvanize those individuals into strong teams that readily subordinated their individual desires to the needs of the group.

The best modern leaders also place a strong value on people. They also realize that references to a "team" ring hollow if the members of the team don't feel valued as people, or if they see the team leader reaping all the glory while they do all the work.

THE IMPORTANCE OF PEOPLE

"For the Lord's portion is his people." (Deut. 32:9) That's the biblical way of saying "People are our most important asset"—not goats, sheep, camels, golden temple ornaments, or even the temple itself!

Peter Senge, in *The Fifth Discipline*, gives a modern update on this passage: ". . . the active force is people. And people have their own will, their own mind, and their own way of thinking. If the employees themselves are not sufficiently motivated to challenge the goals of growth and technical development . . . there simply will be no growth, no gain in productivity, and no technical development."[1]

And many modern leaders, some of whom came of age before Senge, reflect this "people perspective":

❖ "What aspect of running a large corporation is the most daunting? Without a doubt, it's dealing on a day-to-day basis with the human equation—making sure our cast members [employees] are committed and motivated, and that their emotions are engaged in the right ways."[2] These words by Michael Eisner, chairman of The Disney Corporation, are reminiscent of King David's when he took over the throne of Israel: "For who can govern this great people of yours?"

❖ Fred Smith of FedEx runs his company by the watchwords: "People, Service, Profit," in that order. The FedEx *Manager's Guide* states,

"Take care of our people; they, in turn, will deliver the impeccable service demanded by our customers who will reward us with the profitability necessary to secure our future."[3]

❖ Dave Quade, vice president of Foster Products Division of H. B. Fuller, joined his company largely because of the sincere belief in people, which he saw carried out in everyday practice: "Seeing the belief in people and having people involved in decisions, it was like coming to heaven."[4] Sartre wrote, "Hell is other people." But when organized and motivated the right way, they can be heaven as well.

❖ Hal Rosenbluth of Rosenbluth Travel wrote a book called *The Customer Comes Second.* According to Rosenbluth, who comes first? The employees: "If our people don't come first, then they're not free to focus on our clients."[5]

In the *Associates' Handbook* for Wal-Mart, Sam Walton's most-repeated mantra is "Our *People* make the difference." This message is also posted on the backs of the company's trucks and the walls of the warehouses. Any manager who is disciplined for ignoring or abusing people can't say he didn't see the "writing on the wall."

❖ Larry Bossidy, former CEO of Allied Signal, realizes the importance of each and every person: "You've got to make sure employees understand how important they are. As a CEO, you need people more than they need you."[6]

❖ Herb Kelleher knows where his competitive advantage lies: "Southwest is only as good as its people, and we probably spend a disproportionate amount of time concentrating on our people." One measure of that "disproportion" is Southwest's review of 150,000 applications for 4,000 to 5,000 jobs. Kelleher, who believes that "people make the difference," says that "anyone can buy an airplane or lease ticket counter space, or buy computers, but the intangible things—the esprit de corps . . . are the hardest thing for people to imitate."[7] Colleen Barrett, Kelleher's "second-in-command" for many years, has the title, "Manager of People," which reflects the company's perspective.

❖ Jack Welch (known as "Neutron Jack" when he started out as a CEO) became increasingly people-oriented as he matured in his position. He had to, since GE was taking over so many different kinds of businesses. "I spend 60 percent of my time on people stuff, and that's the way it should be. I couldn't produce a show on NBC, I couldn't build an engine . . . So my involvement revolves around people."[8] Welch has put his money (and his body) where his mouth is. He spends a large portion of his time helicoptering to GE's famed Management Development Center in Crotonville to address groups of managers to help them develop into better leaders and to help them develop their own teams.

THE IMPORTANCE OF TEAMS

Since biblical times, people have gotten the most done when they worked cooperatively in teams. Although they didn't actually use the term *team,* the leaders of the Bible realized that a team is more than the sum of its parts. They had not yet heard of the word *synergy,* but they had seen it enough in action to describe it: "Two are better than one, because they have a good return for their work: If one falls down, his friend can help him up . . . Though one may be overpowered, two can defend themselves. A cord of three strands is not easily broken." (Eccles. 4)

Nehemiah realized this when he assembled teams of Hebrews to reconstruct the wall around Jerusalem:

Therefore I stationed some of the people behind the lowest points of the wall at the exposed places, posting them by families, with their swords, spears and bows . . . From that day on, half of my men did the work, while the other half were equipped with spears, shields, bows and armor . . . So we continued the work . . . from the first light of dawn till the stars came out. (Neh. 4)

Nehemiah knew the power of a team with complementary strengths (building and fighting) and an overriding purpose (the protection of their families and the building of a nation).

A modern leader who has likened the building of a team to the building of a wall is Akio Morita, CEO of Sony. Morita observed that the people of a company are like varying stones rather than standardized "bricks," a fact that should be celebrated, not bemoaned: "The manager takes a look at these rough stones, and he has to build a wall by combining them in the best possible way, just as a master mason builds a stone wall. The stones are sometimes round, sometimes square, long, large or small, but somehow the management must figure out how to put them together. . . . As the business changes, it becomes necessary to refit the stones in different places."

When Moses led the Hebrews through the desert, there was a considerable amount of individual sacrifice in the service of the overall team goal of reaching the Promised Land. Morita's and Sony's success have been largely built on the subordination of individual goals to team goals: "The problem with the person who is accustomed to working for the sake of money is that he often forgets that he is expected to work for the group entity, and this self-centered attitude . . . to the exclusion of the goals of his coworkers is not healthy."[9]

Everyone on a team has a separate and important function. Jesus picked his apostles based on their differing skills and backgrounds (some were fishermen, one was a tax collector!). Romans 12 speaks of people with "different gifts . . . prophesying . . . serving . . . teaching . . . encouraging . . . leadership." Ephesians 4:11 says, "It was he (Christ) who gave some to be apostles . . . prophets . . . evangelists . . . pastors and teachers . . ." Everyone on the team possessed "different kinds of gifts and service, but the same spirit." The overriding biblical message? No matter how seemingly humble, no part of the team is any less valuable than any other.

A similar message was delivered by Gordon Bethune in his efforts to revitalize an ailing Continental Airlines. Rather than use the body or a stone wall, Bethune used a watch as his model. In a meeting, he was challenged by an employee who asked why reservations agents should receive the bonus for on-time performance, since they did not affect the airline's punctuality. Bethune collected watches, and realized that, like the human body, they were "miracles of cooperation . . . hundreds of parts fitting together . . . every part of the watch does a job . . . and any part that fails can impair or destroy the function of the entire watch. It's no good to you without the hour hand or the clock face, but it's just as useless without the tiniest screw . . . that holds the mainspring on. . . ." So Bethune held up his watch and asked the employee, "Which part of this watch don't you think we need?" The employee couldn't answer and sat down.[10]

Bethune's logic was very similar to King David's when he justified giving part of the spoils of war to men who had merely given logistical support but had not actually fought on the lines. King David realized that the whole team had contributed to the effort, and by sharing the spoils with all, he was rhetorically asking, "Which of these men don't you think we need?"

Bethune's emphasis on teamwork has been a major ingredient in the successful revitalization of Continental. He says, "An airline is the biggest team sport there is. It's 40,000 people working together . . . toward the same goal . . . Now everybody's on the same team and everyone knows it . . . Everyone knows what the goal is . . . We're all working from the same playbook . . ."[11]

Jack Stack of Springfield Re has a "selfish" reason for wanting to be part of a team (he elected to limit himself to a 19 percent share of the company): "I didn't want to be alone. I was going to be leading the charge up the hill. I wanted to make sure that when I got to the top of the hill and turned around, there was a bunch of people coming with me. It's easy to stop one guy, but it's pretty hard to stop a hundred."[12]

This was the same philosophy that helped ensure the victory of Joab and Abishai, biblical rulers, each of whom was facing an enemy and each of whom knew he might need help. They applied the concept of "flexible teaming": "If the Arameans are too strong for me, come over and help me. And if the Ammonites are too strong for you, I will come and help you." (2 Sam. 10:12)

The name Marc Andreesen does not necessarily conjure up the image of a team leader. Andreesen is the originator of Netscape, and he could be pardoned if he had a "swelled head" like Samson and thought he did it all himself and could keep doing so (but look at what happened to Samson!). But Andreesen's experiences, particularly his battle for market share against Microsoft, have convinced him of the power of teams:

> *When people quit, they tend to leave because they've lost faith in their manager. A management team with a lot of respect can do a much better job of retaining employees, which is why a company like Microsoft, Intel, or Cisco could turn on a dime, do radically different things, and still have those people say, "Okay, we'll follow."*[13]

SELECTING THE TEAM

Most of us remember the experience of choosing sides for kickball during recess. The selection of the teams ("choosing sides") was the primary predictor of how the game would go. No matter how good the "captain" was, if he or she made poor team selections, the game was over before it began. Everyone knew the outcome, and the team that was the victim of such poor selection could only hope for the bell to ring to end the slaughter.

Every year, the National Basketball Association holds a draft of college players. There is a tremendous amount of suspense around this process, because everyone knows a team's fortunes, for the coming year and years to come, hinge on this selection process. No matter how good a coach or leader you are, if you do not select your team wisely, you will be at a severe disadvantage. Red Auerbach, for years the coach of the successful Boston Celtics dynasty, was a master at picking the right players, particularly a young man named Bill Russell from an obscure school in California. But he also picked a group of teammates to complement Russell, each with a particular role to play.

"How you select people is more important than how you manage them once they're on the job," observes Auerbach. "If you start with the right people, you won't have problems later on. If you hire the wrong people . . . you're in serious trouble."[14] Auerbach knew how to select the right mix of superstars and "role players," and how to get them to function as a team.

The Bible is also very explicit about the importance of selecting the right people for a team. Before he picked the twelve apostles, Jesus went out to the mountainside and spent the night praying to God. He knew he had to have just the right team if his message was to be spread throughout the world. When David became king, one of the first things he did was to select a cabinet that was very similar to the cabinets appointed by heads of state today: people with expertise and wisdom to match their responsibilities:

"Joab . . . was over the army; Jehoshaphat . . . was recorder; Zadok . . . and Ahimelech . . . were priests; Seraiah was secretary . . . and David's sons were royal advisors." (2 Sam. 8:15–18) Presumably David's sons were too young and inexperienced to assume a dedicated cabinet post, but he wanted to groom them for further responsibility; one of them was Solomon, who was to become the wisest ruler of Israel.

An important aspect of building teams is complementarity. King David selected his teams of warriors largely based on their complementary strengths. One man, Benaiah, was skilled with a club, which he used to strike down a seven-foot Egyptian brandishing a spear. Those from the tribe of Benjamin were archers and "able to shoot arrows or to sling stones right-handed or left-handed." The sons of Gad "were brave warriors ready for battle and able to handle the shield and spear." (1 Chron. 11–12) Together, this group made up a mighty team with complementary strengths that could be leveraged in any situation.

Gordon Bethune's revitalization team at Continental Airlines was also one with complementary strengths. And, like Jack Welch, who knew he could not produce a TV show, Bethune knew that he could not argue a legal case or fly a plane. He needed the best possible "cabinet team" he could assemble. To help with financing, he hired Larry Kellner, who had worked for a large bank. As EVP of operations, he chose C. D. McLean, who had been responsible for pilot training at Piedmont Airlines. For technical operations, he chose the former director of technical operations at Piedmont.

For chief operating officer, he chose Greg Brenneman, an outside consultant from Bain and Company who knew Continental's problems intimately, perhaps too intimately. Bethune told him, "Greg, it's an opportunity to be chief operating officer of a $6 billion company." And Brenneman replied, "Yeah, the world's worst $6 billion company."

The new "Continental Team" had differing skills, but, like David's "mighty men," they had a similar attitude that united them: an embracing of challenge and risk. "I wanted risk takers; I wanted achievers," says Bethune. "I wanted people who could see past the airline we were to the airline we could become."[15]

A weaker leader would have selected weaker men, who undoubtedly would have lacked the courage to make the bold moves necessary for Continental to revive itself. David Ogilvy, head of Ogilvy & Mather, used to encourage his managers to hire people *better* than they were. Ogilvy would give each new manager a set of Russian nesting dolls, the type where unscrewing the largest doll reveals a slightly smaller doll, until the final doll is a tiny wooden lump. "If each of us hires people who are smaller than we are, we shall become a company of dwarfs," he would explain. "But if each of us hires people who are bigger than we are, Ogilvy & Mather will become a company of giants."[16]

In similar fashion, Paul too advised his young protégés how to select their teams. For example, he advised Titus, his disciple on the island of Crete, to indeed select someone whose qualities surpassed his own:

> *The reason I left you in Crete was that you might . . . appoint elders in every town, as I directed you. An elder must be blameless, the husband of but one wife, a man whose children believe and are not open to the charge of being disobedient . . . not overbearing, not quick-tempered, not given to drunkenness, not violent, not pursuing dishonest gain. (Titus 1:5–7)*

Paul had even more stringent criteria for Timothy's team in Ephesus. In addition to all the traits he had mentioned to Titus, he added that "the overseer must be respectable, hospitable, able to teach . . . not quarrelsome." Deacons had to be "men worthy of respect, sincere, not indulging in much wine." (1 Tim. 3) This no doubt made the selection process a difficult one for these young "coaches." On the other hand, once they found people who met these criteria, their job of actually running the church became much easier.

At first glance, the head of a major airline, a cigar-chomping basketball coach, and an apostle and his two young protégés would seem to have little in common. But all realized the importance of selecting the right people for the team.

THE POWER OF TEAMS

People acting in teams can accomplish amazing goals that an individual, or even a group of individuals, could never have achieved. And there is a large difference between a team and a group of individuals. From a group, Noah assembled a team that had little experience in shipbuilding but a strong dedication to each other and their purpose. Moses forged a ragtag group of ex-slaves into a strong team (of course, it helped that these slaves had previously been divided into tribes or "work groups"). Nehemiah built a wall with teams. Joshua knocked down walls with them. And Jesus turned a small, diverse group of fishermen, tax collectors, and laborers into a team that would convert half the world to their mission.

The people of Israel also experienced periods of dissolution, purposelessness, and selfishness. It was at these times that they degenerated from a team and became a mere "group." They became idol worshipers and ceased to treat each other honorably and ethically. Like "sheep who have gone astray," rather than being unified in a common purpose, they turned "every one to his own way." (Isa. 56:3)

This was the state of the Chicago Bulls when Phil Jackson took over as coach. The Bulls later won six NBA championships, but only after they were able, under Jackson, to function as a team. True, they had the greatest player in the history of the game in Michael Jordan, but it is easy to forget that Jordan was with the Bulls several years before they began to approach greatness by becoming a true team. In fact, during

Jordan's early years with the Bulls, they had difficulty just having a winning season.

The reason? The Bulls were a group, but not a team. The group was dominated by one player with tremendous talents but a lack of team orientation. There was little synergy among the players; the presence of Jordan actually minimized the others' potential and development. In a "crunch" (which was frequently) the other players knew that their main job was to pass the ball to Jordan. If he scored, great. If he didn't, it was no skin off their backs.

When Phil Jackson took over as coach, he turned a mediocre group with one great player into a championship team. He did this by "letting the *me* become the servant of the *we*." He encouraged Jordan to develop his team-oriented skills (defensive play and passing) and to inspire the other players to better performance. He made Jordan into more than just a "star"; he made him a leader. And with Jordan's example, he transformed the Bulls from a purposeless group into a team where everyone (even a substitute who played only a few minutes a game) had a role to play and knew the importance that role played in the championship effort. Like Nehemiah building the wall, Jackson got the Bulls to "work with all their hearts" and to perform "as one man."

Herb Kelleher also enlisted the power of his team when he wanted to improve accident prevention at Southwest Airlines. Other airlines would have formed a small task force and focused on the areas most directly responsible for accident prevention, such as flight crew and pilots. The rest of the "team" would have received some vague memo about the "need for safety."

But Kelleher enlisted everyone in the accident prevention effort, even if their function appeared to have little to do with safety. His message to the entire organization was that "we're a cross-functional team, and the entire team will work together to empower each other to prevent accidents." He had the baggage handlers observe the pilots in flight simulation training, and he had the pilots observe the baggage handlers. When he was done, everyone on the team understood his or her role and the role of everyone else on the team in improving safety and reducing accidents. In the words of Romans 12, Kelleher had created "one body" with "many members" and "differing gifts," all devoted to an overriding goal.

Another organization where a strong leader focuses on "letting the *me* become servant of the *we*" is Disney. Michael Eisner realized that his top executives will work better if they are developed as a team. He also realized the importance of their understanding the roles of the entire Disney "cast."

So Eisner has instituted a program called Disney Dimensions for his top team, which he has dubbed his "synergy boot camp." For eight days, these executives experience every aspect of the company, not from a training room, but firsthand. They play the Disney characters on the grounds of Disney World. They see the beds made in the hotels (and even make a few) and they watch 100,000 meals being cooked (presumably they are not permitted to "ruin the stew" by actually cooking the food—since that is not something that can be trusted to "unskilled labor").

Says Eisner, "They learn what it is like to work in 100-degree heat and 100 percent humidity (shades of the Israelites in the desert here), to clean bathrooms, cut hedges, check out guests, and soothe tired children." The executives keep up this routine from 7:00 A.M. to 11:00 P.M. for over a week.

At first, they dread this experience, says Eisner. "But by the third day, they love it. By the end of the eighth day, they've totally bonded. They've learned to respect what tens of thousands of people do, and they've become close friends at the same time. When they go back to their jobs, what happens is synergy, naturally."[17] The Disney executives may have started out as "reluctant group members," but this experience forged them into a team that willingly, even enthusiastically, sacrificed individual ego for the unity and goals of the group.

King David was also a master team-builder who knew how to increase team spirit by getting all to contribute willingly. David encouraged his followers to "let the *me* become the servant of the *we*" by setting a large example. He wanted his people to donate their efforts and their money to the building of the temple (which would be carried out by his son Solomon). David literally put his money where his mouth was, with no guarantee that others would follow. He had already provided large amounts of gold, silver, and precious stones from the national treasury. His next step in building the team was to donate even more gold and silver from his personal wealth.

This is just what was needed to galvanize the team: "Then the leaders of the families, the officers of the tribes of Israel, the commanders of thousands and commanders of hundreds . . . gave willingly . . . The people rejoiced at the willing response of their leaders, for they had given freely and wholeheartedly . . ." (1 Chron. 29) To forge a team, a leader often must be the "consummate team member," a model willing to selflessly give of his energy and resources so that others are encouraged to contribute.

Jan Carlzon of SAS knew he needed the efforts of every member of the team when he took over Lineflyg, Sweden's mediocre domestic airline and an SAS subsidiary. He could have behaved like a typical CEO or autocratic "king" by coming in and immediately establishing his authority and issuing orders. Instead, he acted like the team-oriented King David; he asked for help from every team member.

Carlzon assembled the group (and a group is all it was at that point) and said, "The company is not doing well. It's losing dollars and suffering from many problems . . . I can't save this company alone. The only chance for Lyneflyg to survive is if you help me— I have some ideas of my own . . . But most importantly, *you* are the ones who must help me, not the other way around."

This was the first step in Carlzon's "group" becoming a team. "We thought you were going to tell us what to do," noted one employee. "But you turned the tables on us."[18] Carlzon had succeeded in "turning the *me* (including himself) into the *we*."

There are many innovative ways to develop a team. We are all familiar with the "executive retreat" at which top management practices teamwork by boosting each other over walls and rappelling down cliffs. Talent Fusion, a digital recruiting firm in Harrisburg, Pennsylvania, has devised an off-site team-building event that is more convenient and costs less: They have a weekly soccer game.

"The game isn't about proficiency in soccer," notes one of the company's executives. "It's about proficiency in team building . . . We talk about strategy, how we're going to win, who's going to do what—all of which is applicable to the business itself. The point is to get people thinking of the team and how to achieve concrete objectives."[19] Like King David and his "mighty men," Talent Fusion holds a business meeting right after the game, when all are hot, sweaty, and enthused. It's a great way to break down barriers and increase team commitment.

But sometimes a leader must give more than gold and silver to get people to act as team. He may have to give up something even more precious—his office. George Colony, CEO of Forrester Research, an Internet research firm, thought his people would work more cooperatively if he took them out of their offices and formed a "pod" in the central computer room. At first, the response was anything but "teamlike."

"Everyone screamed," says a bemused Colony. So he moved out of his plush office and into the pod also. "That new team lit the company on fire," he enthuses. "We shared our tears and our fears, and at the end of the year, we danced on our desks to celebrate our success . . . It's like being in a squad of eight or ten people in the military. You get so you're willing to die for the guy next to you."[20] We don't know whether Colony consulted the Book of Nehemiah (where men were willing to die next to each other to rebuild a wall) or had any knowledge of David's mingling with his "mighty men," but in moving out of his office, he certainly was following their principles of team-building: Give of yourself and put yourself out there with the troops.

But the *me* does not become the *we* without some painful individual sacrifices. The disciples were asked to give up their fathers and mothers, as well as any permanent physical home, to follow Jesus: "Foxes have holes and birds of the air have nests, but the Son of Man has no place to lay his head." (Matt. 8:20) Whoever wanted to be on Jesus' team had to give up a lot.

A. G. Edwards has been a successful brokerage firm for 100 years. They have accomplished this through a team approach very unlike the typical "me first" attitude at most brokerage firms. Taking a page from Phil Jackson and King David, Corporate Vice President Greg Hutchings notes, "Unlike other firms, we do not have a star system. Here it's always putting the team first and the client first . . . you are rewarded for . . . being a team player, unlike other firms where everyone is out for themselves."[21]

A. G. Edwards accomplishes this "team spirit" through their actions, not just empty talk or cheerleading. In a business where "money talks," they shout the "team message" loud and clear by tying all management bonuses to company profits, not the overrides on the earnings of a manager's direct reports. This assures a minimum of backbiting and a unified, company-wide effort, where all are willing to help each other, not just for that sometimes-ethereal "team feeling" but also for group financial success. You won't be asked to give up your mother and father, but if you're willing to sacrifice overrides, you'll make a good "team player" at A. G. Edwards.

GE Plastics was faced with a double challenge when it acquired Borg-Warner Chemicals in a merger: how to preserve the effectiveness of its existing team while integrating the members of the acquired company into the overall team. The corporate cultures were disparate, as were many of the skills. GE Plastics had a younger, more individualistic and aggressive culture; Borg-Warner Chemicals had older employees who were accustomed to a more paternalistic culture.

The solution to integrating these two cultures was to form them into a team with a mission: Renovate five nonprofit facilities in the San Diego area, including a YMCA, a homeless shelter, and a Boys' and Girls' Club. Joel Hutt, manager of marketing communications for GE Plastics, assembled the "troops" and showed them pictures of the run-down facilities. "The director of this 'Y' says fixing up this place will cost $500,000 and take years. Well, I'm here to tell you . . . This GE Army is going to attack this place. We're going to do it in eight hours, and we're going to do it tomorrow!"

Deliberately mixing people from the two companies (and also mixing their skill sets), the teams rebuilt a soccer field, landscaped the grounds, and put in new windows and a retaining wall. (Unlike Nehemiah's team, they did not have to contend with armed attackers trying to prevent them from building!) They used up 11,000 square feet of tile,

2,200 square feet of carpeting, and 550 gallons of paint and planted over 1,000 flowers, bushes, and shrubs.

The renovation of the "Y" and the other community service projects was the turning point in integrating GE Plastics and Borg-Warner. Neither viewed the other as "the competition" or "the outsider" any longer. "We were dirty, tired, grubby and so proud to be part of the whole project," says one employee. "As a former Borg-Warner employee, any questions I had about if this is the kind of company I want to work for . . . these questions were gone."[22]

This project is reminiscent of the team Solomon assembled to build the temple, although Solomon's team was a little larger: 30,000 laborers, 70,000 carriers, 80,000 stonecutters, and 3,300 foremen to supervise this gigantic endeavor. Both Solomon's team and the GE team were galvanized by a strong leader and an overriding purpose.

For both teams, celebration of achievement was important. However, the celebration of the GE team probably did not approach the scale of Solomon's team after they completed construction of the temple: fourteen days of ceremony and feasting. Well, there was less time urgency in those days, and people had more time to celebrate.

CHALLENGES IN TEAM BUILDING

Building a team can be over-romanticized. It is a challenging, messy, often-daunting process. Moses was challenged in the wilderness by rebellious team members who questioned the wisdom of the journey and suggested a return to the security (and slavery) of Egypt. And the entire team deviated from its mission, building a golden calf while Moses was off on the mountain getting divine guidance from his mentor.

In Galatians 5:13, Paul warned the early Christians that they were at great risk when they ceased to act as a team: "If you keep on biting and devouring each other, watch out or you will be destroyed by each other." And the prophet Nahum warned the king of Assyria that his doom was sealed because his team was becoming unproductive and falling apart: "O king of Assyria, your shepherds slumber, your nobles lie down to rest. Your people are scattered on the mountains with no one to gather them." (Nah. 3:18)

Many modern leaders have also hit obstacles as they tried to form and direct teams. Despite most employees' expressed desires to be "part of a real team," many balk when actually asked to participate. When asked which parts of Nestle's approach to change most stymied people, CEO Peter Brabeck-Letmathe answered:

> *You are going to be surprised—it's collaboration. Many people like to work in pyramid structures because pyramid structures are clear. But continuous improvement doesn't really thrive in that kind of environment . . . Frankly, this is the hardest for the people in middle management to accept. They feel we are taking away their hierarchy, that they are losing power.*[23]

Brabeck-Letmathe adds that he is willing to work with those who "don't know how" to collaborate. But those who refuse to work as a team and to accept their place in the team have a limited future with the organization.

Gordon Bethune of Continental echoes this sentiment. "The people who evolved the culture here were from a culture that focused on factionalism," he observes. "Me win. You lose. Most of those people weren't ready to play as team members. We had to make changes."[24]

Another leader who has historically been "team challenged" is Steve Jobs. That would seem logical when you consider that here is a technical and intuitive genius who started out working solo in his garage. He had little experience with corporate organizational life, whether hierarchical or team-oriented. "Jobs's leadership didn't allow for collaboration," notes industry colleague Charles B. Wang. "His colleagues eventually suspended their own judgment when they entered what was termed Jobs's reality distortion field . . . Teamwork cannot be sustained in an environment that shouts down naysayers. If your vision cannot survive attack, it may not be worth defending."[25]

Because of Jobs's drive and technical brilliance, he has received second and third chances at managing teams—at Next, again at Apple, and with other ventures. If Jobs's skill at managing teams grows to the level of his technical competence and strategic vision, there is probably nothing he won't be able to accomplish.

Jack Welch didn't develop GE's team orientation overnight. Many of his managers were used to guarding their own turfs; like the governors in ancient Palestine, they zealously protected their right to people, land, and money. But over time, Welch was able to institute a more team-oriented culture, particularly through his management conclaves held at GE's famed Management Development Center at Crotonville. When the head of appliances had a refrigerator compressor problem, managers from the other businesses saw that he had been the victim of bad luck, and so they chipped in "$20 million here, $10 million there" in the same way that the people of Israel dipped into their pockets to help build the temple.

But not every story of team effort has such happy endings as these. Those of us working inside any type of organization know it's easy to be skeptical when managers and leaders at any level begin talking about "the team" and all its wonderful accomplishments. Too often these statements are inflated, masking dissension, or rewarding those who have actually contributed least to the team's success.

That's why Max De Pree's team accomplishments at Herman Miller are so remarkable. He opened his entire organization to James O'Toole, a management consultant with a keen eye for spotting any posturing and "sugar-coating" by CEOs. O'Toole's initial skepticism was dented when De Pree gave him permission to go anywhere and talk to anyone in the company, manager or worker. It was blasted apart by what he found:

> *The only problem was I couldn't tell one from the other (manager from worker)! People who seemed to be production workers were engaged in solving the "managerial" problems of improving production and quality. People who seemed to be managers had their sleeves rolled up and were working, side by side, with everybody else in an all-out effort to produce the best product in the most effective way.''*[26]

If O'Toole had visited Jerusalem while Nehemiah's team was building the wall or while David's "mighty men" were planning their next escapade, he probably would have spoken similar words. In the best teams, position becomes subordinate to purpose.

DELEGATION

Teams run best when the leader can delegate tasks and authority. One of the first and best delegators was Moses, who learned the hard way that one man, no matter how talented, could not lead single-handedly. Moses was trying to run every aspect of "Children of Israel, Inc." from soup to nuts (at their worst, this was about all that the tribes possessed, but as their fortunes increased, so did their resources and the complexity of governing them).

It took a "consultant" to point out to Moses the futility of trying to run everything himself, and the resulting stress and fatigue he was experiencing. This consultant also happened to be his father-in-law, Jethro, who felt obligated to ask him:

> Why do you sit alone as judge, while all these people stand around you from morning till evening? What you are doing is not good. You and these people who come to you will only wear yourselves out. The work is too heavy for you; you cannot handle it alone . . . select capable men from all the people . . . and appoint them as officials over thousands, hundreds, fifties and tens . . . Have them serve as judges . . . but have them bring every difficult case to you; the simple cases they can decide themselves. (Exod. 18)

Once Moses appointed teams and team leaders, the line outside his tent (which was probably longer than that at any Motor Vehicles Bureau) and his stress level decreased significantly.

Steve Case of AOL had a similar problem when he first started out. Like many entrepreneurs, he tried to do everything and had trouble letting go. He even wrote the ads for AOL and the press releases. "I was involved in every decision," writes Case. We don't know whether Case had as wise an adviser as Moses' father-in-law or whether he came to his own conclusions, but he finally realized that "the only way you're going to create a significant company is to make your role into one where you *guide* things as opposed to do things."[27]

But to be able to delegate, you have to trust your team members to know what their roles are and to be able to perform them (perhaps with a little coaching). Nehemiah knew he couldn't rebuild the Jerusalem wall by himself, so he selected capable leaders ("delegations of trustworthy men") to manage each part of the job: "The Fish Gate was rebuilt by the sons of Hassenaah . . . The Valley Gate was repaired by Hanun . . . The Fountain Gate was repaired by Shallun son of Col-Hozeh." (Neh. 3) And once the job was done, Nehemiah also made sure that his trusted brother, Hanani, was there to protect the gates and the wall along with the commander of the citadel. (Neh. 7)

Perhaps the most skilled biblical delegator was Jesus. He chose his twelve disciples carefully, and sent them out with specific instructions. A good delegator chooses the right person for the task and is very specific about the task and what that team member is authorized to do:

> *When Jesus had called the Twelve together, he gave them power and authority to drive out all demons and to cure diseases . . . He told them, "Take nothing for the journey except a staff—no bread, no bag, no money . . . Wear sandals but not an extra tunic. Whenever you enter a house, stay there until you leave that town. And if any place will not welcome you or listen to you, shake the dust off your feet when you leave, as a testimony against them." (Luke 9:1–5)*

Jesus subsequently sent out seventy-two more delegates with similar instructions. And he sent them out in teams of two for mutual support. And we all know how dramatically and exponentially his followers increased from this original small group.

On the other hand, Dennis Holt, founder of Western International Media, was the "man who couldn't delegate." Holt's single-minded tenacity intimidated his competitors. He was a workaholic who refused to give up any part of the task, and his rivals saw his car parked in front of his office seven days a week. And it wasn't just a "plant"; he was really there working! Unfortunately, Holt was sometimes there for the wrong reason—his inability to delegate. This was "a curse . . . I'm totally hands-on, I don't delegate," he moaned. Finally, he was forced to delegate (but only after his marriage fell apart). He promoted his COO, Michael Kassan, to president. To his delight, he found that even though Kassan lacked media-buying experience, he and Kassan complemented each other well and made an excellent team.[28] Although he had yet to appoint officials over "thousands, hundreds, fifties and tens," he had at least begun the process of delegating responsibility to others besides himself. If he had had a consultant (or father-in-law) like Jethro, perhaps he could have learned to delegate much earlier.

EMPOWERING AND DEVELOPING THE TEAM

Competent leaders know that you cannot just assemble a group of unskilled individuals, call them a "team," and expect them to achieve large organizational goals. You've got to empower the team members, giving them the tools and authority to accomplish their task. And you've got to develop the team, giving it and its members the necessary skills, and constantly giving them the opportunity to upgrade those skills to match the ever-widening tasks.

The apostle Paul gave his young protégé Titus specific instructions on developing his team members at every level: "Teach the older men [senior male executives] to be temperate, worthy of respect, self-controlled, and sound in faith, in love and endurance. Likewise, teach the older women [senior female executives] to be reverent in the way they live, not to be slanderers or addicted to too much wine . . . Then they can train the younger women . . . Similarly, encourage the young men to be self-controlled . . ." (Titus 2:2–6)

Paul's protégé in Ephesus, Timothy, had a different readiness and experience level, and so received different instructions on how to build and develop his team: "Have nothing to do with godless myths and old wives' tales . . . Command and teach . . . Don't let anyone look down on you because you are young . . . Watch your life and your doctrine closely . . ." (1 Tim. 4)

Modern leaders (young or old) also put a large priority on developing their teams. Rosenbluth Travel has an Associate of the Day program. Any employee who is interested in a particular area can "shadow" an executive for the day. Over 100 employees have chosen to spend the day with Rosenbluth himself, learning new skills and observing how an executive conducts himself, structures his day, and works with the team.

At Trilogy Software, each new recruit ("young man or woman" in Paul's terms) is given a sponsor. If the recruit "makes the grade," the sponsor gets a $1,000 bonus. If the recruit fails, the sponsor is fined $4,000. (Paul did not give cash rewards to his young protégés, but rather gave intrinsic rewards for developing their teams, and more authority.)

At Home Depot, store managers are constantly encouraged to empower and develop themselves and their teams. They are given a large amount of leeway in ordering products, setting prices, and hiring people, with a minimum of interference from "corporate."

Bill O'Brien, CEO of Hanover Insurance, one of the top-performing insurance companies of the past decade, realizes that the word *team* rings false if people are not empowered to make increasingly complex decisions or given the skills to do so: "In the type of organization we seek to build, the fullest development of people is on a plane with financial success."[29]

Like Paul, all these organizations realize that a team is only as strong as its individual members, that members must be constantly developed, and that financial rewards can motivate a group but it takes deeper intrinsic rewards to create and empower a true team.

BIBLICAL LESSONS ON TEAM DEVELOPMENT

  ❦ A team is a group of individuals who may have different needs but are pursuing a common, unifying goal.

- An effective team is more than the sum of its parts; an ineffective team achieves less than individuals working on their own might have.

- Acknowledge the unique talents and motivation of each team member.

- A carefully selected team with complementary strengths outperforms a collection of talented individuals who are competing to be the "star."

- A strong leader is empowered, not threatened, by selecting strong team members.

- Remind each team member how his actions contribute to group goals.

- Remind team members that even the most powerful, competent leader can't do it alone and that you need their help.

- Actively reward team-oriented actions and attitudes.

- Expect resistance to team building. Overcome it with verbal encouragement and actions that confirm your commitment to the team approach.

- Delegate to team members according to their strengths and developmental needs.

CHAPTER EIGHT

Courage

*"Do not be afraid, though briers and thorns are all around you and you
live among scorpions."*

—EZEK. 2:6

*Have I not commanded you? Be strong and courageous. Do not be terri-
fied, do not be discouraged."*

—JOSH. 1:9

oshua, Jack Welch, and the Cowardly Lion from *The Wizard
of Oz* may appear to be an unlikely trio, but each in his own
way recognized the value of courage. Time and again,
Joshua exhibited this trait as he knocked down seemingly
impregnable walls and led the Hebrews into battle against seemingly
insurmountable odds. Welch, who spent a large portion of his time
developing leaders at GE's Management Development Center in Crotonville, New York, worked with many technically adept candidates for
top management. He noted that what separated a manager from a leader
was "the instinct and courage to make the tough calls—decisively, but
with fairness and absolute integrity."

The Cowardly Lion is another story. He started out as a nonleader
with no purpose and a ferocious demeanor that hid a total lack of courage. When the members of the "Oz Team" come upon the lion, he is

153

occupying himself with the meaningless task of scaring anyone who happens along his path. Only when he finds meaning through a mutually shared goal and loyalty to others on the team does his true courage come out. As the story progresses, the lion meets many more ferocious characters than the ones he initially tried to frighten. His courage grows as he becomes protective of his team and increasingly dedicated to the team's mission, which is merged completely with his own mission.

Part of the lion's problem, of course, is not so much his need to develop courage as to define it. The lion assumed that because he felt fear, he must not be as courageous as the "King of the Forest" is supposed to be. What he (and most biblical and business leaders) needed to learn is that courage is not the absence of fear but the willingness to act despite feeling fear: "Feel the fear and do it anyway."

The Bible is replete with heroes and leaders who exhibit many kinds of courage: physical, political, and moral. The prototype, of course, is David, the shepherd boy confronting a heavily armored, battle-hardened giant, and who proclaimed to King Saul, "Let no one lose heart on account of this Philistine; your servant will go and fight him." (1 Sam. 17:32) Queen Esther risked her privileged position in the royal palace (and her very life) to save her people from extinction. The prophet Jeremiah was willing to risk death to warn the rulers of his nation of their coming extinction if they did not change their idolatrous ways; he was not put to death, but was subjected to various imprisonments and tortures. Daniel braved a lion's den and the king's wrath rather than deny his beliefs. And Jesus and his disciples were subjected to legal persecution, beatings, ridicule, and death. Courage, supported by inner conviction, is what kept them going.

THE POWER OF COURAGE

Leaders who possess courage have a trait that can permeate and transform everything they do. Courage is often the critical seasoning in the "leadership stew." Without it, no one even wants to taste the stew; even victory can taste bland. With it, every undertaking is an adventure, something to be savored by all whether it succeeds or fails (but with courage, the likelihood of success increases greatly).

The leaders of the Bible were confronted with large but inspiring tasks, and they realized that the need for courage was proportional to the size and importance of these tasks. Therefore, the calls for leaders to have courage are many and frequent:

> *"Be strong and courageous, because you will lead these people to inherit the land I swore to their forefathers." (Josh. 1:6) Keep in mind that this land was swarming with enemies.*
>
> *"Be strong and courageous. Do not be afraid or terrified because of them." (Moses to the people of Israel, Deut. 31:6)*
>
> *"Be strong and courageous, and do the work. Do not be afraid or discouraged." (King David to his successor, King Solomon, 1 Chron. 28:20)*

If these messages seem repetitious, remember that the obstacles faced by these leaders were large-scale and never-ending. They needed constant reminders to be courageous. So does the modern leader. Take away courage from a leader and you are left with a mere manager, or worse, a functionary who uninspiringly enforces the rules of the bureaucracy.

Arthur Martinez saw the need for courage in both himself and his executives when he took over the venerable but ailing Sears retail and catalog operation. Meeting with each applicant for a senior management position, he did not mince words about the size of the challenge, the courage needed to meet it, and the rewards of success. "This is one of the greatest adventures in business history," he told the applicants. "You have to be courageous, filled with self-confidence. If we do it, we'll be wealthier, yes. But more than that, we'll have this incredible psychic gratification. How can you not do it?"[1] This is exactly the courageous attitude that left the followers of Moses, Joshua, and Jesus with little choice but to "get on board."

Sometimes, just to be on a particular leader's team demands that a follower begin with or quickly develop a strong sense of courage. In

Paul's letter to his young "mentee," Timothy, he exhorts him to have courage in his mission: "For God did not give us a spirit of timidity, but a spirit of power, of love, and of self-discipline. (2 Tim. 1:7)

Timothy was young and inexperienced, but no doubt his emerging sense of courage was buttressed by Paul's confident message: "If you're on my team, you are by definition a person of courage." The people on Lou Gerstner's senior team at IBM are more seasoned than Timothy, but the very fact that they're on the team is also an affirmation of their courageous qualities. "If you're on Lou's team, you're a forceful person. The wallflowers don't do very well here," notes a senior vice president of IBM's software group.[2] On both Paul's and Lou's teams, the courage to speak out and act is a requirement.

Another leader to whom the "spirit of timidity" is foreign is Herb Kelleher of Southwest Airlines (no doubt Herb's successor will be equally courageous and audacious). Kelleher has stated, "You have to be willing to take risks for your people. If you won't fight for your people, then you can count on your people not fighting for you."[3] How has Kelleher "fought for his people"? First of all, in the "up-and-down" airline industry, he has never had a layoff.

And then there's his "legal courage." Southwest had lost the first round of a court battle, spending over $500,000 only to have the courts rule that Dallas, Houston, and San Antonio already had adequate air service and there was no need for another carrier such as Southwest. They lost the appeal as well. Kelleher continued to represent the company in court and paid every cent of the court costs out of his own pocket. Says Colleen Barrett, Kelleher's "second in command," "The warrior mentality, the very fight to survive is truly what created our culture."

Paul showed great courage in the Book of Acts. He was striving to build Christianity as a religion in a hostile and uncertain environment. He knew he had a task to complete, and he knew his next stop was to be Jerusalem, but that's really all he knew for certain: "And now, compelled by the holy spirit, I am going to Jerusalem, not knowing what will happen to me there . . . I only know that in every city . . . hardships are facing me." (Acts 20:22–23)

A modern leader who faced a hostile environment and an uncertain journey was Tom Tiller, who at age 29 took over the General Electric range-building plant in Louisville, Kentucky. The range line was losing $10 million per year, one of the six production buildings had been closed, there had been a large downsizing, and the parent company was not about to begin investing more dollars in a money-losing business that seemed to have run dry of innovations.

Tiller's first act was to lay off 400 more employees. But then he decided to "go to Jerusalem." He instinctively knew that he had to look outward to the marketplace for solutions, not inward at an in-grown, money-losing operation. So Tiller chartered a bus and took forty employees on a "caravan" to the Kitchen and Bath Show in Atlanta. They didn't know exactly what they would do or learn there, but they knew they needed to acquire a broader view of their industry and bring back several innovative and actionable ideas.

"We've got to do something, and we've got to do it fast," Tiller exhorted his troops. "We don't have 142 years to do it." Some might have called Tiller's bus expedition foolhardy, not courageous. He had no idea what he might come back with, but he knew he had to go somewhere else and do *something*. If it was the wrong move, he could always try something else. But his pioneering courage paid off. Within eighteen months, GE had three new products designed, built, and delivered. The range division went from a $10 million loss in 1992 to a $35 million profit in 1994.

How courageous is Tom Tiller? When GE was having problems with stove handles that broke off, Tiller made it his priority to design an "unbreakable handle." How did he prove that it was unbreakable? He had his photo taken while he stood under a crane that was holding up a GE range by its handle![4]

Patricia Carrigan was the first female assembly plant manager in the history of General Motors. That alone took a lot of courage. But she was faced with a number of extraordinary problems that tested her courage even further. First there was her background; she had more years in education than she did in business. Also, the Lakewood plant outside of Atlanta had been closed for a year and a half prior to her tenure. Once she revived the plant, grievances were near zero, absenteeism had declined to 9 percent from 25 percent (despite her addition of weekend hours), and sickness and accident costs were cut by two-thirds. Moreover, it was the first plant in GM history to hit the company's "high-quality" standard in its first published audit after start-up.

Carrigan accomplished these goals by exhibiting courage and taking risks. "If you're going to expect an organization to take risks, you have to show some willingness to do that too," she stated. Carrigan initiated a new working approach that literally "tore down the walls" between labor and management. She instituted a training class that gave employees detailed business information and challenged them to devise jointly developed plans for improving business performance. She also formed over a hundred voluntary problem-solving work groups. This took courage in an environment where relations between labor and management had been frequently adversarial. When she left, the union local gave her a plaque for her "leadership, courage, risk taking, and honesty."[5]

In a biblical example, the disciples Peter and John were also men initially "out of their element," except that their problem was the opposite of Carrigan's. Whereas Carrigan had "too much education," they had no schooling at all, only courage and inspiration. Peter and John did not revive a plant, they revived a man, a lame beggar sitting by the temple gate. When they encouraged him to get up and walk, they were immediately brought before the court, which questioned the power by which they had healed him.

Peter and John explained to the court that their faith had enabled them to heal the crippled man, and they did not deny their allegiance to Jesus, in whose name they had healed. "When they saw the courage of Peter and John and realized that they were unschooled, ordinary men, they were astonished." (Acts 4:13) But they were also alarmed. "Then they called them in again and commanded them not to speak or teach at all in the name of Jesus." Peter and John's courageous response? "Judge for yourself whether it is right . . . to obey you rather than God. For we cannot help speaking about what we have seen and heard." (Acts 4:19–20)

Did Patricia Carrigan, Peter, and John feel some fear? Probably. But their courage helped them to act despite it. They became role models for others, not because they were totally fearless, but because they overcame whatever fears they had to act and speak strongly and decisively.

The Bible never says that courage and fear are mutually exclusive. In fact, the most courageous acts take place despite fear. The Book of Hebrews expresses this quite graphically: "Stand firm on your shaky legs . . . those who follow will become strong." The message here is that even when leaders are afraid or vulnerable and others see some of their fear, the courage of the followers actually increases when they see leaders acting in the face of fear or vulnerability.

One leader who justifiably might have had "shaky legs" was New York Mayor Rudolph Giuliani during the World Trade Center disaster. Giuliani, normally a fighter unfazed by public criticism, had been rocked by a bout with prostate cancer and his much-publicized extramarital affair and marital separation. If anyone might have had his "shaky legs" knocked out from under him by the worst terrorist attack on United States soil, Giuliani was a ripe candidate.

Instead, the mayor met the situation with a mixture of courage and compassion. Minutes after the planes hit the World Trade Center, he was on the scene. Like the firefighters and police whose ultimate boss he was, he headed straight for the site of the disaster. When the first tower collapsed, Giuliani was in a temporary command bunker, which he had to hastily evacuate through a haze of dust and silt. But rather than run for his life, the mayor insisted on setting up a news conference. "The mayor was adamant to have communication," noted an assistant. "He was adamant to let it be known that we were not going to cede the city."

Just after this, the mayor did have to run for his life, as the north tower collapsed. But he quickly found another command post in midtown. He stayed in the thick of the action, but also managed to stay above it, meeting with key deputies and commissioners, visiting hospitals, comforting those who lost family members. "There is no doubt that Giuliani is the man you want in charge of this situation," observed a policeman. "In this situation, it is like he is the only one who seems to take command."[6]

Another leader who stood firm on his "shaky legs" is Phil Myers, a hospital account manager for ServiceMaster. "Housekeeping" is not exactly high in the pecking order at a hospital, and Myers had only been on the job two weeks, but he knew he had to respond courageously when the director of surgery mistreated his people. He stormed into her office and pulled all twenty of his staff out of the operating room because she had used foul language and "talked to them like dogs." He told her, "These people are my people. If you've got a problem, yell at me. Don't yell at them."[7] A true leader takes the heat.

Frank Dale took over the *Los Angeles Herald Examiner* when the newspaper itself was on shaky legs, so it would be understandable if he had them too. The newspaper was coming off of a ten-year strike. The front door of the building had been barricaded for years, and people had been killed in the ongoing labor strife. As the new president, Dale had to enter ingloriously through the back door, where he was searched and fingerprinted. His response? He immediately announced to a group of employees, "Maybe the first thing we ought to do is open up the front door." It was exactly the courageous act that was needed. Everyone stood up and cheered. Grown men and women cried.[8]

Were the ensuing weeks easy as the *Herald Examiner* sought to reposition itself in the eyes of the public and its employees? Of course not. But the employees knew that they had a courageous leader who was capable of taking the right actions quickly and early. And they knew they could count on his courage bolstering their own as the fight continued.

In 1997, Peter Brabeck-Letmathe, CEO of Nestle, knew he needed a courageous manager in the company's Mexican operation: "The people in charge were very correct, very decent, doing a fair job. But they didn't have the hunger to win." Brabeck-Letmathe found a new leader. He was not totally fearless, but his hunger and courage were greater than his fear. "He came up with a new plan, a good, judicious plan," recounts Brabeck-Letmathe. "And I remember I looked into his eyes and said, 'Somehow, I know you can do more.'" Brabeck-Letmathe then asked the manager to double the sales volume.

The manager realized the size of the task, so he did not respond instantly or with exaggerated swagger. In fact, "his face turned pale." But then, like Isaiah, he set that face "like flint." ("I have set my face like flint and I know I will not be put to shame—Isaiah 50:7)." "If you have confidence in me," he announced to Brabeck-Letmathe, "I will get it." What happened? "They (the manager's team) became like tigers, each one of them," exults Brabeck-Letmathe. "It was a systemic change—within each person. They decided to go out and fight and win . . . They practically doubled sales in three years. The team that had been too easily satisfied suddenly developed a real fighting spirit."[9]

The leader could not have done this without his team. But the team also could not have achieved this without a courageous, inspired leader.

STANDING FIRM

Repeatedly, the leaders of the Bible are urged to stand firm in their actions and beliefs: "Stand firm then, with the belt of truth buckled around your waist, with the breastplate of righteousness in place . . . take up the shield of faith . . . take the helmet of salvation . . . and the Sword of the spirit." (Eph. 6:14–17)

But what does a company do when two strong leaders have equally firm but opposing beliefs and seemingly equal amounts of courage? Bill Weiss, CEO of Ameritech, knew he was taking a courageous step when, in his early sixties and just a few years before retirement, he began the effort to transform his company from a sleepy, monopolistic local phone company to a forward-looking, competitive, far-reaching telecommunications giant. He courageously demonstrated commitment to this transformation, delivered the message unceasingly, and promised he would let go those who resisted the company's new direction.

As part of this effort, he assembled the "Group of 120," a group of top managers analogous to King David's "mighty men," and asked them to evaluate each other on key leadership qualities as a first step in unifying and improving the team. However, one of the "mightiest men" did not jump on board; in fact, he used all his power and courage to oppose the plan.

Bob Knowling, a general manager from Indiana Bell, was a towering (6′ 3″) former football player who buttonholed many of the other managers to tell them he thought that this aspect of the plan was counterproductive and that he wasn't going to cooperate. Soon, he had ignited a groundswell of opposition. "I can remember one night in a bar," says Dick Notebaert, who was soon to become CEO of Ameritech, "We were going to do appraisals, and this huge guy . . . is in my face saying he's not going to do this appraisal stuff the next day."

Notebaert could easily have "set his face like jello." The appraisals were just one part of the program, and a successful revolt against them could have jettisoned the entire effort. He could have backed down and eliminated the appraisals. But Notebaert took the courageous route. He told Knowling, "Look, I'm not sure this will be good either. I, like you, have never done it before. But the difference between me and you is that I'm going to try it. If I don't like it, I won't do it again, but I am going to try."

Faced with this courage and resolve, Knowling agreed to participate in the sessions. After they were over, he made a statement that rivaled Notebaert's in courage. "I was wrong," he said in front of the entire "Group of 120." He admitted that much of his resistance to the evaluations was symptomatic of his resistance to the whole change effort. He reaffirmed his commitment to the company and to the new direction it was taking, and he asked any others in the room who might be ambivalent to make the same commitment.[10]

Sometimes, when swords clash in honest and courageous disagreement, the light engendered is greater than the heat.

Fred Smith of FedEx is another leader who has constantly stood firm with the courage of his convictions. If he hadn't, the company would literally never have gotten off the ground: Smith hatched the idea of Federal Express as a business school case study. His now-famous "hub and spoke" delivery method (in which all packages are funneled into a central airport and then dispatched to their destinations) was dismissed as unworkable by the professor to whom it was submitted. Smith believed in his idea so much that he sunk his entire life's savings into his new company.

But it has not been continuously smooth sailing for Smith and FedEx. He has had his courage tested several more times along the way. During the Christmas season of 1998, traditionally a "make or break time" for package companies like FedEx, the pilots threatened a strike, claiming their wages were too low and there were too many work rules. FedEx was well aware of the economic damage a strike could cause: Competitor UPS had suffered a similar strike in 1997, during which FedEx had increased its business by 11 percent. It was not looking forward to having the tables turned on it.

Smith was faced with a choice: Grant the pilots' demands and avert any major short-term damage, or stand by his convictions. He chose the latter, gauging that to give in to the pilots might have disastrous long-term effects on the company. Smith had already offered the pilots terms that were at or near the top of the industry, and he did not want to give them the idea that they could hold the company for ransom.

It was a courageous step, and the outcome could have gone either way. Smith risked splitting his company right up the middle (similar to Solomon proposing to divide a baby to settle a "custody dispute" between two women). Thousands of employees demonstrated in support of Smith, saying that he had been fair to all and that the pilots' demands were out of line. In response to the consensus of their coworkers, the pilots backed away from their strike, and FedEx had its best Christmas season ever, united, not divided.[11]

Another leader who has shown the ability to courageously stand firm is George W. Bush. Confronted with the World Trade Center attack less than a year into his administration, Bush ceaselessly trumpeted his resolve to resist the enemy and protect the people and infrastructure of the United States.

After a brief period of "evasive action," Bush decided to return to Washington so that he could orchestrate the U.S. response to the terrorism and to show his own people and the enemy that he would face this crisis with personal courage. Speaking just a few days after the incident, he said:

And you know, through the tears and the sadness, I see an opportunity. And make no mistake about it, the nation is sad. But we're also tough and

resolute, and now's an opportunity to do generations a favor by whipping
terrorism, hunting it down, binding it and holding them accountable . . .
This country will not relent until we have saved ourselves and others from
the terrible tragedy that came upon America.[12]

Bush's statement is reminiscent of Ezekiel 2:6: "Do not be afraid,
though briers and thorns are all around you and you live among scorpions." His courage inspired all those around him—his immediate staff,
the entire country, and the foreign leaders whose help he enlisted in
repulsing the "briers, thorns, and scorpions." Although he did not
quote the Bible exactly, many of Bush's words were in consonance with
the words of Chronicles: "Do not be afraid or discouraged . . . for there
is a greater power with us than with him." (2 Chron. 32:6–7)

Mary Kay Ash founded an amazingly successful and unique company,
but courage has been as essential an ingredient as the fragrances, pow-
ders, and creams her organization sells. It is easy to point to Ash's recent
success, but when she first envisioned her company, her attorney's dis-
couraging message was, "If you are going to throw away your life's
savings ($5,000), why don't you just put it directly in the trash can?"
Her accountant had a similar message.

But Ash had a strong vision backed up by a strong sense of courage.
She put every cent she had into the business and recruited her husband
to be in charge of "administration," a term that must have seemed
laughable when "company headquarters" was the kitchen table. Her
"heart" was tested even further when her husband had a heart attack
and died at that kitchen table a month later.[13]

Her husband's death would have been the final blow to someone
with less courage. Surrounded by the "briers and scorpions" of doubt
and "certain failure," Ash had lost her chief ally and staunchest business
supporter, in addition to her life's partner. But she continued to pursue
her dream. Today, the company she founded has sales of over $1 billion,
employs 3,500 people, and has over 500,000 direct sales consultants. Of
Ash it can truly be said, "You were wearied . . . but you would not say,
'It is hopeless.' You found renewal of strength, and so you did not
faint." (Isa. 57:10)

Shadrach, Meshach, and Abednego exhibited great courage by letting King Nebuchadnezzar tie them up and place them in a fiery furnace to demonstrate their faith in God. The three men proclaimed their faith in their protector, but further stated that, "even if he does not . . . rescue us from your hand, oh King . . . we will not serve your gods." (Dan. 3:17–18) These men had the courage of their convictions, whatever the result.

A modern leader who had the courage of his convictions was Rick Roscitt of AT&T Solutions, a company that started out as a "brainstorm" and went to billions in revenue in just five years. Roscitt decided to launch this division, dedicated to network outsourcing, when the company had no plan to enter this marketplace and very little proven expertise. Moreover, he did it without his getting his boss's support, or even consulting the boss, who was on vacation: "My boss was mad as hell when he came back," recounts Roscitt. "He said we were entering into an arrangement we didn't understand, and that we didn't know what the hell we were doing . . . And you know what? He was right!"[14]

Like Shadrach, Meshach, and Abednego, Roscitt was cast into the fiery furnace of oblivion. He was given little support by the main organization and was treated more like an orphan. But he had a strong sense of courage and belief in himself and his mission. Of course, it helped that a major client, Chase Manhattan Bank, had given him their "blessing"—he had managed the outsourcing of their telecommunications network, and now the bank was asking him to launch a unit dedicated to network outsourcing.

A person with a lot of courage needs only a little encouragement and resources. He also "makes his own luck." After his first successful project with Chase, Roscitt needed a little less courage as the parent company supported his now highly profitable "maverick venture."

A courageous leader sticks to his beliefs, and does not back down even if it appears to others that, short-term, the wrong choice may have been made. Peter and John were asked by the authorities in Jerusalem to stop healing the sick and stop teaching in the name of Jesus. Their answer was that "we cannot help speaking about what we have seen and heard." (Acts 4:20) They could not desert the cause they believed in, regardless of the possible punishment. And miraculously, they were released, since no one could decide what a fitting punishment was for following a particular teacher, however seemingly misguided, if the result was beneficial.

Steve Case of America Online is often painted as the "golden boy" of telecommunications. But at several junctures, Case has been "despised and rejected of men" for what seemed foolish and heretical ideas. Already the head of one of the most successful technology companies in America, Case risked it all in 1997, when he changed AOL's pricing from a usage basis to a uniform monthly charge for unlimited usage.

The response was immediate—and negative. At an industry panel, Case was introduced as "the most hated man in America." They played a busy signal as he walked onstage, an obvious reference to the busy signal many of AOL's subscribers were encountering when they tried to sign on to a network that was now severely overburdened. It seemed like everybody in the United States was now signing on to AOL for twenty-four hours a day, and Case's infrastructure was not prepared to handle it.

Case's response showed great courage. He did not arrogantly write off his critics, nor did he acquiesce and admit that he had followed the wrong strategy. He started off humbly, acknowledging the technical difficulties of implementing the strategy, and the inconvenience to the subscribers. But he did not back down.

Case had the courage to stand up for his strategy and then take the necessary actions to implement it. First, he beefed up AOL's infrastructure. AOL then instructed people to sign off when there was no activity. Thus, after the initial introduction, many people voluntarily stayed off the system until it was equipped to meet the increased demand. Steve Case's decision to go to flat-fee unlimited usage is now seen as prophetic by many of the critics who played the busy signal at the panel. And when his company recently entered a mega-merger with Time Warner, it increased his scope and influence even more.

Like Case's decision to stick with flat-fee usage, Nestle has decided to commit to genetic engineering. Regardless of whether you agree with Nestle's stance on this controversial topic, they have embraced that stance with great courage. And they have not blindly ignored opposing points of view; they have listened, but in the end have not been moved.

Nestle CEO Peter Brabeck-Letmathe observes, "In this world, there are followers and leaders. Leaders have courage—they can stand up against the barrage of public opinion that comes at them and say, 'I have thought about this subject, and I have come to the conclusion that this is the best decision. We are not going to capitulate.' " Whereas other large companies reversed their initial support of genetic engineering, Nestle did not reverse itself or apologize. They asked well-known professors to write their opinions on genetic engineering. Then they reviewed and discussed the information. As Brabeck-Letmathe writes: "We are a global company with global responsibilities. We have to think about the millions in the world who are hungry . . . For these reasons, we took a stand. We will pursue this technology. The reaction from the press and the public has not been happy—but that is why you need nerves of steel in business today. Otherwise, you will never stay the course."[15] Brabeck-Letmathe's strong resolve is reminiscent of the early Christians, who sustained themselves with messages reminding all to be courageous: "Therefore, my dear brothers, stand firm. Let nothing move you." (Paul in 1 Cor. 15:58)

On the opposite side of the corporate and political spectrum, consider the courage of Ben & Jerry's. Ben Cohen and Jerry Greenfield, the two eccentric founders, had an appropriately eccentric plan to make a public stock offering to the residents of Vermont, where the average income is considerably lower than in New York and where the average citizen does not consider himself much of a "venture capitalist." But Ben & Jerry's wanted a stock offering that was accessible to the average person, even in a relatively low-income state.

In most stock offerings, the minimum purchase is $2,000. Ben & Jerry's proposed a minimum purchase of $126! Every stockbroker and adviser they consulted said this venture would fail. They told Ben & Jerry's that you can't raise almost a million dollars in hundred-dollar increments, and that even if you did, you'd never be able to service so many shareholders.

Ben & Jerry's next action took a lot of courage or, to use a non-biblical term, "chutzpah," which roughly translates into "your plan is so outrageous it might actually work!" Acting over the objections of their lawyer, they registered themselves as stockbrokers so they could sell shares themselves. Cohen and Greenfield characterize their effort as truly swimming against the tide, a "huge struggle . . . we were betting the future of the company." But they were no strangers to courage and struggle; early in the company, they were so cash-poor they had resorted to eating ice cream in place of meals. Amazingly, Ben & Jerry's sold out the shares. They were even confronted by disgruntled Vermonters who had been unable to buy any shares—perhaps that took even more courage![16]

We have no record of whether Ben & Jerry's courage during this stock offering was biblically inspired. But there are several passages that relate directly to their experience:

> "If you falter in times of trouble, how small is your strength." (Prov. 24:10)
> "The people to whom I am sending you are obstinate and stubborn." (Ezek. 2:4)

Ezekiel was seeking to warn an entire nation of their impending destruction if they did not change their actions. Cohen and Greenfield went against the advice of their lawyers. Both were faced with formidable opposition, which required great courage to overcome.

COURAGE IN THE FACE OF ADVERSITY

Adversity is a great test of courage. Those with little courage fold in the face of adversity, those with great courage only find their courage magnified when confronted with difficulties. Warren Bennis has stated that "running a business in a bumpy economy is as terrific an education as a young (or presumably middle-aged) person can get. It's not unlike being in a platoon of infantrymen and getting sent to the front lines . . . What the experience teaches you is . . . you learn quickly to make courageous choices."[17]

The heroes of the Bible were created by the courageous choices they were often forced to make. Noah and the flood. Jonah and the whale. Moses and the Red Sea. Queen Esther and Haman. Jesus and Pilate. In each case a great leader became even greater when he or she encountered a difficult obstacle. Anyone can lead in good times. It takes courage to lead in difficult times: "We commend ourselves . . . in troubles, hardships and distresses; in beatings, imprisonment and riots; in hard work, sleepless nights and hunger; . . . through glory and dishonor, bad report and good report." (2 Cor. 6:4–8)

Although Jan Carlzon, CEO of SAS, was not faced with an array of obstacles quite like the above, he had his courage tested repeatedly by adversity of other kinds. When Carlzon tried to launch Euroclass, a new business-class fare, he encountered opposition both within and outside Scandinavia. First he had to hurdle the domestic Board of Civil Aviation, since this idea ran counter to the egalitarianism so prevalent in Sweden. That was relatively easy compared to bucking the resistance of Air France, which put a surcharge on their business-class passengers and demanded that SAS do the same.

Carlzon writes that he wasn't about to abandon his strategy "even if our determination touched off a war between civilian aviation authorities, which is exactly what happened." Air France, a Goliath in the European skies, threatened to stop SAS from flying to France if they did not institute the surcharge. SAS courageously made a similar threat to bar Air France planes from their landing fields.

It was not just "David" versus "Goliath." "We were fighting almost the entire European airline industry," writes Carlzon. After an initial price war, the airlines called in the respective foreign ministers from their countries, who engineered a compromise. SAS would not have to institute a surcharge, while Air France could give business-class discounts to normal-fare passengers.

Carlzon felt this successful, courageous stand against larger rivals was a tremendous morale-booster for SAS and united them in their efforts. He states that committing to action is often a matter of "courage, sometimes bordering on foolhardiness." In another action, he decided to cut fares in an effort to increase ridership. He admits this was not a new idea. Several other airlines had considered reducing fares, done the calculations, and dropped the idea. Carlzon acted on his intuition rather than on a painstaking analysis of the numbers: "I am quite certain that if I had been a more cautious person, I would have failed completely," adding, "We had the courage to act . . . as no one else had . . . Once we dared to take the leap, we gained much more than we ever could have imagined."[18]

Leaps take courage, but the gains can be tremendous whether you are Jan Carlzon taking on Air France, David battling Goliath, Moses challenging Pharaoh to "let my people go" (and then actually going even though he had no "map" and scarce provisions), or Shadrach, Meshach, and Abednego leaping into the furnace.

Of course, leaps mean putting oneself at risk. Some people thrive on risk. One of them is David Johnson, president and CEO of Campbell's Soup, who says, "In a way, what I've preached here is having a group of professionals who put themselves at risk. People who at first go on the high trapeze and perform triple somersaults . . . and do it safely while the crowd watches in amazement. And if your people are really good, you say, 'Take away the nets.' The silence is pervasive as the crowd watches in horror and wonders if you can perform."[19]

Jonathan, King Saul's son, was willing to take a risk to achieve victory over the Philistines (the Philistines seem to be the losingest army in history). Although not perched on the high trapeze, Jonathan and his troops were lodged precariously in a mountain pass, with the Philistines perched on the cliffs on both sides of the pass. Jonathan told his men, "If they come down to us, we will fight them here, but if they call us up, we will climb the cliffs and defeat them there." When Jonathan's men climbed out of their hiding places, the Philistines cried, "Look! The Hebrews are crawling out of the holes they were hiding in." They then shouted, "Come up to us and we'll teach you a lesson." (1 Sam. 14)

The "daring young men" of Israel climbed the cliff and taught the Philistines a lesson. They didn't even need a net. They had courage.

Another leader who took a daring action is Eric Schmidt of Novell. He didn't climb a cliff or swing high on a trapeze. Rather, he told the truth when almost everyone was advising him not to. He acted with courage, and his actions encouraged others to do the same. "When you enter a downturn . . . you have to fight the instinct to be overly cautious . . . Rather, you have to encourage your most creative people to take chances . . . The alternative is to succumb to a culture of fear in which a bleak vision of the future becomes a self-fulfilling prophesy."

On Schmidt's third week on the job, it became evident there would be a $20 million loss for the quarter. Some "leaders" would have soft-pedaled this, or "played with the numbers." Schmidt took a courageous gamble. He decided to announce the loss. The co-chair of Novell, John Young, endorsed this difficult decision. "Later he told me he knew then he'd made the right decision in hiring me. But after that announcement, everyone thought that the company was dead as a doornail." Schmidt's courage didn't stop with an announcement. He took immediate measures to cut costs, develop new products, and make divestitures. Thanks largely to these courageous decisions, he was able to put the company back "in the black" within one year.[20]

Courage often involves speaking one's mind despite strong, powerful opposition. Barry Diller is known today as one of the world's most powerful media and entertainment executives. But he got there through a series of experiences that challenged and gradually built his courage. Diller says it's important to "plunge into the uncomfortable; push, or be lucky enough to have someone push you, beyond your fears and your sense of limitations. That's what I've been doing . . . overcoming my discomfort as I go along."[21]

Early in Diller's career, his boss asked him to read a script and tell the producer what he thought. After he gave the producer his honest opinion, Diller was thoroughly chewed out. Someone with less courage might have concluded he was not cut out for the entertainment industry. However, he learned from this experience and went on to select the scripts for *Raiders of the Lost Ark* and *Flashdance* as well as launching a "big hairy audacious" venture, the Shopping Channel.

One of the biggest tests of courage is the willingness to challenge those in authority, particularly those who have the power to take away your job or diminish your influence. Roger Enrico, CEO of Pepsi-Cola, states, "One of the things we look for when we are assessing people on their way up is, 'Do they have . . . the guts to recommend what might be unpopular solutions to things.' "[22]

Hershey Foods believes in this type of risk-taking so strongly that they have established "The Exalted Order of the Extended Neck." Explains CEO Richard Zimmerman, "I wanted to reward people who were willing to buck the system . . . to stand the heat for an idea they really believe in."[23] Winners have included a maintenance worker who devised a method for cleaning a machine midweek without losing production time, despite other workers' protestations that "it couldn't be done."

One man in the Bible who could easily qualify for "The Exalted Order of the Extended Neck" is Nathan, a subordinate of the mighty King David. Nathan not only had the courage to deliver "negative feedback" to the ruler of the nation (would that Richard Nixon had had such courageous followers), he also knew how to deliver this feedback so that it would be accepted and not denied.

Nathan had watched while King David had sent a man named Uriah to certain death, assigning him to the front lines of the battle, so that he could take Uriah's widow as his own wife. Nathan knew he could not confront the king directly about his misdeeds (at least initially), so instead he told him a parable:

"There were two men in a certain town, one rich and the other poor. The rich man had a very large number of sheep and cattle, but the poor man had nothing except one little ewe lamb . . ."(This was a veiled reference to King David's many wives and Uriah's one wife.)

"A traveler came to the rich man, but the rich man refrained from taking one of his own sheep to prepare a meal for the traveler . . . Instead, he took the ewe lamb that belonged to the poor man and prepared it for the one who had come to him."

David, oblivious to the true identity of the rich man (himself), exploded with anger, "As surely as the Lord lives, the man who did this deserves to die."

Nathan's response, one of the most courageous accusations a subordinate ever gave a boss, let alone a king: "You are the man! You struck down Uriah the Hittite with the sword and took his wife to be your own." David was guilty of murder and adultery, and only Nathan possessed the courage to help him see it, risking imprisonment or death to set his leader and his nation back on the right course. That he was neither imprisoned nor killed is a testimony to his consummate communication skills and his accurate assessment of David's likely response to negative feedback!

Another modern leader who deserves membership in "The Exalted Order of the Extended Neck" is Jack Stack of Springfield Re. The division was about to fail. It was losing $300,000 a year on $21 million in sales. Its 170 workers were demoralized by a backlog of orders and a shop floor that was in a shambles. Even the parent company refused to help, seeing Springfield Re as a lost cause.

Stack's courageous (and perhaps foolhardy) question: Why not buy the plant ourselves? It was the most highly leveraged buyout in corporate history, with eighty-nine parts debt to one part equity, and $90,000 a month in interest payments. Courageous? Yes. A gamble? Perhaps. But Stack had "set his face like flint." Like so many of the leaders (biblical and modern) in this chapter, his courage has helped rescue his organization from "the valley of the shadow of death" and put it back on the road to prosperity.

BIBLICAL LESSONS ON COURAGE

- ✥ Courage is not the absence of fear. It is acting despite the presence of fear.

- ✥ Acts of courage perpetuate additional acts of courage—by both leader and followers.

෯ People are inspired by leaders who are realistic about the obstacles but challenge them anyway.

෯ Stand firm in your beliefs—most honest conflicts can be resolved and the commitment of both parties strengthened as a result.

෯ When it's a "close call" between risk and safety, leaders go for the risk.

෯ When you're hitting difficult short-tem obstacles, remembering your long-term goal creates courage.

෯ Adversity energizes and motivates the courageous leader, but quickly "quenches the fire" of those who lack courage.

෯ People (and turtles) rarely get anywhere without extending their necks.

CHAPTER NINE

Justice and Fairness

"Blessed are they who maintain justice, who constantly do what is right."
—Ps. 106:3

"But let justice roll on like a river, righteousness like a never-failing stream!"

—Amos 5:24

hapter 1 discussed honesty and integrity, which primarily relate to dealings between individuals. Justice and fairness extend into the group arena. Does the leader treat all people with a respect for their basic human rights? Are the rules and procedures applied even-handedly, without favoritism, across all segments of the company?

A corporation is not a democracy, but managers who do not lead with a basic sense of justice and fairness soon find that they will lose the trust and loyalty of their followers. Moreover, they will also gain a reputation with customers, suppliers, and the society at large that, in a crunch, they will use their personal power to make and enforce arbitrary decisions.

LEADING WITH JUSTICE

Will you lead as prescribed in Micah 6:8—"to act justly, to love mercy"? Or will your leadership more closely resemble "you rulers . . . who despise justice and distort all that is right"? (Mic. 3:9)

These passages remind me of an incident that took place early in my career when I was a training manager for a large accounting firm. Our trainers were drawn from the ranks of the accountants, who were removed from their audits for a week to instruct the firm's new recruits. Not all went willingly, but most completed the task loyally and competently once they arrived at the training facility.

We had a very serious exception on one occasion. The instructor obviously saw his week-long assignment as a trainer as a "paid vacation" and also as an opportunity to act irresponsibly and unprofessionally—he was visibly intoxicated when he got up in front of the class on the first day.

As a training manager, it was my job to ensure that quality instruction was taking place and that the new recruits were being oriented to the firm in a positive way. I called the office where the instructor normally worked and spoke to the administrator there, explaining that the person they had sent was drunk in front of the class. He immediately asked me if "a partner had observed this?" I told him that a partner had not been present. The administrator proceeded to inform me that "if a partner didn't see it, it didn't happen." He told me that the instructor should finish out his week of instruction, that they would not speak to him about his actions, and that they would not send a substitute who could act more appropriately.

This was definitely not a situation in which justice was served. The instructor got the message that it's OK to conduct oneself unprofessionally in front of new recruits, and the recruits got the message that there are different sets of rules for different levels of people.

I refrained from quoting the administrator, which would have totally confirmed the recruits' worst stereotypes of large partnerships: the higher up you go, the more leeway you have in bending and breaking the rules.

Some companies, by contrast, actually set up a system to counteract abuses of justice, even by those at high levels. In doing so, they are following the lead of Jehoshaphat, king of Judah, who set up a system of courts and advised the newly appointed judges, "Consider carefully what you do . . . Judge carefully, for with the Lord our God there is no injustice or impartiality." (2 Chron. 19:4–11)

One company that has set up such a system protecting the rights of all is FedEx, and that system is called the Guaranteed Fair Treatment (GFT) process. The process guarantees all employees a trial by their peers (something rather uncommon in most corporations, and one that might have been a good vehicle for the drunken instructor situation described earlier). The appeals process goes all the way to the CEO, where three of five people on the panel can be picked by the employee.

One FedEx manager says that the GFT process is not only a vehicle for justice and fairness but also for better overall management: "The GFT process . . . is a good vehicle for the employee as well as the manager, because if the employee never GFT's the manager, how would you know how you are managing?"[1] In one case, an employee was fired on a technicality and won her case, only to be harassed by her manager. She filed another GFT; in many cases, the employee would have been asked to accept a transfer, but at FedEx, she was allowed to keep her job and the manager was relieved of supervisory responsibility.

Gary Heavin of Curves for Women believes fervently in the long-term power of justice and fairness, and is willing to make short-term economic sacrifices in the interest of fairness. Heavin notes that in most franchising arrangements, the franchisor gets a fixed percentage of the franchisee's revenues. "I thought, 'The people doing really well—why should they pay more?' They'd just get angry and resent us. So I chose a flat fee for all franchisees, according to the law of integrity. I wanted to do the fair thing."[2]

Ironically, Heavin has found that justice and fairness actually "pay" in the long run. "These people who did really well shouted it from the rooftops; they don't hide any revenues from me, and they recruit franchisees—it was the machine that drove us." Heavin, true to his biblical principles, runs his company like David ran his kingdom:

"David reigned over all Israel, doing what was just and right for all his people." (2 Sam. 8:15)

Levi-Strauss has been a strong force for economic and social justice. They were one of the first companies to adopt a socially responsible agenda, stemming all the way back to the San Francisco earthquake of 1906, when they continued the employees' salaries even though they were unable to produce anything.

More recently, Levi-Strauss has offered technical assistance to Ghetto Enterprises, Inc., a small Oakland manufacturer whom they wanted to use as a supplier. As with Ben & Jerry's original experiment using Greyston Bakeries as a supplier, the road was rocky, and ultimately the experiment didn't work. Peter Haas, CEO, doesn't regret this "failed attempt" at justice: "There are many times we stub our toe . . . but that's not for want of trying."

Levi Strauss also monitors the treatment of its workers by suppliers and contractors through its Global Sourcing Guidelines. It sends inspectors to manufacturing facilities to see how they are being treated. As a result, Levi Strauss has terminated business relationships with 5 percent of its contractors and has required improvements (such as paying workers the legally mandated wage or eliminating child and prison-based labor) from 25 percent of the contractors. Says former CEO Walter Haas, Jr.: "Each of us has the capacity to make business not only a source of economic wealth, but also a force for economic and social justice."

Levi Strauss has often "put its money where its mouth is," making financial sacrifices to assure fair treatment of non–U.S. citizens. In Bangladesh and Turkey, contractors were using underage workers. Levi Strauss had what looked like a difficult choice: either discontinue the use of the contractor (in which case all the children would lose their meager means of support) or continue to use a contractor who exploited child labor. Their solution was to have the contractors pay the children's salary while they attended school full-time; Levi Strauss paid for the children's books, tuition, and uniforms. When the children reached working age and had been educated, they were again offered jobs in the plant.[3]

JUSTICE FOR ALL

Leaders with the most vision seek justice for all who are affected by their business, even if (like the children in Bangladesh and Turkey), they are not directly in the line of sight and could be easily ignored. The Bible is very specific about defending the rights of the "alien," the poor, or the disadvantaged.

> *"Administer true justice . . . do not oppress the alien or the poor."* (Zech. 7:10)
> *"Do not take advantage of a hired man . . . whether he is a brother Israelite or alien."* (Deut. 24:14)

Unfortunately, African Americans, whose ancestors were brought here as slaves by force hundreds of years ago, continued to be "economic aliens" until very recently. Levi Strauss sought to integrate these "aliens" into the economic mainstream before it was fashionable and before the law said they "had to." In 1959, several years before the Civil Rights Act, Levi Strauss integrated their plant in Blackstone, Virginia. In contrast to those Southern schools who would later "close their public doors" and become private schools rather than integrate, Levi Strauss insisted they would close their plant if it was *not* integrated. Local officials then asked for separate rest rooms for whites and blacks, as well as separate cafeterias. Then-CEO Walter Haas, Jr., refused. Needless to say, wages for the "Israelites" (the white population) and the "aliens" (the black population) were the same, as the biblical precepts command.

A young leader who wants to make sure no members of his team feel like "aliens" is Mark Elliott, director of data center services at NYCE Corporation. Elliott directs three departments in two different locations. "It could be very easy to treat some better and some worse; one is in a remote location in Michigan," he notes. (Elliott is headquartered in New Jersey.) "If I were to start treating people differently across borders, some people would feel like outcasts, and I don't want that to happen, so I try to allocate resources fairly and pay equal attention to all facilities."

But Elliott also has a "problem within a problem." Within his New Jersey facility, the computer operations department often feels like an "alien outcast"; a group that, although essential to operation, is often looked down upon as the "grunts" who have to work twenty-four hours a day, seven days a week. Because they are also physically separated from the rest of the group, Elliott emphasized computer operations' integral membership on the team by adding nameplates for each individual at the entrance to the operations area.

There was also an "alienation" aspect to the company picnics and holiday parties. Some operations employees missed these events every year because they had to be on duty at the computer center. Elliott wanted to be fair, so now for people who have to work through the picnics and parties he issues theater tickets, gift certificates, and vouchers to restaurants (where the food may be even better than at the picnic). He also puts up the operations employees at hotels when technical or weather emergencies force them to stay late or overnight.

Says one member of the operations group, "We feel part of the organization now, and we didn't before. We felt like stepchildren." Says Elliott, "I try to manage according to the 'justice' theme. I want to be that light in the fog. I want my team to say, 'He's standing there with the light, and he will be fair and lead us to results.' "[4]

Elliott's vision of just leadership echoes the last words of King David: "When one rules over men in righteousness . . . he is like the light of morning at sunrise on a cloudless morning, like the brightness after rain that brings grass from the earth." (2 Sam. 23:4)

Another company where a group of outsiders initially felt mistreated and excluded was Inland Steel. Four young African-American professionals felt that "whenever you were involved in meetings, you always felt like you were not part of the group . . . that you were invisible . . . We were taught by our families to work hard and get ahead, only to find that the doors were closed."

The young managers went to Steve Bowsher, their white manager, because of his reputation for fairness. They complained about lack of opportunity to advance and seemingly "harmless" but racist jokes.

Bowsher felt he had missed the full impact of their comments, probably because he had no experience as an oppressed minority. The only way he could learn how to "do unto others" was to experience what had happened to them.

So Bowsher went to a race relations seminar at the Urban Crisis Center, where the leader, Dr. Charles King, talked about his humiliating experiences in the white world. Ironically, Bowsher experienced some of this exclusion and humiliation himself when the blacks and women in the workshop (now the "majority") ignored him (the white male "minority"). When Bowsher returned to the workplace, he announced to his young black managers, "I've had a traumatic experience . . . I think I can understand you now."

Once he understood and felt the injustice of racism, Bowsher became a crusader for justice. He instituted a mandatory career planning program for all employees so that all felt they had a chance to develop themselves and advance. He gave what he termed "The Sermon on the Mount" to a group of executives, in which he strongly advocated gender and racial equality in hiring and advancement. He recommended that the president of Inland Steel attend Dr. King's workshop, and he brought Dr. King to Chicago to address his team when he took over as president of Ryerson Coil, a subsidiary of Inland.

Bowsher found that racial and gender equality often lead to greater profitability. The formerly unprofitable Ryerson division was profitable within one year after he took over. And the black managers who gave him the "call to justice" now say they feel evaluated based primarily on performance. Tyrone Banks, one of these managers, notes a feeling that, "I have a place here, that my ideas will be appreciated, that my performance will be rewarded."[5] That's true justice.

There is another type of justice emphasized in the Bible: concern for the poor, the sick, and the disabled. In Ezekiel 16, the city of Jerusalem is compared with her "sister," Sodom, whose inhabitants were "arrogant, overfed and unconcerned; they did not help the poor and the needy." This would be an accurate criticism of some modern corporations, but certainly not UPS, which has a community service program for managers. One of the volunteers who had his horizons of justice expanded was David Reid, an operations division manager in Salt Lake City, who worked with disabled residents of a community center.

Reid worked directly with a woman who had cerebral palsy. Her main focus was to be able to tilt her head enough to drive her wheelchair. "It's easy to take things for granted when you see something like that," observes Reid.

And Reid had indeed been taking similar things for granted at his own workplace, resulting in some injustices that he did not appreciate at the time. For example, he had once warned an employee that he might lose his job when he asked for time off to help his wife care for their disabled child. An administrator of the community service program observes, "You can get locked into that 'I've got boxes to move and people to move those boxes' thing, but those people have to move themselves, and those people have to be treated with fairness and dignity to do it well."[6]

Mark Colvard, another UPS manager from Toledo, was assigned to McAllen, Texas, to work with poor Hispanics. He served lunch at a hospice, worked with incarcerated youth, and built an addition onto a house to accommodate a family of seven. He feels he's a better manager now: "I wasn't as open as I am now. I take more time with people." He's also kinder; he had previously turned down a temporary worker's request to go full time because "it wasn't in the budget," but now he "found" the dollars by reducing overtime. The real reason he made the hire? "It was the right thing to do."

Ironically, Colvard's numbers haven't suffered from all this infusion of justice; in fact, they've improved. "I'm closer to my business plan than I've ever been. If my experience in McAllen has anything to do with that, I need to go back."[7]

The Bible also makes special provision for justice to the poor. Deuteronomy 15 states:

Do not be hardhearted or tightfisted toward your poor brothers. Rather be openhanded and freely lend him whatever he needs . . . Give generously to him and do so without a grudging heart; then because of this the Lord will bless you in all your work and in everything you put your hand to.

Gun Denhart of Hanna Anderson has followed this command with her Hannadowns program. Most of us who have or have had young children are familiar with the Hanna Anderson catalog of fine, colorful cotton clothing. Many of us do not realize that Hanna Anderson has a program, Hannadowns, that funnels customers' outgrown clothing directly to people who ordinarily could never afford Hanna Anderson clothing but need clothing desperately.

Any Hanna Anderson customer can return outgrown clothes and receive a 20 percent credit on the purchase price. The clothes are donated to needy women and children such as hurricane victims, religious charities, or women's shelters. If this sounds like a small program, it isn't: 10,000 items a month are returned and donated.

And once again, fairness and justice result in improved numbers. The Hannadowns participants are Hanna Anderson's best customers; they spend three times the money of the average customer. The company received an additional benefit: They were able to hire some of the former residents of the women's shelters, and they have become an "employer of choice," no longer needing to advertise positions.

Says Gun Denhart, "Money is like manure. If you let it pile up, it just smells. But if you spread it around, you can encourage things to grow."[8]

"FAIR SHARE"

The question of "who gets what" has been debated since biblical times. The Bible has several passages that address the issue of what constitutes a "fair share" of the proceeds, harvest, or spoils of war. James 2:1–4 points out that rich and poor alike have rights: "If you show special attention to the man wearing fine clothes and say, 'Here's a good seat for you,' but say to the poor man, 'You stand there' . . . have you not discriminated among yourselves and become judges with evil thoughts?"

Of course, the world is not perfectly fair. It has been pointed out that the law, in its infinite fairness, forbids both rich and poor alike from sleeping under bridges. But there are a number of leaders, many of them very powerful, who subscribe strongly to the concept of "fair share." According to Sam Walton, who was one of the world's richest men: "If American management is going to say to their workers that we're all in this together, they're going to have to stop this foolishness of paying themselves $3 million and $4 million bonuses every year and riding around in limos and corporate jets like they're so much better than everybody else . . . It's not fair for me to ride one way and ask everybody else to ride another way."[9]

During the economic crunch of the 1980s, Henry Schacht, CEO of Cummins Engine, decided the fairest thing to do was for top management to take the largest pay cut. He and his executives took a 12 percent to 15 percent pay cut, while the lowest ranks took only a 2 percent cut. Schacht felt that this was fair, since the executives were the ones most responsible for the company's bottom line, whereas the average worker had little control over it.

This action was in line with the biblical exhortation, "The man with two tunics should share with him who has none . . . be content with your pay." (Luke 3) Two guys with "two tunics" were Ben Cohen and Jerry Greenfield. Actually, they had seven tunics each (their compensation was seven times as much as the lowest paid worker), and they felt that they should limit their pay to this multiple of the lowest salary. "Just because one person has the skill of filling ice cream containers . . . and another person happens to have the skill of talking on the phone and selling ice cream . . . doesn't mean that one person should get paid all that much more than the other one," they maintained.[10]

In addition to giving the employees their "fair share," Ben & Jerry's also wanted to give the community their "fair share" of the profits. So they started giving away 7.5 percent of their profits. When told that this practice might cause the company to fail, they answered that they "set up our corporate philanthropy as a given, like our electric bill or heating bill, we'd just pay it as a cost of doing business . . . We look at our payments to the foundation as a higher electric bill. It's coming out of profits, so it's not preventing us from being profitable. And it's only a small percentage of profits, so it goes up only as our profits go up."[11]

And some of you thought these guys were a couple of anti-capitalistic hippies. What they found is that capitalism, ice cream, and justice can make a pretty good mix.

Herman Miller, the furniture company based in Michigan, felt that handing out golden parachutes for a chosen few was only partial justice. So in 1986, they instituted the "Silver Parachute" for all employees with over two years of service. In case of a takeover, it will be all employees, not just the traditional group of top executives, who will get a "soft landing." Ironically, this not only made the employees feel more secure and better treated, it made the company a less likely takeover target.

Herman Miller is also committed to the Scanlon principles of participatory management, productivity, and profit sharing. Employees are able to become owners, but they *earn* that ownership; it is not a gift. Risk and reward are connected logically and fairly, and 100 percent of the regular employees with one year of service or more are stockholders. Writes Max De Pree, the company's ex-chairman, "The capitalist system cannot avoid being better off by having more employees who act as if they own the place."

Howard Schultz of Starbucks is convinced that one of his key retention and productivity tools is the justice of employee ownership. He feels that it's "no accident that the attrition rate at Starbucks is four to five times lower than the national average for retailers and restaurants . . . I felt very strongly that if people can come to work feeling . . . they have a piece of ownership, however small or large . . . it would give us a huge competitive advantage." He adds, "Success is best if it's shared . . . if we want to inspire our customers, we have to inspire our people. They can't be left behind."[12]

This is the philosophy that helped Joseph devise his "fair share" plan so that his adopted country, Egypt, would not starve in the famine that was afflicting the land. Again and again, Joseph could have victimized the Egyptians. Again and again, he saved them from their own lack of foresight. He wisely set aside a portion of the grain harvest before the famine, and sold it to his countrymen when they ran out of grain, presumably at fair rates of exchange. When they ran out of money, he exchanged the grain for their livestock. And when they ran out of live-stock, he bought their land, but gave it back to them for their use, on the condition that they keep four-fifths of the harvest for themselves and give one-fifth to the Pharaoh.

Joseph could have bled his adopted countrymen dry. But his overall scheme was just and fair—to ensure that they would have enough pro-ductive capacity and consumable resources to be able to survive the famine and prosper again once it was over. And, good politician that he was, he remembered to give "the boss" his fair share as well.

RECTIFYING INJUSTICE

It is one thing for a leader to initially pursue just policies and actions from the outset. But often, a leader must have the courage to confront and reverse injustices, some of which may have been promulgated by his own organization.

At Bear Stearns, Ace Greenberg, chairman of the executive commit-tee, feels that the reversal of injustice must come "from the top" or it won't happen at all. Largely due to Greenberg's leadership, the com-pany has never had a major ethical scandal in an industry more famous for its acquisitiveness than its fairness. Notes Greenberg, "Mark Twain said, 'Fish stink from the head,' right? And it's people up top who set an example of how a business should be run. And if they're sloppy, or throw dollars around and have big expense accounts, I think it perme-ates the whole firm."

Greenberg's antidote is to officially encourage "whistleblowers" to expose injustices and "errors." "We pay them 5 percent of whatever error they uncover, and we pay them on the spot in cash—I have writ-ten checks as large as $50,000 and $60,000."[13] In an environment where "money talks" (and often shouts), these payments are a strong advise-ment to everyone in the firm that "justice will be served" and injustice will be reversed.

Paul O'Neill, former chairman of ALCOA and now secretary of the treasury, also acted promptly when confronted with an injustice. A religious order contacted him and told him that workers in one of his Mexican plants had been overcome by forklift fumes and had to be hospitalized. "I simply didn't believe it," muses O'Neill. "But it turned out they were right."

It turned out that the division president had known about the incident and had performed the required investigatory report, but he then hid the results from the environmental safety group in corporate headquarters. The division president had been with the company for twenty-eight years and had grown the business from $100 million to $1.5 billion, but O'Neill fired him. "Firing people is not fun, but we don't do business this way. A company must live by its values."

And this is not a one-time incident of justice taking precedence over economic gain. O'Neill's philosophy of justice is carried out across all business units and cultures. "We don't pay bribes, even when it is legal to do so," he asserts. And his dedication to justice extends to other areas as well, even when the laws of a country permit injustice. When ALCOA made acquisitions in Hungary, many of the buildings had asbestos. Even though removal of asbestos was not required by law in Hungary, ALCOA spent the money to remove it. "We don't treat people by what the local law is but by what logic says is the right thing; it shows consistency of belief and action," states O'Neill.[14]

Two thousand years ago, another leader asserted the need to obey a higher law—not temporary, man-made, local laws. Jesus, when asked whether the Jews should be obeying Caesar's laws, answered, "Render unto Caesar that which is Caesar's, and unto God that which is God's." (Matt. 22:21) Leaders who are concerned with justice follow their consciences, which are often "higher authorities" when exercised to the fullest.

The Bible advises us that one way to rectify injustice is to "lend freely to the poor." Deuteronomy 15 advises that ultimately "there should be no poor among you" but that while they exist, "I command you to be openhanded toward . . . the poor and needy in your land." One bank that has taken this to heart is South Shore Bank in Chicago, which looks like any other bank from the outside, but distributes its assets with justice. Most banks take their deposits and convert them to credit to fund real estate development in downtown areas that are already over-developed. For over twenty years, South Shore has sought to rectify economic inequality by taking deposits and converting them into credit for development in underserved, needy areas.

The Bible advises us that "David reigned over all Israel, doing what was just and right for all his people." (2 Sam. 8:15) Sounds simple, but it's not easy, whether you're the king of Israel or a modern executive. For example, Weyerhauser was criticized in the press when, seeking to preserve the livelihoods of its employees, it delayed shutting several large mills and reportedly "brooded" about it (as if having a social conscience were an impediment to being a good businessperson). The same leader who delayed these closings also instituted Martin Luther King Day as a holiday for the company, stating, "It's not just a holiday for black people, it's a holiday for all of us to think about our fundamental principles and how to change things that aren't right."[15] Here's a leader who didn't just want to roll logs down a river, but also wanted to help "justice roll like a river."

Xerox is a company whose leadership has a long tradition of commitment to justice. In the racially turbulent 1960s, many companies spent much of their time justifying their discriminatory, exclusionary hiring and promotion policies. Xerox realized that if they were to succeed as a company and function within the Rochester community, they had to be a force for justice within the company and in the greater community. Xerox's leaders, in collaboration with the union, instituted job training programs in the inner city (including one aimed specifically at underemployed women), and gave technical assistance and contracts to a minority-owned manufacturing firm.

But when CEO Peter McCullough took over, he went even further in his pursuit of racial and economic justice. He started a sabbatical program that gave employees paid leaves of up to a full year so they could apply their business skills to projects that would benefit the entire community, not just Xerox. Employees in this program became legal advocates for mine safety and gave job placement assistance to prisoners. In addition, Xerox's Community Involvement Program funneled volunteers into the community to counsel probationers and help run women's shelters.

But in all this "do-gooderism," Xerox did not forget to take a good hard look at itself and the justice and fairness of its policies. It set minority recruitment goals that exceeded federal guidelines. It also identified "pivotal jobs" leading to top management so that women and minorities could be prepared for them and directed to them. By 1991, minorities at Xerox represented 25 percent of all employees, 21 percent of all professionals, 19 percent of officers and managers, and 21 percent of senior executives.[16]

It is not true justice when one nationality or racial group is clustered at the bottom doing the lowest levels of work while another group disproportionately dominates the positions of power. Xerox knew this when it instituted these programs. Pharaoh, a man blind to injustice, paid for this blindness by losing his entire labor force on one memorable night, and his entire army a short while after.

John Lampe was appointed CEO of Firestone during one of its most difficult crises. A large number of the company's tires had shredded while being driven on Ford Explorers on the highway, resulting in 174 deaths and 700 injuries. One of Lampe's first actions was to appear on television to accept accountability and outline the steps that Firestone would take to rectify the situation.

"It wasn't my ambition to be on TV, but customers want to hear from someone who is accountable," notes Lampe. First, Lampe publicly apologized to the families who had suffered deaths or injuries. He changed the manufacturing process at the plant that had made the tires, and spent $50 million to upgrade the facilities. He offered extended warranties (up to four years), free thirty-day test drives, and refunds to any dissatisfied purchasers.

And in a rare and courageous move for a tire manufacturer (whose income largely depends on good relationships with the auto industry, its major consumer), Lampe also challenged the Ford Motor Company to acknowledge its share of the responsibility for the accidents.[17] Lampe's actions and statements were congruent with the pronouncements made thousands of years earlier by the prophet Jeremiah: "Woe to him who builds his palace by unrighteousness, his upper rooms by injustice." (Jer. 22:13) If the leaders of the auto industry had heeded these words a generation earlier and moved quickly to alter the unsafe vehicles they had designed, they might have taken some of the wind out of the sails of the prophet Ralph (Nader).

Lampe's quick response emphasized the necessity of reacting quickly to rectify injustice or to give just rewards to those who have earned them. Ross Perot, head of information technology company EDS, is a firm believer that "justice delayed is justice denied." After a major victory over IBM, Perot didn't even wait until his team had returned to the office. "At EDS we believe in paying for excellence right on the spot, so we rewarded them with the bonuses, the cash, the stock . . . while they're still sweating."[18]

Perot realizes that such acts of swift justice are highly symbolic both for those receiving the direct rewards and to the rest of the company. Jack Stack of Springfield Re recognizes that employees are also highly sensitive to acts and symbols of injustice. "A good manager knows what the guy on the shop floor absolutely can't stand and has disdain for," he observes. "Common sense has to prevail. If I buy a factory one day and show up in a Lamborghini the next, can I then go out and talk about the company being at risk?"[19]

That would seem an obvious injustice, but too many leaders have committed similar ones. Too many biblical leaders attained disproportionate wealth on the backs of their own people. Micah excoriated "you who hate good, who tear the skin from my people and the flesh from their bones." (Mic. 3:1) Nehemiah bemoaned "you who are exacting usury from your own countrymen." (Neh. 5:7) The modern leader would do well to ask himself, "Are my actions just and fair, not just to the shareholders, but also to the employees and society as a whole?" It's not just a matter of morality, it's also a matter of long-term economic success. It's difficult to keep a workforce motivated and loyal if they feel those at the top are taking advantage of them.

JUSTICE REWARDED

Often, those companies and institutions committed to justice are seen as making "sacrifices" that compromise the well-being of their organizations. However, there are a number of examples of organizations that have been able to turn just acts into "win-win" solutions, where they gained not just morally but also economically. The "right thing to do" does not always have to be an additional expense to the organization; sometimes justice can actually help the bottom line, short-term as well as long-term.

Psalm 11 promises that "upright men will see his face." It does not promise immediate or long-term profit for just acts, but that is indeed what has happened to a number of diverse organizations, some of which just wanted to "do good" and others that realized that "doing good" can also mean "doing well."

Vermont National Bank had no way of knowing that its Socially Responsible Banking Fund could also have been named the "Highly Profitable Banking Fund." It just knew it had an idea that resonated with its deepest values and the values of the people of Vermont. The fund was instituted to promote socially valuable, fiscally sound enterprises such as affordable housing, organic farming, small business development, education, and the environment. The goal was explicitly to "balance the scales" of justice and make sure that socially responsible businesses received a chance to develop themselves.

Depositors can earmark their accounts for companies that "make a positive contribution to the environment, their communities, and their employees." Ironically, this venture, which was seen as a risk to profits, has actually increased them. The fund grew from $7 million in the first four months to $87 million in five years. Moreover, it grew $25 million at a time when the total deposits in the state had shrunk by $115 million, and it has consistently grown faster than the growth rate of the entire bank's deposits.

The risk to profits was overrated. David Berge, vice president and director of the Socially Responsible Banking Fund, notes that the loan beneficiaries tend to be more responsible, resulting in fewer defaults than the typical business loan. "Instead of being the last to know that something's gone wrong, we're one of the first." This allows the bank and the beneficiary to work out a solution before a default occurs.[20]

Another business leader who was able to mix justice and profit was

John Shields, the president of the Ohio division of Finast stores. When people looked at downtown Cleveland in the 1980s, they could be pardoned if they were reminded of the Old Testament lines, "Jerusalem will become a heap of rubble, the temple hill a mound overgrown with thickets." (Mic. 3:12) Like many, Shields saw urban decay, but he also saw economic opportunity and a chance to bring economic justice, jobs, and good service to the people of the inner city, many of whom had to take expensive, inconvenient trips to outlying areas to buy their food.

Shields saw the inner city not just as a "mound overgrown with thickets" but as an underserved market. There was an "outstanding business reason" to build new, modern stores, but there was also the opportunity to revitalize the area. Shields oversaw the construction of six new state-of-the-art stores in the inner city. Not only were the neighborhoods better served, but the stores were highly profitable.

Certainly there were some "extraordinary" expenses to set up stores in the inner city, such as additional staff training expenses and the cost of setting up an unobtrusive but effective iron fence around the store to discourage theft. But the effort involved more than just accounting for expenses and trying to make a profit, since it was also an exercise in economic and social justice. The mayor of Cleveland stated that "a good business decision was also the right thing to do for the community. So you have the best of both worlds."

The ultimate testimony to Finast's dedication to fairness and justice? The comments of the residents of the affluent suburbs surrounding the inner city, who were amazed to see better stores there than in upper-class communities like Shaker Heights. "When they go down there, they're stunned," notes Shields. "They say, 'My gosh, this is a nicer store than we have in our neighborhood.' "[21]

New London, Connecticut, was another city in danger of becoming "a heap of rubble" in the 1990s. It had been declining for years due to loss of jobs in the city's primary industry, defense. The housing stock in the city was deteriorating, and 61 percent of the schoolchildren qualified for free or reduced lunches.

The initial force for reviving the city was biblically inspired. Claire

Gaudani, president of Connecticut College, realized that the college had a responsibility to its host city. "We looked to Deuteronomy, which tells us to 'do justice, only justice, that you may thrive.' " Gaudani saw that the city, and the college, could thrive only if economic justice was served. So she revived the New London Development Corporation, which was dedicated to attracting new investment and rebuilding the city's infrastructure. Within three months, she succeeded in convincing Pfizer to build a $280 million research facility employing 2,000 people.[22]

"Do justice, only justice, that you may thrive." That's why Ben & Jerry's uses Greyston to bake its brownies and instituted a new flavor, Rain Forest Crunch, which is a product designed around a social mission to preserve the South American rain forest. It's why Anita Roddick makes the campaign to save the whales an integral part of her business plan, not just a cause to which she donates. It's why Mark Elliott treats his computer programmers on a par with the more visible, front-desk employees. It's why Jack Stack gives his employees shares in the company.

These and other leaders are taking to heart the question posed by Edward Simon, the president of Herman Miller: "Why can't we do good works at work? . . . Business is the only institution that has a chance . . . to fundamentally improve the injustice that exists in the world."[23]

BIBLICAL LESSONS ON
JUSTICE AND FAIRNESS

- ❧ If people perceive that they are being treated unfairly, they will stop performing or they will act like those who are perceived as favored.

- ❧ The most credible companies are committed to justice not just in the workplace but in the communities where they are located.

❧ The most credible leaders believe in fairness to all individuals and groups and act in consonance with these beliefs even when this is uncomfortable or difficult.

❧ A concern for the economically or socially disadvantaged can help not just a leader's credibility but also a company's profitability.

❧ A leader who operates on principles of fairness inspires better employee performance, loyalty, and retention.

❧ It's not enough to pursue justice. A leader also needs to reverse injustices and issue deserved rewards quickly.

CHAPTER TEN

Leadership
Development

"Praised be the Lord, who has allowed me to see a successor on my throne today."

—KING DAVID, 1 KINGS 1:47

"Look at the land with your own eyes, since you are not going to cross this Jordan. But commission Joshua, and encourage and strengthen him, for he will lead this people across."

—DEUT. 3:27–28

o paraphrase an old parable about a fish: Give me a leader for a generation and I will perpetuate the organization for a generation. Help me to develop leaders in every generation, and I will perpetuate the organization forever.

We consider corporations like IBM, Procter & Gamble, and General Electric to be long-standing organizations because they have been in existence for perhaps a century; much of their success has been due to the continuity of leadership that they have experienced. The "organization" called Judeo-Christianity has been around for almost sixty times as long, and largely for the same reasons—the ability to constantly renew its mission and find the right leaders to execute the mission.

But whether you're in modern Los Angeles or ancient Palestine, leaders do not just appear—they need to be developed. Noel Tichy writes that organizations can develop leaders at every level only if other leaders teach them both the theory and the practice, especially the latter, because you can read many books on how to walk on water or lead people across the desert without increasing your competence in either area. Tichy calls this mechanism—whereby one generation of leaders develops the next one—the "leadership engine."[1]

But the "engine" is anything but automatic. The most successful, long-lasting organizations make a conscious effort to develop leaders in every generation. King David started to develop his "inner circle" long before they were needed and before he even took power. Pursued by Saul, he escaped to a cave, where "all those in distress or in debt . . . gathered around him, and he became their leader." (1 Sam. 22:1–2) Later, many of these men would become members of David's cabinet and the future leaders of Israel. When leadership development and succession planning were performed conscientiously, the nation prospered. When these practices were performed poorly or neglected, the nation suffered through a succession of leaders who lost sight of the mission, oppressed the people, and reverted to idol-worship.

The worst curse, which occasionally came to pass, is uttered in Isaiah 3:4: "I will make boys their officials, mere children will govern them."

THE IMPORTANCE OF LEADERSHIP DEVELOPMENT

The leaders of the Bible, as well as today's most astute business and civic leaders, wanted competent, mature leaders with the right priorities and values following in their shoes (or sandals). That we now have over a billion followers of Judaism and Christianity and millions of synagogues and churches with a well-organized, planned leadership process is a testimony to their legacy.

But there are some corporations that are just as "religious" about continuous leadership development, many of them among the most successful companies in their industries. GE under Jack Welch (and also undoubtedly under his successor, Jeffrey Immelt) was totally vigilant that its officials not be "boys," but rather fully developed leaders who had undergone "trial by fire" and achieved the difficult goals set for them.

"I want a revolution, and I want it to start at Crotonville," said Welch, referring to GE's famed Management Development Center, begun in 1956 and recently renamed the Jack Welch Management Development Center. Crotonville has traditionally been the place where GE's new ideas and the battle plans for implementing them have been generated.

Many CEOs pay "lip service" to their organization's leadership development efforts, perhaps connecting briefly by conference call or sending a canned video message at the beginning of a session. But Welch put his helicopter where his mouth was. He flew to Crotonville every two weeks, where he engaged in freewheeling "learning experiences" with his executives, and didn't miss a session in his sixteen years as chairman.

Many familiar with Jack Welch's hard-nosed, bottom-line approach initially doubted his commitment to executive development. At the beginning of his tenure, many of his division heads were diverting funds allocated for executive development to other areas of their budget, including the "bottom line." Welch made sure that executives who cooperated with the executive development efforts were rewarded and that those who did not suffered consequences.

Although a cult of personality grew up around Welch, he realized that GE's success was largely due to careful executive development and succession planning, with lots of good leaders in the pipeline in case anything ever happened to him or another key player. The day after he had suffered a heart attack, he was pleased that GE stock actually went up $1. When the press intimated that he had no apparent successor, he responded, "That is far from the truth . . . It's like an obsession. I'm always talking with Paolo Fresco (GE's vice chairman), even when we're out for a drink. 'What's so-and-so like; can he take a balanced view of things; or to what extent does he bring in new ideas?' It's on my mind constantly, and finding the right person is the most important thing I can do for my group at the moment."[2]

Welch's most fervent wish echoed the plea of Moses: "May the Lord . . . appoint a man . . . so the people will not be like sheep without a shepherd." (Num. 27:16–17) Welch's efforts at Crotonville and elsewhere to continually develop his executives assured him that there would be no shortage of competent shepherds.

Andrew Grove of Intel is another executive who reinforced his commitment to leadership development with extra dollars in an executive's bonus. Like Welch, Grove truly enjoyed the process of teaching his potential successors. Grove went into the classroom to teach several times a year. "I've always had an urge to teach, to share with others what I've figured out for myself. It is that same urge that makes me want to share the lessons I've learned."[3]

Grove insisted that every executive at Intel do some teaching. He believed that you can learn to make the tough decisions only from people who have been there, not from outside consultants. It's not as old as GE's or the Bible's, but during his tenure Grove did develop a good, solid "leadership engine."

Larry Bossidy, former CEO of Allied Signal, also realized that development of new leaders is not only a key to profitability, it's also very satisfying in terms of feeling like you've left a legacy, not just an income statement. "How am I doing as a leader? The answer is how the people you lead are doing. Do they learn? Do they manage conflict? Do they initiate change? You won't remember when you retire what you did in the first quarter of 1994 . . . What you'll remember is how many people you developed."[4] Bossidy is so committed to, and so rewarded by, the leadership development process that he has founded a company completely devoted to executive development.

None of us, particularly top executives, likes to dwell on this topic, but we are all going to die someday. In March 1996, a plane carrying a group of top executives on a trade mission crashed in Bosnia, leaving their organizations in differing states of preparedness for executive succession. Asea Brown Boveri's president and CEO died, and the company could come up with only an interim replacement. Bechtel had no replacement at all for P. Stuart Tholan, president of Bechtel Europe, Middle East, and Southeast Asia. But Foster Wheeler, a $4.5 billion engineering and construction company in New Jersey, had no such gaping holes because they had done careful succession planning for unanticipated events.

The U.S. government has a succession plan in place in case of the death, impeachment, or resignation of our top executives. We have become all too familiar with it through the cases of John F. Kennedy, Richard Nixon, Spiro Agnew, and Bill Clinton. But it exists for a reason, and smart companies ensure that they too have a succession plan in place that addresses all contingencies, even the "unthinkable."

In practice, this means that a company should be constantly assessing all of its "high potentials" so that in an emergency or planned move, all are placed where they can make the maximum contribution and be most fully developed. This also may mean "prodding" the CEO, since no one likes to confront the possibility of their own disappearance or death.

One leader who confronted and accepted his disappearance and death long before it took place was Jesus. He consciously prepared his followers to take up their complementary responsibilities after he was gone, giving specific instructions as well as inspirational motivation. He even gave his "executives" new names befitting their new roles. To the disciple formerly known as Simon, he said, "And I tell you that you are Peter [which means *rock*], and on this rock I will build my church." (Matt. 16:18)

A modern example of someone who knew the importance of developing and appointing a successor is Roberto Goizueta of Coca-Cola. "To Goizueta, succession was the logical culmination of a program he designed to develop and promote talented people. He saw the decision to delegate authority as one of his three main tasks . . . And he saw designating a successor as the ultimate act of delegation."[5]

"In the beginning" of biblical leadership, leadership development and succession planning were not done consciously. Much of the activities took place naturally and spontaneously. The experience of Noah and the flood, for instance, makes any "Outward Bound" or similar "outdoor education" experience seem like a leisurely float down a babbling brook (which indeed many of them are). But as time passed, the nation's leaders began to realize that they would survive as a people and a culture only if they had strong leaders who could defend them against outside threats (Philistines, Egyptians, lions, and wolves) and internal decay (loss of purpose, idol-worship, excessive jousting for power).

Particularly with the institution of the monarchy (but even before), it was imperative that systems be put into place to assure the competency, purposefulness, and morality of top leadership, and also that there was a "leadership engine" capable of producing the next generation of leaders. Then as now, it was important to develop a system of mentoring and role modeling and to provide developmental assignments to prospective leaders, whether they were royalty or not.

Noel Tichy has written, "A person may have all the traits of a leader, but if he or she doesn't personally see to the development of new leaders, the organization won't be sustainable."[6] The "organization" that began with the Bible has sustained itself for almost sixty centuries; modern corporations would do well to borrow some of its techniques.

MENTORS, COACHES, AND ROLE MODELS

One of the most vivid images from the Bible is that of Moses mentoring Joshua in the "tent of meeting." These sessions are particularly intriguing because we do not know for certain what each might have said to the other. We only know that when Moses went into the tent, "the pillar of cloud would come down and stay at the entrance," and that "his young aide Joshua son of Nun did not leave the tent." (Exod. 33:9–11) Now I ask you, if your boss's office was constantly surrounded by a pillar of cloud, would you want to leave or would you want to stick around to make sure you received all the mentoring you could?

And we can be sure a lot of mentoring was taking place in that tent, probably not just simple job coaching ("Make sure you have at least twenty-five good trumpeters when you approach Jericho") but much deeper discussions on how to motivate individuals and large groups, battle tactics, and techniques for maintaining group cohesion in the face of obstacles and difficulties (how high is that wall?). Moses wasn't just "teaching skills," he was grooming Joshua to lead the tribes of Israel. Moses knew it, Joshua knew it, and the people of Israel knew it. The very act of mentoring was increasing Joshua's power and credibility.

For a modern-day version of Moses' tent, let's segue to the Cayman Islands vacation home of Roger Enrico, another place you would probably not want to leave if you were an aspiring executive at PepsiCo. Enrico had risen to the top circle of executives and was considering leaving PepsiCo to teach at the university level. Wayne Calloway, CEO, and Paul Russell, PepsiCo's vice president of executive development, had a better idea: If Enrico wanted to teach, why couldn't he teach what he knew best, the business of PepsiCo, to the people who most wanted to learn it, the upcoming executives of PepsiCo? This fit in perfectly with the corporate mission at the time, since it was estimated that PepsiCo would need 1,500 new executives in the next few years, who would have to be imported if they couldn't be developed. (The idea of importing "foreign" executives into Pepsi was about as attractive as the Israelites recruiting the Philistines to maintain the temple in Jerusalem.)

From early in the morning until late at night for one week, Enrico met with nine executives to share knowledge and ideas about how the company had been run, how it could be run, new products, and other important issues. All participants had to come up with a "stretch dream project," return to the workplace to work on the project, and then meet with Enrico again to review progress. Ten workshops were run in eighteen months, and several very profitable corporate initiatives (such as the Family Meals campaign) were launched. The program became a mainstay of PepsiCo's leadership development efforts.[7]

Dick Stonesifer of GE Appliances was an executive who made mentoring and coaching into a two-way process. Before he asked anyone to expose their weaknesses or failings to him, he exposed his development needs to them. Many of us have responded to our bosses' requests to give them 360-degree feedback, but how many of us have ever seen the entire feedback report? Stonesifer projected his feedback up on the wall (both the brutal criticism and the ebullient praise) so his entire team could see it, after which he asked them for help on remedying his deficiencies.

Stonesifer then asked his people (in small groups) to share their data directly with each other and to brainstorm suggestions for the improvement of each person. Stonesifer was very blunt about the uselessness of many 360-degree processes, and he wanted to make sure his was a good use of company resources and time. "In the end, this is the only way to get leaders to develop others," he said. "We all know what we do well or poorly. The issue here is: Am I going to help or am I going to bitch about you over by the water cooler?"[8]

We don't know how candid Moses was with Joshua about his own strengths and weaknesses, or whether he made Joshua discuss his personal weaknesses with the other members of his team. After all, this was several thousand years ago, and assessment techniques were not as sophisticated. But we do know that Joshua, like Dick Stonesifer's legions, received a strong dose of useful advice and candid feedback. This enabled him to knock down some pretty daunting obstacles and march into a territory literally known as the "Promised Land."

Mentor/coach selection is very important, however. Your initial excitement at being assigned to a development program might be dampened if you found out that your mentor was Ahab or Jezebel. Or Samson, who could try to "teach" you brute strength but whose political sophistication was rather low. Unfortunately, none of these would have been a good candidate for being coached either. Samson, Ahab, and Jezebel were perfect examples of the "Peter Principle"—people who had risen to their level of incompetence. They were essentially undevelopable. The only direction for them was out, and they knew it.

Paul Russell of PepsiCo points out "the importance of the person you put in front of an audience as the leader" and adds that, no matter how highly placed, mentors must be "icons—world class people that everyone looks to as the leader or expert." Holding up an unethical person (no matter how successful) or an incompetent person (no matter how ethical) as a role model will only result in cynicism.

Kermit Campbell, CEO of Herman Miller, is a strong believer in the power of mentoring and developing leaders. He brought his thirty top operating managers together so they could develop a strategy for action. In the process, they developed each other as well. "The participation was very intense, and it kept feeding on itself, and by the time the half-day was complete, we had, as a group, gone to a much higher level than we had ever achieved before. That's what I feel I should be doing as a CEO, taking each of us to a higher plane."[9]

Two leaders who took each other to a higher plane were Esther and Mordechai. Esther had quite unexpectedly become the queen of all Persia, when only the day before she had been just an attractive Jewish adolescent. Mordechai, the "mentor," had the advantage of more life experience and access to the world outside the palace. Esther had the advantage of her great beauty (which had grabbed the king's attention and loyalty), her position inside the palace, and a pretty clever head on her shoulders. Unlike Ahab, Jezebel, and Samson, she was supremely "developable."

And working with her mentor, she accomplished the following, which would look good on any young manager's (or queen's) performance appraisal.

* Became the first and only Jewish queen of Persia
* Reversed a decree that would have resulted in the genocide of her people
* Persuaded the king to offer her half of his kingdom
* Asked instead for the preservation of her people, and succeeded
* Succeeded in having her mentor led triumphantly around the city on a horse by his worst enemy
* Succeeded in having her people's worst enemy removed permanently from the organization

Neither Esther nor Mordechai could have achieved these goals without the other, which is the essence of mentoring.

Norman Brinker is a restaurateur who knows the value of mentoring and coaching from both ends. He started out as a protégé of Robert

Peterson of Jack-in-the-Box, a fast-food chain. After receiving a share of the company there, he opened Brink's, which he sold, then acquired Steak 'n' Ale, which went public in 1971 with twenty-eight restaurants. Five years later he sold it to Pillsbury for $100 million and bought Chili's.

In 1993, Brinker suffered a near-fatal polo accident. Ron McDougall, president of Brinker International, was able to pick up the routine CEO duties adequately. But what was missed most was Brinker's mentoring ability. He had developed a reputation for attracting good people, giving them challenging assignments. He gave his protégés leeway to run their own businesses while still offering them guidance when needed.

Brinker's protégés now run large successful chains like TGI Friday's, Outback Steakhouse, and Spaghetti Warehouse. Much of that success can be traced back to Brinker's coaching and mentoring ability.

Brinker's relationship with his protégés is reminiscent of Elijah's and Elisha's in the Old Testament. When Elijah was about to be taken to heaven, he asked his protégé Elisha, "Tell me, what can I do for you before I am taken from you?" "Let me inherit a double portion of your spirit," Elisha replied. (2 Kings 2:9) Elisha could have asked for anything: goods, money, powerful position. But what he asked for is what mentors have the power to give to their protégés—the benefit of their knowledge and life experience. When we give our protégés even a *single* portion of our spirit, we increase their ability to achieve organizational and personal goals, and we help the organization as well. It's a win-win. And to that we can also add a "win" for the mentor, who usually grows from the experience and gets a tremendous sense of "generativity" by helping another person achieve his or her goals.

Talk to a mentor and a protégé independently, and you'll often find that they are both committed to the same goals. When Noel Tichy asked Larry Bossidy what his goals were, the answer was "customer satisfaction, integration of activities and processes, and make the numbers/meet the commitments." When he asked Bossidy's protégé, Mary Petrovich, the same question, he got the same answer.[10]

But Bossidy left Petrovich free to devise her own methods for reaching the goals. Brinker did the same for his protégés. Mordechai did the same for Esther. That's the difference between coaching someone and telling them exactly what to do. The former develops leaders; the latter only creates a clone of the original.

DEVELOPMENTAL ASSIGNMENTS AND ACTION LEARNING

Most management experts agree that traditional seminars have their place, but that most learning takes place back on the job through actual job assignments, or through "action learning"—experiential exercises aimed at solving real-life problems that have immediate relevance to the company. Noel Tichy observes that "winning leaders . . . push people not just to memorize the organization's values but to wrestle with them, to internalize and use them." He advocates putting people "in progressively more difficult situations where they have to make decisions, and then give them feedback and support."[11]

Jay Conger adds that "challenge, hardship and derailment," if experienced at the right time and in the right amounts, also create and strengthen leaders. Burt Nanus and Warren Bennis believe that "nearly all leaders are highly proficient in learning from experience," and Morgan McCall observes that "it's what a person has to do, not what he or she is exposed to, that generates crucial learning."

In the Bible, anyone who wished to lead needed to be properly instructed, but the closest thing to a seminar room was the tent in which Moses mentored Joshua. Most of the development took place through challenging assignments that usually involved a great deal of "action learning."

Earlier, we discussed Timothy, a young apostle whom Paul dispatched to the church in Ephesus. Paul knew that this assignment would force his young protégé to stretch, but he felt he had picked the right developmental assignment for him. He advised Timothy to "stay there in Ephesus, so that you may command certain men not to teach false doctrines any longer nor to devote themselves to myths and endless genealogies." (1 Tim. 1:3–4) Anyone entrusted with such a difficult assignment would need words of encouragement, which Paul added soon after outlining the task: "Timothy, my son, I give you this instruction in keeping with the prophecies once made about you, so that by following them you may fight the good fight, holding on to faith and a good conscience." (1 Tim. 1:18–19)

Moses realized that if Joshua was to lead the nation of Israel, he needed a series of progressively responsible developmental assignments. One of these was to lead a reconnaissance mission to explore the Promised Land prior to invading it. He instructed Joshua to "see what the land is like and whether the people who live there are strong or weak, few or many . . . What kind of towns do they live in? Are they unwalled or fortified? How is the soil? Is it fertile or poor?" (Num. 13:18–20)

All Moses was asking of Joshua was that he perform a comprehensive agricultural, political, military, and socioeconomic survey in unfamiliar territory in the midst of a hostile enemy. How's that for a developmental assignment? It's the type of mission that literally separates the men from the boys, the fainthearted from the courageous. And Joshua was up to the task; he was also one of the few who came back believing the Israelites could successfully take over the land despite the strength of the opposing forces. His leadership skills would be further developed as he tried to convince the majority of the people that this task could be accomplished and that they should not give up by returning to Egypt.

Daniel's developmental assignments were to read the writing on the wall and survive the lions' den; Shadrach, Meshach, and Abednego had to undergo the fiery furnace. David's developmental assignments included an apprenticeship as a shepherd (an entry-level position in which he honed his organizational skills and sharpened his combat skills by killing lions who threatened his sheep) and a truly "stretch" assignment for which he courageously volunteered: the killing of the combat champion of the Philistines.

It is not surprising that the most successful modern organizations also develop their leaders through action learning and developmental assignments. In 1994, KPMG handpicked thirty-five initial participants (high-potential partners) in their Leadership 2000 program, which was designed to develop the company's future top management. Rather than sit passively through the traditional leadership seminar, the executives were put through a "trial by fire" in which they were asked to:

1. Play the role of the CEO speaking on a controversial topic to a hostile audience (the action learning included actual lights and cameras to duplicate a press conference).
2. Commit to development activities back on the job, such as spending a week in a client's office interviewing and shadowing the client's upper management, or chairing the annual partners' meeting for a particular line of business.

This type of learning and the follow-up assignments had significant and measurable results. One-half of the group was given more responsibilities, and many were appointed to key task forces. All reported feeling more confident in their leadership roles. Two years later, KPMG decided to add another class of thirty-six, and to intermix the two classes so that the ideas and energy were magnified.[12] Perhaps it is a coincidence, but Jesus formed a group of apostles of almost identical size ("the Seventy-Two") when he wanted to expand the message of his church.

Jack Welch was a firm believer in action learning. Before a session of GE's Executive Development Course, he sent out a memo to the participants, in which he asked them to think about and be prepared to discuss the following situation:

Tomorrow you are appointed the CEO of GE:

❖ What would you do in the first thirty days?
❖ Do you have a current "vision" of what to do?
❖ How would you go about developing one?
❖ Present your best shot at the vision.
❖ How would you go about "selling" the vision?
❖ What foundations would you build on?
❖ What current practices would you jettison?"[13]

These are probably similar questions to the ones that Moses asked Joshua in the tent, or that David posed to Solomon before transferring the crown. One thing is certain: Neither Welch nor any of these biblical leaders would trust pure "book learning" or lectures to prepare the leaders of the future. Action learning was key if the organization was to create a strong new generation of leaders.

In running his "Building the Business" top-level executive development sessions for PepsiCo, Roger Enrico incorporated both action learning and developmental assignments. At the end of the first five-day workshop, all participants were asked to return to the workplace to initiate or continue work on real projects, which would then be discussed and analyzed when they returned for a three-day follow-up workshop several months later.

Gary Wendt, CEO of GE Capital, annually would take several hundred top performers and their spouses to China, India, or some other "exotic" site, which also just "happened" to be an area envisioned as a new market for GE. In this expedition, Wendt and his executives would soak in the area's culture, probe for growth opportunities, and form relationships with key businesspeople and politicians. Although pleasurable, this was not a "junket" dedicated to the serious pursuit of drinking, eating, and playing. Such an approach would be too close an approximation to the revelry surrounding the worship of the Golden Calf. These "tours" were more like developmental learning events—windows to the future—than hedonistic celebrations that merely dissipate the organization's energy and distract it from its purpose.

If leaders are created from difficult or challenging experiences, it should be no surprise that the trying experiences of the people in the Bible were the forge out of which a host of new leaders were created. Jay Conger and Beth Benjamin cite a number of challenges that, if negotiated successfully, lead to the development of even stronger leaders.[14] Each of these can be matched with a number of biblical leaders:

❖ Managing difficult relationships with supervisors or key staff (Daniel and Nebuchadnezzar, Joseph and Pharaoh, David and Absalom)

- ❖ Playing for high stakes (Moses and the ten plagues, Esther risking her life to save her people)
- ❖ Facing extremely harsh business situations (Noah and the flood; Joseph and the famine; Job, who lost seven thousand sheep, three thousand camels, five hundred yoke of oxen, and five hundred donkeys yet who maintained his integrity and rose to prosper once again)
- ❖ Struggling with complexity of scope or scale (Solomon building the temple)
- ❖ Having the wrong background or lacking a needed skill or credential (David, poor shepherd boy, defeating Goliath and then becoming the king of Israel)
- ❖ Having to make a sudden, stark transition (Moses having to leave Egypt with little notice and no clear map to his destination; the disciples giving up their nets and following Jesus)

Former chairman of British automaker Rover, Sir Graham Day, concurs that difficult experience is often the best teacher. His organization had become too complacent in a turbulent market and was beginning to lose ground. "Rover's need to establish what we now term a learning organization came from the imperative to secure the company's survival. Executives reported significant learning experiences stemmed from hardships and learning from other people, both the revered and the hated."[15] Moses learned a lot from his father-in-law, Jethro, but he learned even more from his joustings with Pharaoh; without a Pharaoh, there would never have been a need for a Moses.

Manfred Kets De Vries has referred to developmental assignments as "doing a Timbuktu"—sending an executive in need of development to a remote outpost with a number of difficult challenges.[16] If De Vries had been writing in biblical times, he probably would have referred to "doing a Crete," "doing an Egypt," or "doing a Babylon." Most of the Bible's leaders were shaped not by theoretical learning but by challenging, often harrowing experiences in which they were forced to take dramatic actions to preserve lives and achieve group goals. They and their mentors intuitively knew that "the only real training for leadership is leadership."

ORDERLY SUCCESSION

The transition from Moses to Joshua was an orderly one. Moses hand-picked Joshua, mentored him, and gave him challenging developmental experiences. Apparently there was no rival for the leadership of the organization, so there was none of the competition for the throne that can result in dissension and internal weakness.

On the other hand, the transition from David to Solomon was disorderly and rancorous, definitely not the model for effective succession planning. David, Solomon, and the nation were extremely fortunate that Solomon was able to govern at all, and that the nation survived.

David had many sons by his many wives (which can make succession planning in a "family business" very complicated). The first in line to succeed David on the throne was Amnon. However, Amnon was not a paragon of personal morality. Highly attracted to his half-sister, Tamar, he feigned illness, asked her to tend to him, and raped her. King David was furious, but failed to take any action in response.

Tamar's brother, Absalom, fumed about this for two years. Finally, he lured his half-brother Amnon to a sheep-shearing, where he had his attendants kill him.

Where first we had an incestuous rapist about to ascend the throne, we now have a murderer. But ruthless and ambitious executives sometimes make tactical errors. Absalom could not wait until his father David had died, and so he challenged his authority. He gained the loyalty of a group of tribal leaders, and he gathered them at Hebron to challenge his father politically and militarily.

David was highly conflicted about the attempted early accession of his own son, but he gathered his forces and put down the rebellion; in the process he suffered the loss of a son whom he had loved. He next designated Solomon ("Shlomo" in Hebrew, derived from "Shalom," the word for peace). He laid hands on Solomon, anointed him with oil, and symbolically placed the cornerstone of the temple for him. He also probably heaved a tremendous sigh of relief that after all the mayhem he still had a few sons left and that this one seemed capable of ruling with a kind and wise, yet firm, hand.

It's not always a "straight line," but as the Bible progresses, the leadership transitions generally become more planned and less random, more peaceful and less violent, culminating in the orderly passage (despite turbulent conditions) from Jesus to his disciples. Modern companies also need planned, peaceful leadership transitions if they are to last more than a generation or two.

Samuel Curtis Johnson of S. C. Johnson arranged a smoother transition than David's by "dividing up the kingdom" among his three offspring according to their desires and abilities. Helen Leopold-Johnson now heads the recreational goods business, Curt Johnson the industrial unit, and Herbert Fisk Johnson the largest unit, consumer products, which includes such brands as Drano, Windex, and Raid.

How did Johnson accomplish this without the wholesale succession mayhem of "David and Sons"? There was a tradition of peaceful executive continuity and cooperation. As Helen Leopold-Johnson notes, "My grandfather set the tone in the 1920s, and my father came with international growth and technology. Each generation brings something different."

The offspring were given appropriate developmental assignments, such as Johnson Bank, considered a "good farm team" for the children. The family also set up a council of advisers, which helped them divide up the responsibilities (similar to the Twelve Tribes of Israel) and provided a systematic mechanism for resolving disputes (no fratricide here!). "We all came with slightly different strengths," notes Helen Leopold-Johnson. "You're not in it for yourself, and it doesn't matter which piece is bigger than the other . . . If one of us goes berserk, there's a plan to remove that person."[17]

Jack Welch's "obsession" with a smooth transition came from the firsthand knowledge that a contentious process often resulted in organizational damage. When he himself had been chosen, the candidates were subjected to a four-year head-to-head competition, and the company had become too internally focused. "Things were . . . becoming very political . . . camps were being formed in the company. Pray to God that doesn't happen again."[18]

Welch didn't just "pray," he planned. He made a list of the top candidates best prepared to succeed him, and every May and November the directors reviewed the files of the top fifteen managers for strengths, weaknesses, and future assignments. He was trying to avoid a succession process that became "a bloody dustup" of "poor preparation, out-of-control egos, and bad choices."

When Bill Taylor became CEO of CIGNA at age 44, the selection of his successor may not have appeared to be a priority. But Taylor realized that the age of a CEO is irrelevant in succession planning, since emergencies and unplanned events can, and frequently do, arise. He made succession planning and management development two of his top priorities, discussing the qualifications of two to three replacements regularly at board meetings and in-depth once a year. He also wrote a letter "to be opened in the event of my death or disability," which recorded what had actually been said at these meetings; he realized that in the scramble for power, the data might be subjectively interpreted or distorted. Taylor made sure that succession planning extended down several layers of the organization, to include business heads and high potentials, with a particular emphasis on young managers who would be the lifeblood of the organization and who would be the most likely to become the next CEO.[19]

David Packard of Hewlett-Packard also realized the importance of systematic succession planning, particularly in a company closely identified with the personalities and policies of its current leaders. "The object is to build sufficient strength into the organization so that the future of Hewlett-Packard Company is not dependent upon any one or two or three people, including Bill [Hewlett] and myself."[20] These two leaders were not about to fall into the trap of France's Louis the XIV, who proclaimed, "Apres moi, le deluge," which roughly translates into, "After me, the company's up for grabs." Nor did they want to use as their credo King David's initial succession philosophy: "After me, whoever is still standing."

Becton Dickinson realized the need for a more formal succession process when Ray Gilmartin suddenly left to become CEO of Merck (whose succession plan for the internal candidates also went awry, since Gilmartin was an outsider). Becton Dickinson was left with a difficult transition problem because Clateo Castellini, the heir apparent, had announced his intention to retire and return to his native Italy. Moreover, Castellini had little board experience. Becton Dickinson learned from experience and instituted a more formal succession planning process in which twice a year all candidates for higher office are reviewed and any "heirs apparent" are given board experience.

David had appointed all the leaders of his cabinet with an eye toward their executive development and potential, as Jesus had done with the disciples. It was no accident that this carefully picked group of twelve men was soon able to develop many times that number of leaders to spread the message and power of the organization. Once "the Twelve" became "the Seventy-Two," an inexorable process was set in motion. And Jesus made sure they had plenty of "board experience."

This "multiplier effect" was used by Ameritech in its "Each One Teach One" developmental program, which helped it make the transition from a "Baby Bell" to a diversified high-technology giant. Beginning with its top core of executives (the "Group of 120"; seventy-two wasn't quite enough), the company launched a process to change the culture of the remaining 65,000 employees. They brought in 1,000 managers—fifty at a time—for four-day workshops in which the new mission was communicated. The managers returned to their units to teach those who worked for them and to initiate projects that operationalized the new goals and values. The result? A bottom-line improvement of $700 million.[21]

Executive development and succession cannot be left to "a wing and a prayer"; it must be carefully planned. There is no "leadership engine" without a group of "engineers" who build it and keep it on course. As Federal Express explains:

> *Our aim is to infuse our managers with the theory and philosophy and beliefs that the company has held to and practiced and benefited and grown from for over twenty-five years. We want to infuse these ideas into our leaders and have them go out and do the same to their employees.*[22]

Jay Conger feels that corporate succession planning needs to be more like the military, where there is a structured and ongoing dedication to developing the organization and the individual executives needed to lead it. For an effective succession vehicle, we might also look to the people of the Bible. The transition from leader to leader was sometimes smooth and sometimes rocky, but they managed to find and develop the right leaders at the right time, keep the organization's mission and vitality intact, and keep their "leadership engine" well-oiled and powerful.

LETTING GO/LEAVING A LEGACY

Perhaps the biggest test for leaders is their ability to "let go," surrendering the reins of power to well-prepared successors. Mature leaders realize when the time is near for them to leave the stage, and they anticipate this by gradually transferring the trappings and the reality of power to their protégés.

Moses had angered God because he impulsively struck a rock in anger, and so his departure was hastened and he was not allowed to lead the Israelites into the Promised Land. Surely this was not an easy hand-off for Moses, but he handled it in a mature manner. His eyes filled with tears as he climbed Mount Nebo to view the land he would not enter, but when he descended, he graciously transferred the mantle of power to Joshua, neither protesting nor interfering with Joshua's actions and staying behind to die in the desert. Before he did so, he blessed the tribes and he blessed Joshua as well: "So Joshua . . . was filled with the spirit of wisdom because Moses had lain hands on him. So the Israelites listened to him and did what the Lord had commanded Moses." (Deut. 34:9)

That's an example of a clean, smooth transition. But some leaders do not let go so easily. David Ulrich notes that "when leaders linger, staying on boards, keeping offices, consulting . . . very often these well-intentioned efforts backfire" and adds that a CEO should leave with honor and dignity, transferring "relationship equity" to the new CEO and "getting out of his own way . . ."[23] Moses did not stay on Joshua's board, nor did David keep his office in the palace when Solomon acceded to the throne. They got out of the way.

Jack Welch promised, "The day I go home, I'll disappear from the place and the person who comes in will do it their way."[24] It's hard enough following in a giant's footsteps without having those enormous shoes still hovering over your head as well.

Ecclesiastes 2:21 reminds us that succession is particularly difficult when "a man must leave all . . . to someone who has not worked for it." That's why it's important to give the new leaders developmental assignments so that they can prove themselves on the battlefield and earn the right to the position.

But surrender of power can still be difficult for many leaders. Henry Ford rejected almost every recommendation of his son, Edsel, to the point where the discouraged Edsel developed a cancerous stomach ulcer. At Edsel's funeral, his bitter widow approached her father-in-law and said, "You killed my husband." William Paley of CBS fired his successors, and Peter Grace one-upped Paley by firing his successor from his deathbed on trumped-up harassment charges.[25]

As we've noted, some of the biblical successions were rancorous, too. David felt heir-apparent Absalom was too aggressive in pushing for the throne before David was ready to yield it, resulting in a disastrous civil war and the death of Absalom. But most of these turbulent transitions were followed by periods of stability and more orderly transitions. No one transition was disastrous enough to destroy the organization. That's because, when push came to shove, most of these leaders came to care more about the survival of the larger organization than they did about their own individual achievements or position.

Top executives (both corporate and biblical) have often been known for their strong egos, without which "things don't get done." But as a wise leader matures, the drive that pushed him to "make a name for himself" by achieving individual feats yields to a concern for "generativity"—the nurturing of the next generation of leaders. Organizational survival becomes more important than personal achievement and adulation.

When the torch is not passed in an orderly, planned way (or when it is passed to persons deliberately selected because they are weaker or less competent than the current leader), the organization's continued survival will be in jeopardy. "[T]he ultimate test for a leader is not whether he or she makes smart decisions and takes decisive action, but whether he or she teaches others to be leaders and builds an organization that can sustain its success even when he or she is not around."[26] True leaders put ego aside and strive to create successors who go beyond them.

At the end of PepsiCo's leadership development program, Roger Enrico asked all the participating executives to envision not how high they would rise but rather the legacy they would leave at the end of their careers. For organizations that remain successful over the long-term, that legacy is often the creation of leaders who surpass their predecessors. The directors of KPMG's leadership development program felt they had made a major contribution to the firm because "when the time comes to turn over the leadership of the firm, we feel we will have played an important role in passing the baton to a more capable pair of hands."[27]

And lest you feel that it would be "impossible" to find a more capable pair of hands than your own, consider the words of Jesus Christ, whom many believe to be the very embodiment of perfection. He expressed supreme confidence in his followers' ability not just to "do what I have been doing" but to "do even greater things than these."

BIBLICAL LESSONS ON LEADERSHIP DEVELOPMENT

- ❧ Conscious and conscientious development of competent, caring leaders is critical to organizational survival.

- ❧ Your personal legacy will not survive unless you entrust it to a successor who has been well developed and shares your mission and business philosophy.

∞ Constantly assess your leadership "bench strength," because accidents and unplanned events can deprive you of potential leaders.

∞ Coaching and mentoring are keys to the development of tomorrow's leaders.

∞ Developmental assignments are the best way to prepare a leader for more responsibility.

∞ Learning by doing (action learning) carries more impact than verbal transfer of information.

∞ Orderly successions help ensure that an organization will survive and stay true to its mission; contentious or unplanned successions can endanger the organization and its mission.

∞ The best leaders "let go" gradually, so that the next generation of leaders can be developed and eventually take over.

∞ The best leaders subordinate their own egos to the ongoing success of the organization. They wish and actively plan for their successors to surpass them.

Notes

CHAPTER 1

1. Robert Levering and Milton Moskowitz, *The 100 Best Companies to Work for in America* (New York: Plume/Penguin, 1994), pp. 226–227.
2. Robert Knowling, "Why Vision Matters," *Leader to Leader*, Fall 2000, p. 38.
3. Richard Daft, *Leadership: Theory and Practice* (Fort Worth, Tex.: Dryden Press), p. 168.
4. Levering and Moskowitz, *The 100 Best Companies*, p. 336.
5. Thomas J. Neff and James M. Citrin, *Lessons from the Top* (New York: Currency/Doubleday, 2001), p. 330.
6. Levering and Moskowitz, *The 100 Best Companies*, p. 97.
7. Bill Capodagli and Lynn Jackson, *Leading at the Speed of Change* (New York: McGraw-Hill, 2001), pp. 59–60, 79.
8. Janet Lowe, *Warren Buffet Speaks* (New York: Wiley, 1997) pp. 68–69.
9. Neff and Citrin, *Lessons from the Top*, p. 311.
10. Ibid., p. 25.
11. Ibid., p. 22.
12. Janet Lowe, *Jack Welch Speaks* (New York: John Wiley & Sons, 2001), p. 65.
13. Daft, *Leadership: Theory and Practice*, p. 200.
14. Robert F. Dennehy, "The Executive as Storyteller," *Management Review*, March 1999, p. 42.
15. Peter Krass, ed., *The Book of Leadership Wisdom* (New York: John Wiley & Sons, 1998), p. 248.
16. Neff and Citrin, *Lessons from the Top*, p. 251.
17. Ibid., p. 375.
18. Lowe, *Jack Welch Speaks*, p. 65.
19. Telephone interview with Gary Heavin, August 2001.
20. Suzy Wetlaufer, "Organizing for Empowerment: An Interview with AES's Roger Sant and Dennis Bakke," *Harvard Business Review*, January–February 1999, p. 112.
21. Jeffrey L. Seglin, *The Good, The Bad, and Your Business* (New York: John Wiley & Sons, 2000), p. 13.
22. Lowe, *Jack Welch Speaks*, pp. 35–36.

23. Peter Senge, *The Fifth Discipline* (New York: Currency/Doubleday, 1990), p. 143.

CHAPTER 2

1. James O'Toole, *Leadership from A to Z* (San Francisco: Jossey-Bass, 1999), p. 95.
2. Stuart Crainer, *The 75 Greatest Management Decisions Ever Made* (New York: AMACOM, 1999), p. 44.
3. *General Electric Annual Report*, 1997.
4. Robert Levering and Milton Moskowitz, *The 100 Best Companies to Work for in America* (New York: Plume/Penguin, 1994), p. 291.
5. Ibid., p. 79.
6. Ben Cohen and Jerry Greenfield, *Ben & Jerry's Double Dip* (New York: Simon and Schuster, 1997), p. 167.
7. Geoffrey Colvin, "Larry Bossidy Won't Stop," *Fortune*, January 13, 1997, pp. 135–137.
8. Emily Duncan, "The New Reality," *Leader to Leader* [quarterly publication of The Drucker Foundation], Winter 2000, pp. 9–11.
9. Anita Roddick, "Leader as Advocate: Building the Business by Building the Community, An Interview with Anita Roddick," *Leader to Leader,* Summer 2000, p. 21.
10. Thomas J. Neff and James M. Citrin, *Lessons from the Top* (New York: Currency/Doubleday, 2001), p. 145.
11. Lee G. Bolman and Terrence E. Deal, *Leading with Soul* (San Francisco: Jossey-Bass, 2001), pp. 231–232.
12. David Bollier, *Aiming Higher* (New York: AMACOM, 1996), p. 172.
13. Robert F. Dennehy, "The Executive as Storyteller," *Management Review*, March 1999, pp. 42–43.
14. Gordon Bethune, *From Worst to First* (New York: John Wiley & Sons, 1998), p. 160.
15. C. William Pollard, "Mission as an Organizing Purpose," *Leader to Leader*, Spring 2000, pp. 17–21.
16. "Bonuses Aren't Just for Bosses," *Fast Company*, December 2000, p. 74.
17. Telephone interview with Gary Heavin, August 2001.

CHAPTER 3

1. Robert Levering and Milton Moskowitz, *The 100 Best Companies to Work for in America* (New York: Plume/Penguin, 1994), p. 458.

2. David Bollier, *Aiming Higher* (New York: AMACOM, 1996), p. 216.
3. Thomas J. Neff and James M. Citrin, *Lessons from the Top* (New York: Currency/Doubleday, 2001), p.261.
4. Gordon Bethune, *From Worst to First* (New York: John Wiley & Sons, 1998), p. 140.
5. *The Excellence Files*, video produced by Enterprise Media, Cambridge, Mass., 1997.
6. Suzy Wetlaufer, "Organizing for Empowerment: An Interview with AES's Roger Sant and Dennis Bakke," *Harvard Business Review*, January–February 1999, p. 121.
7. Ben Cohen and Jerry Greenfield, *Ben & Jerry's Double Dip* (New York: Simon and Schuster, 1997), p. 51.
8. Neff and Citrin, *Lessons from the Top*, p. 231.
9. John Grossman, "A Whirlwind of Humanity," *Sky*, January 1997, pp. 96–101.
10. Richard Daft, *Leadership: Theory and Practice* (Fort Worth, Tex.: Dryden Press, 1999), p.352.
11. "Radical Ways of CEO Are a Boon to Bank," *Wall Street Journal*, March 20, 1995, B1–B2.
12. Neff and Citrin, *Lessons from the Top*, p.155.
13. Telephone interview with Gary Heavin, August 2001.
14. Stuart Crainer, *The 75 Greatest Management Decisions Ever Made* (New York: AMACOM, 1999), pp. 86–87.
15. Levering and Moskowitz, *The 100 Best Companies*, pp. 278–280.
16. Ibid., p. 56.
17. Ibid., p. 324.
18. Ibid., p. 408.
19. Warren Blank, *The 108 Skills of Natural Born Leaders* (New York: AMACOM, 2001), p. 62.
20. Neff and Citrin, *Lessons from the Top*, p. 334.
21. Ibid., p. 318.
22. Telephone interview with Gary Heavin, August 2001.
23. Levering and Moskowitz, *The 100 Best Companies*, p. 312.
24. Ibid., p. 131.
25. Lee G. Bolman and Terrence E. Deal, *Leading with Soul* (San Francisco: Jossey-Bass, 2001), p. 225.
26. Levering and Moskowitz, *The 100 Best Companies*, p. 156.
27. Bolman and Deal, *Leading with Soul*, p. 226.
28. Pamela Coker, "Let Customers Know You Love Them," *Nation's Business*, August 1992, p. 9.

CHAPTER 4

1. Patrick Lencioni, "The Trouble with Humility," *Leader to Leader*, Winter 1999, p. 44.

2. Richard Daft, *Leadership: Theory and Practice* (Fort Worth, Tex.: Dryden Press, 1999), p. 74.
3. Ibid., p. 221
4. Brian De Biro, *Beyond Success* (New York: Perigee, 1997), p. 189.
5. Thomas J. Neff and James M. Citrin, *Lessons from the Top* (New York: Currency/Doubleday, 2001), p. 66.
6. Frances Hesselbein, Marshall Goldsmith, and Richard Beckhard, eds., *The Leader of the Future* (San Francisco: Jossey-Bass, 1996), p.106.
7. Neff and Citrin, *Lessons from the Top*, p. 273.
8. Ibid., p. 292.
9. Ibid., p. 149.
10. Ibid., p. 140.
11. Ibid., p. 312.
12. Ibid., p. 108.
13. Stuart Crainer, *The 75 Greatest Management Decisions Ever Made* (New York: AMACOM, 1999), p. 94.
14. Robert Levering and Milton Moskowitz, *The 100 Best Companies to Work for in America* (New York: Plume/Penguin, 1994), p. 374.
15. Suzy Wetlaufer, "Organizing for Empowerment: An Interview with AES's Roger Sant and Dennis Bakke," *Harvard Business Review,* January–February 1999, p. 119.
16. Robert Townsend, *Up the Organization* (New York: Knopf, 1970), p. 115.
17. Rekha Balu, "How to Bounce Back from Setbacks," *Fast Company*, April 2001, p. 156.
18. William J. Steere, "Sustaining Growth," *Leader to Leader,* Spring 2000, p. 37.
19. Neff and Citrin, *Lessons from the Top*, p. 191
20. Steven Covey, "Three Roles of the Leader in the New Paradigm," in Hesselbein, Goldsmith, and Beckhard, *The Leader of the Future*, p. 156.
21. Telephone interview with Gary Heavin, August 2001.
22. Charles Pollard, "The Leader Who Serves," in Hesselbein, Goldsmith, and Beckhard, *The Leader of the Future*, pp. 244–248.

CHAPTER 5

1. David Bollier, *Aiming Higher* (New York: AMACOM, 1996), p. 207.
2. Thomas J. Neff and James M. Citrin, *Lessons from the Top* (New York: Currency/Doubleday, 2001), p. 176.
3. Robert Levering and Milton Moskowitz, *The 100 Best Companies to Work for in America* (New York: Plume/Penguin, 1994), p. 204.
4. Ibid., p. 233
5. Erika Germer, "Huddle Up!" *Fast Company,* December 2000, p. 86.

6. "Leading Through Rough Times: An Interview with Novell's Eric Schmidt," *Harvard Business Review*, March 2001, pp. 119–120.

7. "The Business Case Against Revolution: An Interview with Nestle's Peter Brabeck," *Harvard Business Review*, February 2001, p. 117.

8. Sam Walton with John Huey, *Made in America* (New York: Bantam Books, 1993), pp. 200–213.

9. Levering and Moskowitz, *The 100 Best Companies*, p. 177.

10. Bollier, *Aiming Higher*, pp. 169–182.

11. Suzy Wetlaufer, "Organizing for Empowerment: An Interview with AES's Roger Sant and Dennis Bakke," *Harvard Business Review*, January–February 1999, p. 117.

12. Jay Conger, "The Necessary Act of Persuasion," *Harvard Business Review*, May–June 1998, p. 93.

13. Ibid., pp. 94–95.

14. Richard Daft, *Leadership: Theory and Practice* (Fort Worth, Tex.: Dryden Press, 1999), p. 165.

15. Tom Peters, "Leadership Is Confusing as Hell," *Fast Company*, March 2001, p. 138.

16. Neff and Citrin, *Lessons from the Top*, p. 346.

17. Ibid., p. 291.

18. Ibid., p. 177.

19. Ibid., p. 360.

20. Andrew Grove, "Strategic Inflection Points," *Leader to Leader*, Winter 1999, pp. 17–18.

21. Gordon Bethune, *From Worst to First* (New York: John Wiley & Sons, 1998), p. 158–159.

22. William J. Steere, "Sustaining Growth," *Leader to Leader*, Spring 2000, p. 37.

23. *Fast Company*, December 2000, p. 72.

24. Levering and Moskowitz, *The 100 Best Companies*, p. 80.

25. Robert F. Dennehy, "The Executive as Storyteller," *Management Review*, March 1999, pp. 40–41.

CHAPTER 6

1. David Bollier, *Aiming Higher* (New York: AMACOM, 1996), p. 171.

2. Thomas J. Neff and James M. Citrin, *Lessons from the Top* (New York: Currency/Doubleday, 2001), p. 171.

3. Ibid., p. 106

4. "Leading Through Rough Times: An Interview with Novell's Eric Schmidt," *Harvard Business Review*, March 2001, pp. 119–120.

5. Neff and Citrin, *Lessons from the Top*, p. 145

6. Ibid., p. 312

7. Robert Levering and Milton Moskowitz, *The 100 Best Companies to Work for in America* (New York: Plume/Penguin, 1994), p. 155.
8. Suzy Wetlaufer, "Organizing for Empowerment: An Interview with AES's Roger Sant and Dennis Bakke," *Harvard Business Review,* January–February 1999, p. 120.
9. Neff and Citrin, *Lessons from the Top*, p. 172.
10. "Leader as Social Advocate: Building the Business by Building the Community, An Interview with Anita Roddick," *Leader to Leader,* Summer 2000, p. 21.
11. Levering and Moskowitz, *The 100 Best Companies*, p. 270.
12. "Smart Steps," *Fast Company*, March 2001, p. 95.
13. Neff and Citrin, *Lessons from the Top*, p. 59.
14. Levering and Moskowitz, *The 100 Best Companies*, p. 486.
15. Neff and Citrin, *Lessons from the Top*, p. 331.
16. Ibid., p. 44.
17. Ibid., p. 312.
18. Levering and Moskowitz, *The 100 Best Companies*, p. 192.
19. Robert Knowling, "Why Vision Matters," *Leader to Leader*, Fall 2000, p. 38.
20. Gordon Bethune, *From Worst to First* (New York: John Wiley & Sons, 1998), p. 141.
21. Neff and Citrin, *Lessons from the Top*, p. 238.
22. Levering and Moskowitz, *The 100 Best Companies*, p. 223.
23. Bollier, *Aiming Higher*, p. 220.
24. Tom Peters and Nancy Austin, *A Passion for Excellence* (New York: Random House, 1985), p.267.
25. Levering and Moskowitz, *The 100 Best Companies*, p. 454.
26. Ibid., p. 420.
27. Noel Tichy, *The Leadership Engine* (New York: Harper Business, 1997), pp. 113–114.

CHAPTER 7

1. Peter Senge, *The Fifth Discipline* (New York: Currency/Doubleday, 1990), p. 139.
2. *Harvard Business Review Interviews with CEOs* (Boston: Harvard University Business School Press, 2000), p. 243.
3. Robert Levering and Milton Moskowitz, *The 100 Best Companies to Work for in America* (New York: Plume/Penguin, 1994), p. 122.
4. Ibid., p. 138.
5. Ibid., p. 398.
6. Deepak Sethi, "Learning from the Middle," *Leader to Leader*, Summer 2000, p. 6.

7. *The Excellence Files* (video produced by Enterprise Media, Cambridge, Mass., 1997); Thomas J. Neff and James M. Citrin, *Lessons from the Top* (New York: Currency/Doubleday, 2001), p. 192.

8. Neff and Citrin, *Lessons from the Top,* p. 345.

9. Peter Krass, ed., *The Book of Leadership Wisdom* (New York: John Wiley & Sons, 1998), pp. 284–285.

10. Gordon Bethune, *From Worst to First* (New York: John Wiley & Sons, 1998), p. 125.

11. Ibid., p. 181.

12. *Managing People: 101 Proven Ideas* (Boston: Inc. Magazine, 1992), pp. 141–142.

13. "Marc Andreesen: Act II," *Fast Company*, February 2001, pp. 114–118.

14. John Maxwell, *Developing the Leaders Around You* (Nashville: Thomas Nelson, 1995), p. 152.

15. Bethune, *From Worst to First,* p. 170.

16. Maxwell, *Developing the Leaders Around You,* p. 47.

17. *Harvard Business Review Interviews with CEOs,* p. 242.

18. Jan Carlzon, *Moments of Truth* (New York: Harper & Row, 1987), p. 11.

19. "Not Just for Kicks," *Fast Company*, March 2001, p. 70.

20. Tony Schwartz, "If You Work Twenty Hours a Day, Your Product Will Be Crap," *Fast Company*, December 2000, pp. 326–327.

21. Levering and Moskowitz, *The 100 Best Companies,* p. 115.

22. David Bollier, *Aiming Higher* (New York: AMACOM, 1996), pp. 268–279.

23. "The Business Case Against Revolution," *Harvard Business Review*, February 2001, p. 119.

24. Neff and Citrin, *Lessons from the Top,* p. 58.

25. Krass, *The Book of Leadership Wisdom,* pp. 151–152.

26. Max De Pree, *Leadership Is an Art* (New York: Doubleday, 1989), p. xxii.

27. Neff and Citrin, *Lessons from the Top,* p. 74.

28. David Baron, *Moses on Management* (New York: Pocket Books, 1999), p. 102.

29. Senge, *The Fifth Discipline,* p. 144.

CHAPTER 8

1. Richard Daft, *Leadership: Theory and Practice* (Fort Worth, Tex.: Dryden Press, 1999), p. 335.

2. Mark Boslet, "Big Blue After Lou," *The Industry Standard*, June 4, 2001, pp. 56–61.

3. Thomas J. Neff and James M. Citrin, *Lessons from the Top* (New York: Currency/Doubleday, 2001), p. 191.

4. Noel Tichy, *The Leadership Engine* (New York: Harper Business, 1997), p. 129.

5. James Kouzes and Barry Posner, *The Leadership Challenge* (San Francisco: Jossey-Bass, 1995), p. 37.

6. Jennifer Steinhauer, "Giuliani Takes Charge, and City Sees Him as the Essential Man," *The New York Times*, September 14, 2001, p. A2.
7. Tichy, *The Leadership Engine*, p. 136.
8. Warren Bennis and Burt Nanus, *Leaders* (New York: Harper Business, 1997), p. 35.
9. "The Business Case Against Revolution," *Harvard Business Review*, February 2001, pp. 117–118.
10. Tichy, *The Leadership Engine*, pp. 125–126.
11. Neff and Citrin, *Lessons from the Top*, p. 278.
12. Excerpts from president's remarks on investigation into attacks, *The New York Times*, September 14, 2001, p. A8.
13. John Maxwell, *Failing Forward* (Nashville: Thomas Nelson, 2000), p. 6.
14. Bill Capodagli and Lynn Jackson, *Leading at the Speed of Change* (New York: McGraw-Hill, 2001), p. 5.
15. "The Business Case Against Revolution," p. 118.
16. Ben Cohen and Jerry Greenfield, *Ben & Jerry's Double Dip* (New York: Simon and Schuster, 1997), pp. 93–100.
17. Warren Bennis, "The Voice of Experience," *Fast Company,* May 2001, p. 86.
18. Jan Carlzon, *Moments of Truth* (New York: Harper & Row, 1987), p. 77.
19. Neff and Citrin, *Lessons from the Top*, p. 185.
20. "Leading Through Rough Times: An Interview with Novell's Eric Schmidt," *Harvard Business Review*, March 2001, pp. 116–123.
21. Richard Daft, *Leadership: Theory and Practice* (Fort Worth, Tex.: Dryden Press, 1999), p. 381.
22. Ibid., p. 382.
23. Robert Levering and Milton Moskowitz, *The 100 Best Companies to Work for in America* (New York: Plume/Penguin, 1994), p. 174.

CHAPTER 9

1. Robert Levering and Milton Moskowitz, *The 100 Best Companies to Work for in America* (New York: Plume/Penguin, 1994), p. 123.
2. Telephone interview with Gary Heavin, August 2001.
3. David Bollier, *Aiming Higher* (New York: AMACOM, 1996), pp. 339–351.
4. Interview with Mark Elliott, September 2001.
5. Bollier, *Aiming Higher*, pp. 111–121.
6. Brent Bowers and Deidre Leipziger, eds., *The New York Times Management Reader* (New York: Times Books, 2001), pp. 185–186.
7. Ibid., pp. 186–187.
8. Bollier, *Aiming Higher*, pp. 28–35.
9. Levering and Moskowitz, *The 100 Best Companies*, p. 479.
10. Ibid., p. 48.

11. Ben Cohen and Jerry Greenfield, *Ben & Jerry's Double Dip* (New York: Simon and Schuster, 1997), p. 103.
12. Thomas J. Neff and James M. Citrin, *Lessons from the Top* (New York: Currency/Doubleday, 2001), p. 262.
13. Ibid., p. 153.
14. Ibid., p. 245.
15. Levering and Moskowitz, *The 100 Best Companies*, p. 485.
16. Bollier, *Aiming Higher*, pp. 352–365.
17. David Welch, "Meet the New Face of Firestone," *Business Week*, April 3, 2001, pp. 64–66.
18. Bowers and Leipziger, eds., *The New York Times Management Reader*, p. 72.
19. *Managing People: 101 Proven Ideas* (Boston: Inc. Magazine, 1992), p. 148.
20. Bollier, *Aiming Higher*, p. 10.
21. Ibid., p. 66.
22. Claire Gaudani, "Doing Justice," *Leader to Leader*, Fall 2000, pp. 9–11.
23. Peter Senge, *The Fifth Discipline* (New York: Currency/Doubleday, 1990), p. 5.

CHAPTER 10

1. Noel Tichy, *The Leadership Engine* (New York: Harper Business, 1997), p. 6.
2. Janet Lowe, *Jack Welch Speaks* (New York: John Wiley & Sons, 1998), p.198.
3. Tichy, *The Leadership Engine*, p. 46.
4. Ibid., p. 41.
5. Dennis C. Carey and Dayton Ogden, *CEO Succession* (Oxford: Oxford University Press, 2000), p.15.
6. Tichy, *The Leadership Engine*, p. 43.
7. Ibid., pp. 133–143.
8. Ibid., pp. 296–297.
9. Robert Rosen, *Leading People* (New York: Viking, 1996), p. 192.
10. Tichy, *The Leadership Engine*, p. 85.
11. Ibid., pp. 121, 169.
12. Frances Hesselbein, Marshall Goldsmith, and Richard Beckhard, eds., *The Leader of the Future* (San Francisco: Jossey-Bass, 1997), pp. 254–257.
13. Tichy, *The Leadership Engine*, p. 46.
14. Jay Conger and Beth Benjamin, *Building Leaders* (San Francisco: Jossey-Bass, 1999), p. 69.
15. Randall H. White, Philip Hodgson, and Stuart Crainer, *The Future of Leadership* (Lanham, Md.: Pitman, 1996), p. 111.
16. Manfred Kets De Vries, *The Leadership Mystique* (London: Prentice Hall, 2001), p. 283.

17. Brent Bowers and Deidre Leipziger, eds., *The New York Times Management Reader* (New York: Times Books, 2001), p. 220.
18. Lowe, *Jack Welch Speaks*, p. 198.
19. Carey and Ogden, *CEO Succession*, pp. 33–34.
20. Julie Fenster, ed., *In the Words of the Great Business Leaders* (New York: John Wiley & Sons, 2000), p. 309.
21. Tichy, *The Leadership Engine*, p. 124.
22. Conger and Benjamin, *Building Leaders*, p. 123.
23. Dave Ulrich, Jack Zenger, and Norm Smallwood, *Results-Based Leadership* (Boston: Harvard Business School Press, 1999), p. 214.
24. Lowe, *Jack Welch Speaks*, p. 202.
25. De Vries, *The Leadership Mystique*, pp. 118–119.
26. Tichy, *The Leadership Engine,* p. 3.
27. Hesselbein, Goldsmith, and Beckhard, *The Leader of the Future*, p. 258.

Index